PATHS IN
THE SNOW

'Jem Bloomfield provides an insightful and interesting exploration of scriptural and literary echoes in the first Chronicle of Narnia. Always intelligent, often intriguing, and at times an arresting read.'
Michael Ward, University of Oxford, author of *Planet Narnia: The Seven Heavens in the Imagination of C. S. Lewis*

'This is a book that will delight all Narnians. Jem Bloomfield leads us on a charming yet erudite ramble through the land of Narnia, pointing out many of the literary and theological references Lewis wove consciously or unconsciously into his tale. Added to this, he investigates the importance of various social issues, such as the significance of handshakes, the vital importance of tea, a mid-twentieth-century debate on the nature of time – and how Edmund's greedy consumption of the White Witch's Turkish Delight can be viewed in the context of post-war rationing and parental warnings never to take sweets from strangers. Bloomfield's diverse approach is refreshing and enlightening: I read the book in one huge gulp and enjoyed every page of it.'
Katherine Langrish, author of *From Spare Oom to War Drobe: Travels in Narnia with my Nine-Year-Old Self*

'Diligently researched and passionately argued, this literary re-reading of one of the best-loved children's stories of the twentieth century is crammed with beguiling, often surprising, insights into the creation of the Land of Narnia.'
Brian Sibley, writer and broadcaster, author of *Shadowlands: The True Story of C. S. Lewis and Joy Davidman*

'This is a rich and rewarding book, an indispensable guide for anyone wanting to gain a deeper understanding of C. S. Lewis's much-loved novel. Jem Bloomfield superbly demonstrates how Lewis's many diverse literary interests, both medieval and modern, helped to shape the world of Narnia. Setting *The Lion, the Witch and the Wardrobe* in the context of its times, he also explores in fascinating detail its connections to twentieth-century debates about everything from food rationing to Bible translation. Thoroughly well-informed, accessible and entertaining, this is a book no fan of Narnia should be without.'
Eleanor Parker, University of Oxford, author of *Winters in the World: A Journey Through the Anglo-Saxon Year*

PATHS IN THE SNOW

A literary journey through
THE LION, THE WITCH
AND THE WARDROBE

JEM BLOOMFIELD

DARTON·LONGMAN+TODD

For the members of Narnia Club
and the congregation of Beeston Parish Church

First published in 2023 by
Darton, Longman and Todd Ltd
1 Spencer Court
140 – 142 Wandsworth High Street
London SW18 4JJ

ISBN: 978-1-915412-30-0

A catalogue record for this book is available from the British Library.

Printed and bound in Great Britain
by Bell & Bain, Glasgow

CONTENTS

INTRODUCTION

'as clerkes fyndyn wretyn/ in here book'
(anonymous medieval carol)

This book arose from two experiences over recent years. The first was the lockdown in the UK during the first months of the global Coronavirus epidemic. Amongst the chaos and emergency of those first weeks, when almost everything seemed uncertain, many churches were grappling with twin problems of taking care of their vulnerable members and offering some sort of spiritual ministry. The online world, which had been a greater or lesser part of our experiences before the pandemic, now became the medium through which many of us engaged with the world outside. (Those of us who were not nurses, delivery drivers, or other members of the essential workforce.) A range of solutions were hastily put together to allow Christians to continue to share worship and fellowship in those isolating times. Some involved online services through Zoom or Facebook, and others the more old-fashioned technologies of dropping packages on people's doorsteps.

In seeking something I could do as a member of a ministry team in a Midlands parish, I had an idea. I would produce a sort of remote Christian book club, and so I reached for a familiar text. A lot of the congregation, I thought, would already have a copy of *The Lion, the Witch and the Wardrobe*, and most would be roughly familiar with the outlines of the story. There wouldn't be time – or mental energy – to all tackle a new book together, but we could find value in revisiting a Christian classic. Week by week, I recorded some thoughts on each chapter on my phone. The viewing numbers showed that some of our congregation were listening, and it became a regular part of life in those early months. Sitting at the desk in my bedroom, with the phone on top of a pile of books, chatting to the church members whom I couldn't see, and who couldn't yet reply, but whom I could visualise from our years together in the parish. Occasionally people would post a comment on the online recordings, and they made some really thought-provoking suggestions. Slowing down to read the chapters one by one, and commenting on them in turn, showed more and more depth to the book. There always seemed to be more to find and ponder on the other side of the turned page. It was only months later that the choice of *The Lion, the Witch and the Wardrobe* seemed especially apt, when I realised that the novel started with some children stuck inside a house, and told the story of the world they found inside.

The second experience was a year or so later, when life at the university where I worked was returning to some cautiously recognisable version of normality. Not normal, by any means, with the masking and the distancing and the more drastic restrictions appearing here and there. Nonetheless, it was a long way from being inside the house for everything but a couple of hours a day. Alongside my regular teaching, I set up a group to read through and discuss the Narnia novels. Again, I thought it would be a relatively accessible option for students, especially for first-years, and those second-years who had only known online university life so far. The books would provide an opportunity for literary and theological reflection at whatever level the members felt comfortable.

INTRODUCTION

Perhaps I, slightly selfishly, wanted to start hearing the other side of the conversation which had been so one-sided in lockdown. The group turned out to be more popular than I had expected, and the restrictions on the number of people who could meet in rooms meant we had to convene some ad-hoc meetings outside in the first term.

This group also became a regular part of the week, and one of its highlights for me. The regular members ranged from first-years just arrived at university and tackling their first essays, to PhD students busy on research which would produce book-length studies. Their favourite academic topics also varied, from linguistics to art history, from Classics to medieval studies. Some were Christians, some were not. The weekly discussions took us down lines of thought which I could not have anticipated. Why did the Pevensies end up speaking pseudo-medieval English when no one else in Narnia did? Where did Mrs Beaver's sewing machine come from? Did the White Witch use a stone knife on Aslan because she was unable to handle iron? We became used to each other's particular interests, and expertise in spotting significant moments or words in the text. Some of the members, we joked, were always ready to form the Royal Society for the Prevention of Cruelty to Susans.

This Reading Group – or 'Narnia Club' as it was quickly dubbed by its members – continues. We're still reading through a novel a term, and meeting to discuss a couple of chapters each week. We're still picking out small details and scrutinising them for whatever meanings they might reveal when we hold them up to the light. However, the group led me to put some of my thoughts about *The Lion, the Witch and the Wardrobe* into more ordered form on paper, and the result was this book.

There are many excellent books on C. S. Lewis more generally, and the Narnia novels more specifically. In recent years I've particularly enjoyed – and learned a lot from – Rowan Williams' *The Lion's World* and Katherine Langrish's *From Spare Oom to War Drobe*. This book is not an attempt to cover all the aspects of Narnia stories. Instead, it focuses on a particular aspect of them: how these novels work as literature. This approach involves various aspects, such as looking at their historical context, and the changing meanings of particular words or images in them. The most frequent aspect of this literary approach is my favourite: focusing on the connections between Narnia and other stories.

This is perhaps not the most obvious element of the magical world of Narnia, nor the one which immediately enchants the reader. Probably very few of us, on our first introduction to *The Lion, the Witch and the Wardrobe*, followed the adventures of the Pevensie children, exclaiming with excitement at the apparent references to the works of E. Nesbit or the clear textual connection to the Scottish poet William Dunbar. It could even be objected that the more attention we pay to the traces of other books in Narnia, the less we will be absorbed by the story itself. Adding footnotes and chasing up literary echoes certainly can distract us from immersion in the fantastical world of Narnia, and – more seriously – from the emotional and spiritual experiences which that world can involve. Nonetheless, I think the connections between the world of Narnia and other texts is an essential element of the books' meanings, and one which can deepen, rather than limit, the experiences they point us towards.

My first argument in favour of reading Narnia via its literary connections is a simple one: C. S. Lewis was himself a professional reader and writer about books. He was a fellow of Magdalen College in Oxford for many years, and later accepted the Chair of Mediaeval and Renaissance Literature at Cambridge. He was also a prodigiously well-read person, even for a professor of literature. He wrote landmark works on topics like literary allegory, the world-view of medieval and Renaissance poets, and the literary history of the sixteenth century. This exceptional extent of reading and literary appreciation is demonstrated by the range of texts which seem to have left their mark on Narnia. Scholars have found echoes of the eighteenth-century satirist Jonathan Swift and the Renaissance epic poet Edmund Spenser, as well as more recent writers such as Oscar Wilde and Evelyn Waugh.

Lewis's broad and deep reading is not itself an argument for approaching Narnia via literary connections. But it points to something significant about the Narnia books: the way they are visibly constructed from other texts. An obvious comparison might be made with the fantasy works of Lewis's friend and colleague J. R. R. Tolkien. His Middle-Earth was the result of years of imaginary world-building, stretching back for decades before the books were published. This makes itself felt in the feeling of depth and age in the stories: Middle-Earth has an atmosphere of the ancient which most other fantasy works lack (and which many later novelists have attempted to reproduce.) It is a fantasy world with its own prehistory, linguistic development and even archaeology. In contrast, Lewis's fantasy tales have a brightness and vividness which grab both the attention and the emotions, but they don't have the same feeling of depth to the world. It is evident to later readers (and no doubt many at the time) that Lewis was not simply writing a less carefully thought-through version of Tolkien's immersive epic style of fantasy, but rather creating in a different mode. If that's the case, it makes sense to read that mode of fantasy on its own terms. When we encounter a Classical faun, an ice-witch, talking animals and Father Christmas in the same story, we can either write the combination off as a flaw or a minor quirk of the author, or we can explore what it means to have placed those disparate figures within the same fictional landscape. Examining the connections between Narnia and other texts isn't taking us further away from the magic, by treating the books as lifeless examples of a literary theory. Instead it is paying closer attention to something distinctive and vital in the workings and meaning of Narnia.

My second argument for a literary reading of Narnia centres on the spiritual and theological complexities of the novels. Though the religious significance of the stories are not always evident in a young person's first experience of Narnia – many readers have been delighted or horrified in later life to realise they had been spending so much of their fantasy life within Christian symbolism – this is an integral part of the novels. Generations of Narnia enthusiasts have found the religious meanings as compelling and inspiring as the fantastical setting and the narratives of adventure. Their effect is not limited to young readers, either, as the academic and theological scholarship which surrounds Lewis's work will testify. Rowan Williams, previously the Archbishop of Canterbury and the Master of Magdalene College, Cambridge, did not read the Narnian stories until he was a student, but his writing testifies to the powerful effect they had upon him. 'I can only confess', writes Williams, 'to being repeatedly humbled and reconverted by Lewis in a way that is true of few other modern Christian writers'. The spiritual significance of the Narnia novels is clearly an essential element to understand about them, and one which I hope to elucidate in this book as well. Once again, this might seem an argument for avoiding the approach I have been arguing towards. It might seem that paying such close attention to literary connections is to concentrate on small textual details at the expense of the grand narrative. Examining the way one passage echoes a medieval carol and another shows influence from a fairy tale could appear to be distracting our attention from the real meanings of that passage. Especially since those meanings within the story might point us towards higher and deeper meanings in religious terms. The scholar concerned with tracking textual connections could look like someone mistaking the details of the windowpane for the world to be seen through the glass. However, I don't think that is quite true. Nor do I think it is a coincidence that Lewis, the famous preacher and apologist, wrote religious novels which display such evident connections to other books. Stories were not only important to Lewis as a professor of literature, they were also a vital part of his experience of Christianity. Indeed, it was via stories and myths that Lewis found his way back to Christian faith. Through discussions with Tolkien and other friends, he became convinced that the mythology he loved so deeply was not evidence that Christianity was just another myth like all the others. Rather, mythologies were means by which gleams and fragments of the ultimate truth made their way into human culture. Christianity was, in a sense, a myth, but it was a myth which God had created using history and humanity as the narrative and images. It was the one true myth, which all the others refracted.

This fact suggests we should look carefully at the combination of fantastical fiction and religious meaning in the Narnian novels. Stories and myths were deeply important to Lewis, not just as a means of encoding facts or truths which could be stated in more straightforward ways, but as a means of drawing closer to the experience and mystery of God. If Lewis believed that Christianity was the 'true myth', and that other mythologies and folktales contained traces of the meaning which was revealed in Christ, then there is no definitive line to be drawn between narratives which should be read and those which should be ignored. True narratives can lead us away from greater truths, and false myths can contain glimmers which point us towards the shining source of light. To me, this means that it is well worth considering the way the Narnian novels touch other tales and stories. Tracing the mass of interwoven mythological and literary narratives which Lewis loved so well, and which led him back to the Christian faith, will take us to the heart of Narnia.

THE ROBIN AND THE DRAGON

There is an example which should help to illustrate what this kind of reading can show us in practice. It involves a relatively minor moment in *The Lion, the Witch and the Wardrobe*, but one in which we can see how Lewis's literary and religious ideas wind themselves round each other. In the early chapters of the book, the Pevensie children find their way into Narnia all together, discovering that Mr Tumnus' cave has been trashed and he has been arrested by the Secret Police sent by the White Witch.

> They were all wondering what to do next, when Lucy said, 'Look! There's a robin, with such a red breast. It's the first bird I've seen here. I say! – I wonder if birds can talk in Narnia? It almost looks as if it wanted to say something to us.'[1]

Lucy asks the bird if it can tell them where Tumnus has been taken, and, though it doesn't speak, the robin leads them further into the woods and down a hill. After they have been following it for a while, Edmund expresses a reservation to Peter:

> 'We're following a guide we know nothing about. How do we know which side that bird is on? Why shouldn't it be leading us into a trap?'
>
> 'That's a nasty idea. Still – a robin, you know. They're good birds in all the stories I've ever read. I'm sure a robin wouldn't be on the wrong side.'[2]

Edmund goes on to object again, that even if the robin is on Tumnus' side, how do they know that the fauns are the right side and the White Witch is on the wrong side. The novel is unequivocal about the fact that Edmund is in the wrong: his questioning of the robin soon leads to his suggesting that they might want to side with the White Witch. But, as a number of my Narnian Reading Group pointed out when we discussed this passage, Edmund is being entirely logical. The children have found themselves in the middle of an apparent civil war between two sets of creatures, and it is only sheer chance that Lucy happened to meet a member of one side, and Edmund one of the other side. Since the robin can't talk, they don't even know which side it is allied to, let alone whether that means they should follow it or not. Still, follow it they do, and the book seems to approve their choice (not least because doing so leads them to the snugness and cheer of a meal with the beavers.)

This objection to the robin could be brushed away, on the grounds that rigorous logic is hardly very useful to children who have stumbled through a wardrobe into a land of fauns who hold tea parties. Robins are good because the children instinctively feel they're good. However, a parallel text is hinted at by Peter's reference to robins being good 'in all the stories I've ever read'. Though he does not specify further, there is one particular fictional robin which I think can expand our understanding of this encounter.

The Secret Garden by Frances Hodgson Burnett was published in 1911, and was an established children's classic by the time Lewis was writing in the 1940s. It tells the story of a young orphan called Mary who comes to live at Misselthwaite Manor in Yorkshire. Her unloving childhood has made Mary spoiled and unpleasant, but her experiences of nature and friendship at the Manor eventually bring out her more positive traits, and allow her to help others in turn. One of the book's central images is the secret garden of the title, a walled enclosure full of roses which was shut up and lost by the Manor's owner when his wife, who loved the garden, died. Mary's healing progress inward, into herself and the garden, is accompanied by a robin. He is described at several points as acting as if he were communicating with her, and he becomes the means by which she discovers the garden:

> But just at that moment the robin, who had ended his song, gave a little shake of his wings, spread them, and flew away. He had made his visit and had other things to do. 'He has flown over the wall!' Mary cried out, watching him. 'He has flown into the orchard—he has flown across the other wall—into the garden where there is no door!'[3]

The image of the robin who comes and goes from this secret, walled-off garden becomes the focus of suspense and mystery in the early part of the novel. Having shown her the garden's existence, the robin next leads Mary to the key:

> and as the robin hopped about under them she saw him hop over a small pile of freshly turned-up earth. He stopped on it to look for a worm. The earth had been turned up because a dog had been trying to dig up a mole and he had scratched quite a deep hole. Mary looked at it, not really knowing why the hole was there, and as she looked she saw something almost buried in the newly turned soil.
>
> It was something like a ring of rusty iron or brass, and when the robin flew up into a tree near by she put out her hand and picked the ring up. It was more than a ring, however; it was an old key which looked as if it had been buried a long time. Mistress Mary stood up and looked at it with an almost frightened face as it hung from her finger. 'Perhaps it has been buried for ten years,' she said in a whisper. 'Perhaps it is the key to the garden!' [4]

INTRODUCTION

Developing the idea that the robin will be her means of finding the garden, Mary jokingly speaks to it:

> 'You showed me where the key was yesterday,' she said. 'You ought to show me the door today; but I don't believe you know!'
>
> The robin flew from his swinging spray of ivy on to the top of the wall and he opened his beak and sang a loud, lovely trill, merely to show off. Nothing in the world is quite as adorably lovely as a robin when he shows off—and they are nearly always doing it.
>
> Mary Lennox had heard a great deal about Magic in her Ayah's stories, and she always said what happened almost at that moment was Magic. One of the nice little gusts of wind rushed down the walk, and it was a stronger one than the rest. It was strong enough to wave the branches of the trees, and it was more than strong enough to sway the trailing sprays of untrimmed ivy hanging from the wall.
>
> Mary had stepped close to the robin, and suddenly the gust of wind swung aside some loose ivy trails, and more suddenly still she jumped towards it and caught it in her hand.[5]

It is the handle of the door into the secret garden. This excursion into Burnett's Yorkshire landscape helps expand our vision of the passage where the Pevensies follow their own robin. It suggests a possible origin both for Lewis's inclusion of a helpful robin, and for Peter's belief that robins are good and should be followed. It does more than that, however. The echo of *The Secret Garden* layers other ideas into this early chapter of *The Lion, the Witch and the Wardrobe*. Although they do not yet know it, the robin is leading them towards talking animals who are on the side of Aslan. That side is opposed to the magical winter of the witch, since, in the words of the old rhyme recited by Mr

Beaver, 'when he bares his teeth, winter meets its death/ And when he shakes his mane, we shall have spring again'. This robin is leading the Pevensies towards the sprouting foliage of spring, just as Mary's robin leads her to the secret garden which she will restore to verdant growth. Indeed, a later passage from *The Secret Garden* strikes the same note of ecstatic delight in spring as the Narnians feel:

> 'Things are crowding up out of the earth,' she ran on in a hurry. 'And there are flowers uncurling and buds on everything and the green veil has covered nearly all the grey and the birds are in such a hurry about their nests for fear they may be too late, that some of them are even fighting for places in the secret garden. And the rosebushes look as wick as wick can be, and there are primroses in the lanes and woods, and the seeds we planted are up.[6]

As the power of the Witch weakens in Narnia, Lewis provides a similar passage of description:

> Only five minutes later he noticed a dozen crocuses growing round the foot of an old tree – gold and purple and white. Then came a sound even more delicious than the sound of the water. Close beside the path they were following a bird suddenly chirped from the branch of a tree. It was answered by the chuckle of another bird a little further off ... wherever Edmund's eyes turned he saw birds alighting on branches, or sailing overhead or chasing one another or having their little quarrels or tidying up their feathers with their beaks ... There was no trace of the fog now. The sky became bluer and bluer ... In the wide glades there were primroses.[7]

Speaking to the robin, and following where he leads, begins the Pevensies' actions in Narnia on the side of life and spring.

INTRODUCTION

Mary's own story connects the idea of growing plants and personal healing, both of which are brought by Aslan's return. There is also a strong Christian resonance in the idea of a lost and bitter human finding the way back into a magical garden, which may have appealed to Lewis. After all, the Fall saw humankind banished from Eden in Genesis, and Christ's redemption is often described as restoring them to the blessings of the garden. Preachers and artists have made much of the fact that when Mary Magdalen first sees the risen Jesus, she mistakes him for a gardener.

The seventeenth-century preacher Lancelot Andrewes declared that by making that mistake 'she was in the right'. He continues:

> For in a sense, and a good sense, Christ may well be said to be a gardener, and indeed is one ...

1   A gardener He is then. The first, the fairest garden that ever was, Paradise, He was the gardener, it was of His planting. So, a gardener.
2   And ever since it is He That as God makes all our gardens green, sends us yearly the spring, and all the herbs and flowers we then gather, and neither Paul with his planting, nor Apollos with his watering, could do any good without Him. So a gardener in that sense.
3. But not in that sense alone; but He it is that gardens our 'souls' too, and makes them, as the Prophet saith, 'like a well-watered garden' weeds out of them whatsoever is noisome or unsavory, sows and plants them with true roots and seeds of righteousness, waters them with the dew of His grace, and make them bring forth fruit to eternal life.

But it is none of these, but besides all these, nay over and above all these, this day if ever, most properly He was a gardener. Was one, and so after a more peculiar manner might take this likeness on Him. Christ rising was indeed a gardener, and that a strange one, Who made such an herb grow out of the ground this day as the like was never seen before, a dead body to shoot forth alive out of the grave.

I ask, was He so this day alone? No, but this profession of His this day begun, He will follow to the end. For He it is That by virtue of this morning's act shall garden our bodies too, turn all our graves into garden plots, yea shall one day turn land and sea and all into a great garden, and so husband them as they shall in due time bring forth live bodies, even all our bodies alive again.[8]

Aside from the intoxication of Andrewes' style, which was much admired by writers such as T. S. Eliot and Lewis himself, we can see an important combination of ideas in this passage. In teasing out all the implications of an image like Christ as gardener, Andrewes connects it on a cosmological level, with the creation of the Garden of Eden, a personal level, with Christ the 'gardener' of our souls, and on a natural level, with Christ as the bringer of the spring each year. A similar association of ideas appears in *The Lion, the Witch and the Wardrobe*, where Aslan's very arrival in Narnia begins to make the snow thaw and the plants appear above the soil. This sense of the appearance of Christ as analogous to (or accompanied by) the arrival of spring appears in Christian readings of the Song of Solomon. This set of ecstatic love poems is interpreted in both Jewish and Christian traditions as a mystical allegory of the yearning for God's presence. One especially well-known passage, which has been set by musicians like the Tudor composer Thomas Tomkins and the Restoration composer Henry Purcell, runs thus:

INTRODUCTION

> My beloved spake, and said unto me, Rise up, my love, my fair one, and come away. For, lo, the winter is past, the rain is over and gone; The flowers appear on the earth; the time of the singing of birds is come, and the voice of the turtle [dove] is heard in our land; The fig tree putteth forth her green figs, and the vines with the tender grape give a good smell. Arise, my love, my fair one, and come away. (2:10-12)[9]

Aslan's association with the green shoots of spring and the singing of birds is thus not simply because these things are nice, and a bit of a cliché in writing about the English countryside. It is part of a Christian tradition which associates the arrival of the Beloved with the new season, and connects Mary Magdalene's mistake over Christ's identity with the idea of the garden of Eden and the gardener of the resurrection. Lewis's novel fuses these metaphorical ideas together and installs them in the workings of his fantasy universe, so it is literally the arrival of the Messiah which causes spring to happen. There is no actual garden in Narnia, but the way Aslan's arrival heralds the end of the long winter imposed by the Witch connects the idea of redemption to the image of flourishing flowers and birds.

The parallel I've drawn between the robin which the Pevensies follow, and the robin of *The Secret Garden*, isn't essential to following the narrative at this point. We won't lose anything from the plot if we don't wonder which stories Peter might be thinking of when he trusts the robin, or if we don't remember a girl in Yorkshire trying to find her way into the garden. However, these connections do expand the symbolism of the novel. They draw in other images and resonances which add a depth and richness to this relatively brief passage. Drawing that connection also allows us to consider the theological themes implicit in these images, such as the way redemption and the new growth of spring are imaginatively linked.

Another example, from the medieval Scottish poet William Dunbar, gives a broader and more diffuse perspective on Lewis's literary and theological imagination. Dunbar was a fourteenth-century poet and priest, though some of his verse is considerably more forthright (not to say crude) than a modern audience might expect. Lewis was particularly fond of his poem on the subject of Easter Day calling it 'language of thundering and unanswerable greatness' and stating that from the first line to the last '[it] defies the powes of evil and has the ring of a steel gauntlet flung down'.[10] The refrain means 'the Lord is risen from the tomb', and the first and third verses run like this:

> Done is a battell on the dragon blak,
> *Done is a battle on the dragon black*
> Our campioun Chryst confountet hes his force;
> *Our champion Christ confounded all his force*
> The yettis of hell ar brokin with a crak,
> *The gates of hell are broken with a crack*
> The signe triumphall rasit is of the croce,
> *The triumph sign is raised up, of the cross*
> The divillis trymmillis with hiddous voce,
> *The devils tremble with their hideous voice*
> The saulis ar borrowit and to the blis can go,
> *The souls are borrowed, and to the bliss can go*
> Chryst with his blud our ransonis dois indoce:
> *Christ with his blood our ransom does endorse*
> Surrexit Dominus de sepulchro.
> *Surrexit Dominus de sepulchro*
>
> He for our saik that sufferit to be slane,
> *He that, for our sake, suffered to be slain*

INTRODUCTION

And lyk a lamb in sacrifice wes dicht,
And like a lamb in sacrifice was done to death
Is lyk a lyone rissin up againe,
Is like a lion risen up again
And as gyane raxit him on hicht;
And like a giant raised himself on high
Sprungin is Aurora radius and bricht,
Sprung is Aurora, radiant and bright
On loft is gone the glorius Appollo,
Aloft is gone the glorious Apollo
The blisfull day depairtit fro the nicht:
The blissful day has left behind the night
Surrexit Dominus de sepulchro.
Surrexit Dominus de sepulchro

Anyone familiar with Narnia will be struck by a poem which celebrates the resurrection with the image of a lion rising up again. A reread of *The Lion, the Witch and the Wardrobe* might also note the presence of Giant Rumblebuffin, and the fact that Rumblebuffin smashes the gates of the White Witch's castle to let out the creatures whom Aslan has brought back to life. Closer attention to the breaking of the Stone Table would notice that it happened at the moment of dawn, when the sun rose from the sea, whilst the two Classical gods mentioned by Dunbar are Aurora, goddess of the dawn, and Apollo the sun-god. These images are not original to Dunbar: the Bible refers to the Lion of Judah, and medieval sermons and paintings depicted the breaking of the gates of hell to release the captives. It cannot be proved that Lewis was inspired by this particular poem, rather than gathering the same images himself from other sources (though they do all occur together in a poem we know he admired). However, there is something very Narnian about the way they are bundled together in this poem, with biblical titles jostling against medieval doctrines and

Classical allusions. Dunbar's enthusiastic, even wild, layering of images and symbols on top of each other, to produce an ecstatic proclamation of the risen Christ, has a lot in common with Lewis's approach in *The Lion, the Witch and the Wardrobe*. I believe Dunbar gives up both a glimpse into Lewis's sources of inspiration, and a hint as to how we could read his novel.

PATHS IN THE SNOW

These are the kinds of connections and echoes I'll explore in the following chapters. Literary resonances which deepen our understanding of the meanings which suffuse Narnia. They're not all of the same kind. Some are from earlier texts which I think have influenced Lewis. Dunbar's poem, for example, is one which we know Lewis read and admired. Certain lines of it seem to have left a mark on the imagery and even the plotting of the later part of *The Lion, the Witch and the Wardrobe*. Other connections can be drawn with texts from Lewis's own era, even from a couple of years after he published the first Narnia novel, because they illuminate an aspect of the cultural and historical world he was writing in. I draw a parallel, for example, between Narnia and J. B. Priestley's *An Inspector Calls*, which plays with mid-century ideas about time and causality, drawing on the theories of J. W. Dunne, which were popular with intellectuals and writers of the era. Lewis was not necessarily alluding to Priestley's play specifically, but I discuss it because it shows the theme of time being handled in a way which casts light on the puzzle of Narnian time.

There are even some texts from some time after Lewis's era which I mention in order to draw contrasts with what happened in the genre which he did so much to shape (though these are relatively rarer). The feasts in the *Harry Potter* novels, for example, seem to be descended from the convivial meals of *The Lion, the Witch and the Wardrobe*, and yet have a rather different cultural meaning because of the time and place when they were written. Finally, there are echoes and allusions to a text which might seem so obvious and dominant in Narnia as to need no discussion at all: the Bible. These are worth examining and teasing out, because the specific verses and scenes which Lewis chooses to rework in Narnia give the fantastical world much of its shape and meaning. His choice, for example, to place the Deeper Magic *before* the dawn of time is an allusion to the idea of the Logos at the opening of John's Gospel and affects his depiction of Aslan as saviour. It can be just as important when Lewis chooses to omit or change an element of a scene, such as when Susan and Lucy ask to stay up with Aslan because they cannot sleep. Lewis's borrowings from the Bible are by no means straightforward, and the artistry with which he selects and interweaves details is a central part of the novel.

In the end, each tracing of an echo or a reference is intended to bring us back to the text of *The Lion, the Witch and the Wardrobe*. I have only included parallels and connections which seem to me to enrich our understanding of the text, to reveal shades of meaning which were not obvious before. This book is intended to carry on the process which I have enjoyed so much sharing with my parish and with the Narnia Club: of exploring the landscape of Narnia in deeper detail, and by doing so, being drawn more deeply into the mysteries which can be glimpsed over its horizons.

PRACTICAL NOTES

This book will be best enjoyed by readers who have either committed the entire text of *The Lion, the Witch and the Wardrobe* to memory, or have a copy to hand whilst reading. You will probably want to remind yourself of crucial moments, or look up specific lines. My discussion of the book moves forward chapter by chapter, but I sometimes refer to other chapters or later plot points. This means that you really need to have read Lewis's novel first: otherwise there is a risk of bafflement or even plot spoilers. In each chapter I don't attempt to summarise or comment on the whole plot, but rather pick out details and connections which strike me as worth investigating further. For this reason some chapters are much longer than others, and some much shorter. I hope this doesn't mean I give your favourite passages of the book short shrift, but if I do, I hope it encourages you to find a friend or family member and explain to them at length what I have missed out. At least then they will benefit from my omission. When referring to a text not written in modern English, I have usually provided a translation. The cut-off point is roughly the turn of the seventeenth century; I have assumed that most readers do not need a translation of Shakespeare or the King James Bible, but that they will need one for earlier texts. The translations are my own unless noted otherwise, though (as with any translation) they are informed and influenced by much better versions by other writers. In making the translations I have not attempted to produce a smooth or satisfactory version in modern English, but instead to give a decent rendering which enables the reader to recognise the words in the original text. In each case I thought it would be more useful to point the reader towards the text as best I could, rather than trying to replace it and assure them that the modern version includes everything they need. In this book, more than most, it seemed useful to demonstrate the oddness and potential interest of other texts.

CHAPTER ONE

LUCY LOOKS INTO A WARDROBE

A TAIL OF THE ELDER TIMES

> Once there were four children whose names were Peter,
> Susan, Edmund and Lucy. This story is about something that
> happened to them when they were sent away from London
> during the war because of the air-raids.[11]

T he first sentences of *The Lion, the Witch and the Wardrobe*
contain the first literary echo of the novel, and deftly set
up a tension which will last through the entire series.
These two sentences hint things about the worlds, and the
time, which the Narnia novels will explore. 'Once, there were
four children … ' has an unmistakable ring to it. It is one we're
familiar with from our childhood. It is the formula to begin a
fairy tale. 'Once upon a time, there was a beautiful princess … '
'Once, on the shores of a loch … ' 'Once, under the tallest oak
tree in the forest … ' The word establishes a particular mood
at the beginning of a book. It invites us to listen in the way we
used to as children, to settle in and enjoy a story. It also prepares
us to hear about certain kinds of things: magic, heroism, fate,
talking animals, wicked stepmothers, fabulous treasures,
shape-shifting. It brings with it a whole set of expectations and
memories which will enable us properly to understand the
things that will happen in the following story. We won't be able
to predict what happens, necessarily, but we will be able to
appreciate it properly according to the understood rules of the
form. 'Once' is a powerful word. In this case, it places us in a
world of children's fiction and suggest a connection to a specific
and very famous example of that genre. 'Once there were four

children whose names were Peter, Susan, Edmund and Lucy', has the ring of another well-known literary text's opening lines:

> Once upon a time there were four little Rabbits, and their names were— Flopsy, Mopsy, Cotton-tail, and Peter. They lived with their Mother in a sand-bank, underneath the root of a very big fir-tree. 'Now my dears,' said old Mrs. Rabbit one morning, 'you may go into the fields or down the lane, but don't go into Mr. McGregor's garden: your Father had an accident there; he was put in a pie by Mrs. McGregor.'[12]

Several key themes of *The Lion, the Witch and the Wardrobe* are here immediately: a world in which animals can talk, a character who crosses over the divisions between two worlds, and the risk to life and limb which happens after that transgression. That may sound rather facetious, but C. S. Lewis took the stories of Beatrix Potter very seriously. His approach to literature, as expressed in his essays on books and his critical treatise *An Experiment in Criticism*, did not allow the relegation of 'books for children' into a separate and lesser category of writing. Indeed, in that treatise he suggests at one point that children's experience of literature can be as genuine and true as that of adults, commenting that in some self-consciously cultured households 'the only real literary experience ... may be occurring in a back bedroom where a small boy is reading *Treasure Island* under the bed-clothes by the light of an electric torch'.[13] In another essay he insisted that *The Tale of Peter Rabbit*, from which the quotation above is taken, was as valid a piece of data for the literary scholar as any other work, mentioning his response to a literary theory which a student had proposed:

> Applying the elenchus after my fashion I inquired whether her theory would cover *The Tale of Peter Rabbit*. After a silence

of some minutes, she asked me if I thought there was any use in introducing such an example into a serious literary discussion.[14]

He evidently did think it was worthwhile. For Lewis to begin a novel which reiterated the doctrine of the atonement and other mysteries of Christian faith by alluding slyly to *Peter Rabbit* would be simply following his own literary principles.

The sentence which starts with 'once', opening up a vista of fairy-tales, magical happenings and talking animals, is followed with one in a rather different tone. 'This story is about something that happened to them when they were sent away from London during the war because of the air-raids.' This sets up another kind of fictional time. It is chronologically specific, refers to recent military and political history, and provides a dateable range for the narrative. The novel was published in 1950, five years after the end of the Second World War. This means it does not qualify as historical fiction in conventional terms, since it deals with events which are not only within living memory but really quite recent. At least, that is the case for adults. Most child readers of *The Lion, the Witch and the Wardrobe* (or children to whom it was read) would have a less certain perspective. After all, a five-year-old would not remember the war at all, a ten-year-old would have been born during it, and a fifteen-year-old would have some secure (if brief) memories of the world before the war. Thus, for some small readers it would have ended before they could remember, and for others it would be a defining memory which they could barely peer beyond. The matter-of-fact language of 'during the war' and 'when they were sent away ... because of the air-raids' certainly assumes that the audience have the same sort of knowledge as the author: the narrative does not pause to explain which war is being discussed, or anything about the programme of evacuation which took children (and sometimes their mothers) into the country away from built-up areas in danger of German bombing. Thus the opening of the story juxtaposes two very different kinds of time. Firstly, the whimsical, fairy-tale tale of 'once'. A world in which time is not structured in the same way as in our world. It makes little sense to ask whether Cinderella went to the ball before or after the attempted invasion of Britain by the Spanish Armada. That is not the kind of story being told. Nor, in fact, does it make much more sense to ask whether Cinderella went to the ball before or after Goldilocks wandered into the house of the Three Bears. Time in this mode is not chronological, events are suspended in an eternal 'once'. Secondly, there is the everyday and historical time of the air raids and the evacuation programme. It is reasonably recent, findable in newspapers and has had an effect on the current situation. (A drastic effect, in some ways, as we will notice in a later chapter discussing food rationing.) The narrative presents us with these two kinds of time in the first two sentences, and we may not yet realise how different they are. Lucy is soon going to pass from one mode of time to another, and when she gets back both she and her siblings will discover that the two modes do not translate easily into each other. On a larger scale, the Narnia novels present the reader with the challenge, and the quest, of how to inhabit the two kinds of time themselves.

INTO THE WOODS

In the meantime, as Lucy first finds her way into Narnia, there is an echo of a literary work to rival *The Tale of Peter Rabbit*: the *Divine Comedy* of Dante Alighieri. Dante was an Italian poet, though many would say he is *the* Italian poet, given the range and influence of his writings. He composed his most famous work, the epic *Divine Comedy,* in the early fourteenth century, and it relates the story of the poet himself travelling through the realms of the afterlife. Its three books, *Hell*, *Purgatory* and *Paradise*, are packed with characters from recent religious and political history, and figures whom the poem's readers would have recognised undergo symbolic punishments or enjoy symbolic rewards which suit the lives they lived on earth. It is a rapid and vivid work, which had a huge influence on renaissance literature. The very beginning of the epic tells of how Dante began his voyage into the worlds beyond ours:

> Nel mezzo del cammin di nostra vita
> mi ritrovai per una selva oscura
> ché la diritta via era smarrita.

> *In the middle of this road of life we travel*
> *I found myself within a shadowy wood*
> *Where the right path was lost*[15]

This is not unlike what has happened to Lucy. Like the Italian poet, this English schoolgirl blunders her way unknowingly from the mundane world into an unknown wood, where they will both meet a guide. (The great Roman poet Virgil in his case, the faun Tumnus in hers.) As well as the general setting of the wood, which might be equally suited to Shakespeare's Athenian lovers or the fairy-tale *Hansel and Gretel*, there is a verbal echo which hints at a Dante connection. That second line, '*mi ritrovai per una selva oscura*' ('I found myself in a shadowy wood') uses the word 'ritrovai' for Dante's experience. In Italian it means more or less 'I found', with a similar range of meaning to its English equivalent: one can 'find' an object like a book or a ring, one can 'find' oneself in a place by realising where one is, and one can 'find' something to be the case ('I found it boring', 'I find it too cold', etc). In fact another version of the same verb appears in the third stanza, when Dante has explained that the wood was so threatening and terrible that even the memory of it is unpleasant:

> ma per trattar del ben ch'i' vi trovai,
> dirò de l'altre cose ch'i' v'ho scorte.
>
> *But to relate the good which I found there,*
> *I'll also tell the other things I saw.*

We're ready to hear about his adventures including the good which Dante '*trovai*', or found, after he had '*ritrovai*' himself in the wood. I have focused on this word with such pedantry because its English equivalent crops up repeatedly in Lucy's discovery of Narnia. 'Soon she went further in and found that there was a second row of coats hanging up behind the first one' … 'Next moment she found that what was rubbing against her face and hands was no longer soft fur, but something hard and rough and even prickly', 'a moment later she found that she was standing in the middle of a wood at night-time'.[16]

In pointing out the parallels between Dante 'finding' himself in a wood, and Lucy 'finding' herself in one, I'm not suggesting that Lewis deliberately picked this word from the opening of the *Inferno*, and 'hid' it in his novel as a clue. I think it is much more likely that Lewis, having used Dante's opening image as a model for his own character's blundering into the magical wood, was unconsciously reminded of the phrasing of the poem. Lucy's repeated 'finding' of things is a trace, a dimly visible imprint of the original work which had an effect on the Narnian story. I would speculate that when Lewis came to write the scene, these words just seemed to fit his character's experiences and feelings. They felt imaginatively and creatively 'right'. Only on comparing the two texts later is a reader likely to notice the apparent borrowing of textual detail. For a writer like Lewis, who was so widely read and so steeped in medieval and Renaissance literature, the creative process was always likely to draw on the earlier works in literary tradition. His imagination had been shaped and fed by that tradition. In fact, it is entirely possible that Lewis did not have Dante's *Divine Comedy* in mind when he wrote the scene of Lucy wandering through the wardrobe into Narnia. That may seem a self-defeating suggestion, when I have just spent quite some time arguing that situation, plot and even individual verbs associate the two works. However, that would not mean that there is no connection between Narnia and the *Inferno*. It would simply mean that Lewis's memory and imagination were working in combination, so that when he created a scene of a character moving from our world to another world, he instinctively drew on Dante's great work. This is a point worth stressing for the chapters which follow: in tracing the apparent literary allusions in *The Lion, the Witch and the Wardrobe*, I am not suggesting that Lewis sat down and drew up an elaborate plot of where he would hide quotations from older texts. Nor am I suggesting that when we have identified an allusion, we have 'solved' the text. Recognising the potential influence of Dante on this scene does not mean that Lucy is 'actually' Dante's poet-wanderer, or that Narnia is 'actually' the Inferno. One meaning does not replace or overwrite the other. Instead, we can read Lewis's book with a richer awareness of its literary surroundings, and of the tradition it participates in. We might compare this to a painting, where the depth and texture of the shadows makes the figures in the foreground stand out more brightly and dramatically.

This raises the question of how our reading of Narnia might be affected by the recognition of this echo from Dante. I think it sets up a framework for interpreting the story in a couple of ways. Firstly, it emphasises the fact that Lucy will encounter a world of moral choices and consequences. The Pevensies will be thrown into the middle of a conflict where they need to literally choose sides, and face peril because of the decisions they have made. This is not evident at the moment when Lucy steps into the wardrobe, but the echoes of Dante offer these implications. Secondly, the resonances with the *Divine Comedy* emphasise the huge scope of the plot which the children will participate in. Dante's epic covers the whole of hell, purgatory and heaven, culminating in a vision of God. There is a similarly epic scope to the Narnia novels: the children initially become involved in the liberation of the country called Narnia, then other books add other countries and even a Creation and Apocalypse. Even before the narrative moves beyond the bounds of Lantern Waste and Cair Paravel, the Pevensies encounter Aslan. The stakes of this story are very large indeed, and questions of ultimate reality, as well as questions of good and evil, are woven through the narrative. It may be that neither of these points seems particularly astonishing, and that anyone reading *The Lion, the Witch and the Wardrobe* today is already expecting children's fantasy novels to be about young characters who are involved in saving whole worlds and in meeting divine beings. However, it is worth pointing out that this had not been the norm for fantasy before Lewis's generation. Especially in the case of children's fiction, the stakes had usually been much lower than the metaphysical scale on which Lewis and his Pevensies operate. Farah Mendlesohn and Michael Levy describe this change in post-war children's fantasy, noting that Narnia 'epitomised and encoded' a change to stories concerned with whole worlds and their salvation.[17] One of the major developments visible in *The Lion, the Witch and the Wardrobe* is the combining of children having a whimsical adventure in the countryside, a tale of talking animals, and the cosmological backdrop of works like *The Divine Comedy* and *Paradise Lost*. In other words, it is possible that the echoes of Dante (and of medieval romance) which I think we can hear in Lucy's journey through the wardrobe seem to add little to our experience of the book, only because they been part of something which fundamentally changed the entire genre.

THE LITTLE GIRL AND THE FAIRIES

Having jumped ahead to Lucy's finding herself in Narnia, I'd now like to retrace her steps and pause just before she found the wardrobe. This is slightly out of the novel's sequence, but there are some minor but telling details which we can easily hurry past on the way to that portal. Lucy, with the other Pevensies, wanders through some rooms of the Professor's house. On first reading (or on fifth) these might not seem that important. She does not pay that much attention to them, and the story never returns to these empty rooms and corridors. The point of them is simply that Lucy is getting mildly lost, and that she might happen upon something interesting in the depths of the old place. However, on rereading them closely, I think something more is going on here. It's an image which recurs in various forms later in the series. Lucy herself has to 'free' the Dufflepuds in *The Voyage of the Dawn Treader* by a walk through a similar empty, upstairs corridor of the house of the wizard. In *The Magician's Nephew* Polly and Digory stumble across the magical experiments of Uncle Andrew whilst exploring the attics above their house.

In this case, Lewis describes the rooms thus:

> The first few doors they tried led only into spare bedrooms, as everyone had expected that they would; but soon they came to a very long room full of pictures, and there they found a suit of armour; and after that was a room all hung with green, with a harp in one corner.[18]

After this comes 'a whole series of rooms that led into each other and were lined with books – most of them very old books and some bigger than a Bible in a church'.[19] This, at least, is a hopeful image for anyone paying attention to the literary echoes resonating in Narnia: to get there the Pevensies have to walk through rooms crammed with old books. If we see these rooms as bringing them (unknowingly) closer to the adventures in Narnia, there is a touch of the Gothic in the long gallery of portraits and a suit of armour. It hints that the children exploring the big, almost empty house, might come across strange and threatening secrets. The room 'all hung with green, with a harp in one corner' is slightly more obscure. Nonetheless, I believe it provides a strong suggestion about what is about to happen to one of the children. In order to explain it, we must look at an anonymous medieval poem about a queen stolen by the fairies.

The poem known as *Sir Orfeo* was written around the turn of the fourteenth century, in the language now known as 'Middle English'. It tells the story of a noble king, who is the greatest harp-player ever known, and whose wife Heurodis is stolen away by the king of the fairies. The king puts his lands in the hands of a steward and goes out to live in the wilderness to lament his lost love. After much wandering and harp-playing, he sees his wife riding in a company of mysterious ladies. He follows them through a cliff, and into the lands of the fairies. Arriving at the castle of the fairy king, he sees a collection of people who have been stolen by the fairies, and exist in a sort of suspended animation. When Orfeo has played his harp for the fairies, the king is so pleased that he offers him anything he wants. Orfeo chooses Heurodis as a reward, and returns with her to our world. When he returns to his own lands, he has been living in the wilderness for so long that no-one recognises him. His steward, however, sees the harp he is playing, and Orfeo explains that he found it in the wilderness next to a dead body. The steward laments at the death of his king, whereupon Orfeo reveals himself and rewards the man for his loyalty. The poem ends with a statement that this song was made by harpers in Brittany, and a wish that God will save everyone present just as he has brought Orfeo out of his troubles. Readers with a taste for Classical mythology will probably have recognised that this poem, which has a king called 'Orfeo' who visits another world to recover his lost love 'Heurodis', is a medieval reworking of the myth of Orpheus and Euridice. This is a rather more cheerful version, since it ends with virtue rewarded and happiness restored, but the outlines of the story are very similar. The city of the fairy king, with its unnerving picture of people stolen away from our world, occupies a similar position to Hades in the classical myth.

I mention this poem because it combines the two elements which we see in the room the Pevensies wander through shortly before Lucy enters Narnia: the colour green and the harp. The poem opens thus:

> We redeth oft and findeth y-write –
> *Often we read, and find written*
> And this clerkes wele it wite –
> *And these scholars know this very well*
> Layes that ben in harping
> *That stories that are in song*
> Ben y-founde of ferli thing:
> *Are made about marvellous things*
> Sum beth of wer, and sum of wo
> *Some are tales of war, and some of woe*
> And sum of joie and mirthe also,
> *And some of joy and mirth also*
> And sum of trecherie and gile,
> *And some of treachery and guile*
> Of old aventours that fel while,
> *Of old adventures that happened long ago*

And sum of bourdes and ribaudy –
And some of jokes and ribaldry
And an ither beth of fairy.[20]
And many are about fairy things

'Fairy things', incidentally, does not mean the kind of fairy generally popular in children's books in the nineteenth and twentieth centuries. As many people fond of fantasy novels will know, and as will have been clear from the brief outline of *Sir Orfeo* above, the word 'fairy' has had a range of meanings over the years. The Victorian fairies, tiny, dainty creatures like miniature children with gossamer wings and a predilection for hiding in flowers, are a relatively recent creation. Though they do draw on an older tradition of literary ideas about fairies: Shakespeare, after all, in *A Midsummer Night's Dream*, gave Titania fairy attendants called things like Mustard-Seed and Cowslip who could steal honey from bees. However, the fairies of the medieval tradition which we find in *Sir Orfeo* are human-sized and much less whimsical. They have a king and a kingdom, complete with lands and castles and retinues of fairy knights. They seem to have some magical abilities, such as travelling long distances, appearing and disappearing suddenly, and possibly being able to ride through solid rock; but these are not equated with the insubstantial quality of Victorian fairies, or of ghosts. A group of fairy warriors who can appear apparently by magic in an orchard are also a physical threat to those who might attack them. These kinds of fairies (as Ronald Hutton has pointed out) are less like the 'fairies' which the post-Victorian imagination conjures up, and more like the high elves of J. R. R. Tolkien's novels.

The harp which the Pevensies found in the empty room finds a parallel in the mention of 'lais that ben in harping' in the opening of this poem (even though 'harping' here means more generally 'song'). It goes on to mention that Breton musicians 'token an harp in gle and game' (took up a harp in music and fun), and made this poem.[21] The same motif blurs into the story itself, since the tale immediately tells us that 'Orfeo mest of ani thing/ Lovede the gle of harping' (Orfeo loved the music and joy of harping more than anything else) that he rewarded good harpers at his court, and that he loved to play the instrument himself. Indeed, 'he lerned so, ther nothing was/ A better harper in no plas' (he learned to play so well that there was no better harper anywhere) and that 'he myght of his harping her/ He shulde thinke that he wer/ In one of the joys of Paradys' (anyone who heard Orfeo play the harp would think that he was enjoying the delights of heaven).[22] At this point, 'harping' seems a most suitable word for the poem's obsession with the instrument.

The harp is a central symbol of *Sir Orfeo*: it is the means by which the poem says it was itself composed, it is the past-time of the central character, it is the only object he takes into the wilderness, it is the means by which he wins his wife back, and it is the token by which he tests his steward on returning. I think the harp in the green-draped room is hinting at the presence of *Sir Orfeo* alongside the Pevensies' explorations in the Professor's house. Lucy is about to accidentally wander into the world of Narnia, just as Heurodis is taken to the fairies' land. In something of a twist, it will not be her who becomes the property of the sinister ruler of this land, but rather the boy who went in after her. Edmund will need rescuing rather than Lucy. The colour of the room also provides a suggestion of the uncanny in a specifically medieval way. Green appears in many medieval texts when fairies or otherworldly creatures are about. In *Sir Orfeo*, when the king was found his way into the fairy kingdom, it is described as 'a fair cuntray/ As bright so sonne on somers day/ Smothe and plain and al grene' (a fair country, as bright as the sun on a summer's day, smooth and level and all green).[23] Of course there is nothing inherently remarkable about a landscape being described as green, but other texts associate the colour with fairies. Mostly famously, one of the title characters of *Sir Gawain and the Green Knight* is entirely that colour. When this mysterious knight arrives at Camelot during the Christmas feast and challenges King Arthur's knights to an adventure, the poem describes both his great size and his unusual tint:

> And his lyndes and his lymes so longe and so grete,
> *And his loins and his limbs so long and so great*
> Half etayn in erde I hope þat he were,
> *I think he must have been half a giant*
> Bot mon most I algate mynn hym to bene,
> *But I certainly must declare him to be the biggest man*
> And þat þe myriest in his muckel þat myȝt ride;
> *And the finest of that size that ever rode a horse*
> For of bak and of brest al were his bodi sturne,
> *For his body was strong at his back and his front*
> Both his wombe and his wast were worthily smale,
> *His stomach and his waist were trim and small*
> And alle his eatures folȝande, in forme þat he hade, ful clene;
> *And all his features were in proportion, neatly*
> For wonder of his hwe men hade,
> *His colour surprised everyone*
> Set in his semblaunt sene;
> *As he appeared to them there*
> He ferde as freke were fade,
> *He held himself boldly*
> And oueral enker-grene.
> *And overall he was entirely green*
> Ande al grayþed in grene þis gome and his wedes:
> *This man and his clothes were coloured green*

LUCY LOOKS INTO A WARDROBE

Up in Scotland, another poem about the fairy realm by the late medieval poet William Dunbar, involves a group of noble ladies all dressed in green, some bearing harps:

> And ober one of thir, in grene arayit,
> *And every one of them, dressed in green*
> On harp or lute full merily thai playit,
> *On harp or lute they played very merrily*
> And sang ballettis with michty notis clere:
> *And sang ballads with strong, clear notes*
> Ladyes to dance full soberly assayit,
> *Ladies set to a stately dance*
> Endlang the lusty ryvir so thai mayit,
> *And made merry along the lovely river*
> Thair observance rycht hevynly was to here;
> *Their customary ceremony was heavenly to hear*

Near these ladies, the poet sees several of the classical gods, including Neptune, Janus and Bacchus. Amongst them he notices 'Pluto, the eldritch incubus, In cloke of grene, his court usit no sable' (Pluto, the elvish incubus, In a green cloak, no-one in his court wears black). Pluto, the god of the underworld, is not only described as an 'elvish incubus', linking him with folkloric fairy-like creatures and wicked spirits, but as wearing a green cloak. More than this, Dunbar mentions that whilst one might expect a figure like Pluto to wear sable, in fact no-one at his court does. (With an implication that green is the appropriate colour for the courtiers of the elvish lord of the underworld.) The green hangings in the harp room look almost like a danger signal, in the context of these poems.

By the end of this chapter, then, Lewis's text is resonating with echoes from earlier works. His young heroine has walked through empty rooms which hint at fairies, high adventure, the underworld and kidnapping. She has found herself in a wood which suggests that a descent into a bleak and terrible realm will result in a vision of holy glory. She has been named in a way which suggests there may be talking animals somewhere about the place. As these traces of texts from Renaissance Florence, medieval England and the Victorian Lake District become just visible around her, Lucy walks further into Narnia and meets someone.

CHAPTER TWO

WHAT LUCY FOUND THERE

At the end of the last chapter, Lucy had found her way into Narnia and met a remarkable person. We will consider Mr Tumnus at some length below, but before Lucy can enquire about his identity or even name, he asks her a crucial question. ' ... should I be right in thinking that you are a Daughter of Eve?' In order to explore the significance of that question, and why the book shows Tumnus enquiring about Lucy rather than the other way round, I shall start from another part of the English landscape.

HAVE YOU EVER HEARD ME SAY THAT WORD ...

Puck of Pook's Hill was published in 1906 by Rudyard Kipling, a writer more famous these days for his *Jungle Book* and *Just So Stories*. It begins with two children in the English countryside on Midsummer Eve, performing a scene from *A Midsummer Night's Dream*. They have come out for a picnic, and to enjoy the summer afternoon, but after they have recited their bit of Shakespeare, someone else joins them: 'The bushes parted. In the very spot where Dan had stood as Puck they saw a small, brown, broad-shouldered, pointy-eared person with a snub nose, slanting blue eyes, and a grin that ran right across his freckled face.'[24] This person turns out to be Puck himself, accidentally called out of the countryside by the fact that they have been performing a play which involves him on Midsummer Eve. He tells them that the place they are standing in, by Pook's Hill, is his own land. 'Pook's Hill' is actually a version of a much older name: 'Puck's Hill', and he is the creature whom Shakespeare wrote about in the play.

In that play, another fairy gives a brief description of the spirit in question:

> Either I mistake your shape and making quite,
> Or else you are that shrewd and knavish sprite
> Call'd Robin Goodfellow: are not you he
> That frights the maidens of the villagery;
> Skim milk, and sometimes labour in the quern
> And bootless make the breathless housewife churn;
> And sometime make the drink to bear no barm;
> Mislead night-wanderers, laughing at their harm?
> Those that Hobgoblin call you and sweet Puck,
> You do their work, and they shall have good luck:
> Are not you he? [25]

The Puck who appears to these children is rather like the mischievous creature of Shakespeare's play, but he also seems to be much older and more magical. He tells stories of when pagan gods were brought to Britain, and talks about the reign of Elizabeth I as if it were very late in his sense of time. Puck allows the children to see the people and events that have passed across the English landscape, and the book becomes a series of chapters devoted to these figures. A Roman centurion, a stone-mason and a medieval knight all appear in front of them, weaving a history of the land around them which both invests it with magic and laments that the enchantment has mostly gone from it.

The first hint that Narnia might have something to do with the enchanted England conjured up by Kipling comes when Puck explains why he has arrived and points to the landscape:

> 'Is it?' said their visitor, sitting down. 'Then what on Human Earth made you act Midsummer Night's Dream three times over, on Midsummer Eve, in the middle of a Ring, and under

– right under one of my oldest hills in Old England? Pook's Hill – Puck's Hill – Puck's Hill – Pook's Hill! It's as plain as the nose on my face.'

He pointed to the bare, fern-covered slope of Pook's Hill that runs up from the far side of the mill-stream to a dark wood. Beyond that wood the ground rises and rises for five hundred feet, till at last you climb out on the bare top of Beacon Hill, to look over the Pevensey Levels and the Channel and half the naked South Downs.'[26]

The name of the area near them – the Pevensey Levels – is almost the same as the surname of Peter, Edmund, Susan and Lucy. Since *Puck of Pook's Hill* is all about the things which have happened in that region across the years, the word keeps cropping up throughout the book. One of the chapters is called 'Old Men at Pevensey', and Puck met the Norse god Weland in a sleet storm on the Pevensey Levels, to take only a couple of examples. This is joined by a stronger verbal echo when Puck is telling them about the magical inhabitants of the land, and one of the children uses an unfortunate term:

'Wait awhile,' said Puck. 'You don't grow an oak in a year— and Old England's older than twenty oaks. Let's sit down again and think. I can do that for a century at a time.'

'Ah, but you're a fairy,' said Dan.

'Have you ever heard me say that word yet?' said Puck quickly.

'No. You talk about "the People of the Hills", but you never say "fairies",' said Una. 'I was wondering at that. Don't you like it?'

'How would you like to be called "mortal" or "human being" all the time?' said Puck; 'or "son of Adam" or "daughter of Eve"?'

'I shouldn't like it at all,' said Dan. 'That's how the Djinns and Afrits talk in the Arabian Nights.'

49

'And that's how I feel about saying – that word that I don't say. Besides, what you call them are made-up things the People of the Hills have never heard of – little buzzflies with butterfly wings and gauze petticoats, and shiny stars in their hair, and a wand like a schoolteacher's cane for punishing bad boys and rewarding good ones. I know 'em!'[27]

This is only a passing mention in *Puck of Pook's Hill*, but the titles 'son of Adam' and 'daughter of Eve' become a big part of the plot of *The Lion, the Witch and the Wardrobe*. Mr Tumnus first greets Lucy as a 'daughter of Eve', though the term rather disconcerts her, and it becomes clear that only sons of Adam and daughters of Eve have a vital role in lifting the curse which Narnia labours under.

The connections between the two books go deeper than a place name and a similar turn of phrase, though. Both stories involve children stumbling accidentally into a world of magic and adventure in the depths of the English countryside. In the case of *Puck of Pook's Hill*, the children meet characters from the past who tell them about adventures, whilst in *The Lion, the Witch and the Wardrobe* they take part in the adventures as main characters. The comparison with Kipling's tales highlights something in Narnia which might easily be overlooked: the magical world which the children find is a version of England. Despite the profusion of mythological figures from different traditions which inhabit Narnia, the country itself is relatively similar to the one the Pevensies inhabit. It has woods, hills and rivers, rather than deserts, steppes or olive groves. The thaw which comes in the middle chapters is recognisably the spring of the British Isles, or at least of northern Europe, and the flowers which emerge from the snow can be seen in the woods of those regions. Though Mr Tumnus lives in a cave, it is a cosy Edwardian-sounding cave with armchairs and bookshelves, and the tea he serves includes sardines and buttered toast. When the novel's climax takes place at the Stone Table, the characters are in the kind of Stone Age monument which can be found all around these islands. All of which is not to insist that Narnia 'belongs' in some sense to Britain or British readers, but to emphasise the odd familiarity of the landscape which the Pevensies traverse. They disappear through the wardrobe into an unfamiliar place, full of fantastical creatures and spells, but it is also a version of their own country.

The tales in *Puck of Pook's Hill* deliberately enchant the English countryside, showing their young listeners how much extraordinary history can be traced by telling the stories which have criss-crossed one area, and how much magic and legend have accrued around them. The Pevensies' journey through Narnia also invests that landscape with magic and conflict, though under another name.

This matters for Lewis's book because what happens in Narnia implicitly poses a challenge to the reader. It is striking that when Lucy explores the newly-discovered wood and lamppost, she meets a creature who regards her as strange and fantastical. Mr Tumnus, with his horns and hairy legs, is an odd sight for Lucy and the reader alike. But we become aware that he is scrutinising her at the same time. The name which he applies to her, 'daughter of Eve', sounds archaic and faintly legendary, but it does not come from Narnia. In an odd turn inside-out, Mr Tumnus suggests that there is something rather more mysterious and magical about being a little girl than there is about being a Classical faun. Any girl reading *The Lion, the Witch and the Wardrobe*, he implies, comes of a more ancient and heroic lineage than he does, and is heir to titles which a mere Narnian cannot claim. After all, when Lucy becomes a queen at Cair Paravel, she is not crowned because she and her siblings have conquered Narnia, nor because they have saved it by driving out the White Witch. The progress of the

PATHS IN THE SNOW

novel makes clear that being a queen of Narnia is the outcome of being a daughter of Eve. Various critics have pointed out the unpleasantly colonialist overtones of a narrative template in which a troubled land needs European characters to 'discover' it, master its culture and magics/technologies, and then establish themselves as its saviours. This pattern can be seen repeated from the mountains of *King Solomon's Mines* to the deserts of *Dune*. However, this recognition can also obscure a more basic element in Lewis's novel here: it calls the identity of its readers into question. Whilst they are busy wondering at fauns, witches and talking beavers, it quietly poses the question of who they think they are, and whether they have thought through what that means. Children's literature is full of apparently ordinary young characters who turn out to have a high and heroic destiny foretold of them: Harry Potter and Lyra Belacqua are only two of the most obvious recent examples. It is surely one of the attractions of this trope that ordinary readers can imagine themselves into the role. Harry Potter, though unusually unfortunate in his family situation, is not unusual in most ways. If he can wake up one morning, discover he has the ability to speak to snakes, and be informed that he is the most famous boy in the wizarding world, it is tempting for a young bookworm to suspend their own disbelief long enough to consider the same thing happening to them tomorrow. But Lewis goes one step further. Unlike Harry Potter or Lyra Belacqua, Lucy Pevensie is genuinely no more the Chosen One than the reader is. If they had stumbled through that wardrobe into Narnia, they would have counted as a son of Adam or a daughter of Eve. Whether the reader consciously recognises the fact or not, this brings them somewhat closer to the fantasy world itself. At the same time, it implicates their identity in Mr Tumnus' question as to what Lucy actually is.

Thus the parallels between *The Lion, the Witch and the*

Wardrobe and *Puck of Pook's Hill* suggests a source for a couple of minor details of the novel, but they also highlight elements of how Narnia works. Kipling's book is more obviously about the English landscape and the fantastical things which are embedded in its history. The appearance of his Puck stresses the idea that walking through the countryside may involve walking alongside magical and mysterious elements, and suggests that the boundary may be crossed accidentally. The same suggestions occur, in less obvious ways, in Lucy's initial discovery of Narnia. But Lewis's borrowings have been reshaped in ways that mean the reader finds their own world, and their own self, questioned.

PIPES AND SLIPPERS

Having arrived, via Pook's Hill, at Mr Tumnus, it is worth discussing this remarkable figure at more length. He is perhaps second only to Aslan as a character who stays in the memory of Narnian readers. He is the first person Lucy meets in Narnia, and Pauline Baynes' memorable illustrations combined with Lewis's vivid description to produce one of the defining images of the novel. He may, indeed, be easier to visualise than Aslan, because the lion bears such a weight of significance and the faun is described so specifically.

When Lucy (and the reader) first enter Narnia, they are drawn into it by a figure who is both domestic and strange. Tumnus is demonstrably non-human, with his goat's legs, his tail and his horns, but he is also carrying familiar objects like an umbrella and a pile of parcels. When he invites Lucy back to his cave, he offers her the cosy and familiar delights of an English tea table: sardines, hot buttered toast and little sugared cakes. Edmund may meet a pale, unearthly queen with a magic goblet and a box of Turkish Delight but Lucy's first fantastical figure meets her halfway between her world and the rest of Narnia. Fan culture suggests there is something appealing about this halfway point, as demonstrated by the ambience rooms on YouTube based on Tumnus' cave and the fan fiction which centres on him. Educational schemes which make use of *The Lion, the Witch and the Wardrobe* show a similar pull towards the cave in Lantern Waste. For example, Christin Ditchfield's *A Family Guide to The Lion, the Witch and the Wardrobe* suggests that parents help their children connect with the book's moral and spiritual teaching by engaging in various practical activities to 'continue the adventure'. These include holding a tea party in the style of Mr Tumnus, and the book includes recipes for tea and scones, and advice on visiting 'an authentic British tearoom'.[28] The 'Hearth Magic' scheme of work for home-schooled children by Amber Hellewell also suggests that students could make 'enchanted tea' whilst exploring the character of Mr Tumnus.

The literary comparison I would like to make in the case of Mr Tumnus is another English classic associated with the idyll of a vanishing countryside. Kenneth Grahame's *The Wind in the Willows* was first published in 1908, a few decades before Lewis's work. It had become an established children's classic by the mid-twentieth century. As many readers will not need to be informed, *The Wind in the Willows* tells the story of animals who live in the English countryside: the timid, domestic Mole in his underground home, the dashing water-rat Ratty, with his striped blazer and rowing boat, the grumpy but good-hearted Badger who lives in the depths of the snowy wood, and the frivolous Mr Toad who lives in his ancestral Toad Hall and squanders his time and money on the latest fad. Though their adventures are children's stories, and feature animals who talk, they are also a recognisable depiction of social types in Edwardian England, which I think illuminates the odd mode of fiction which they present. They are fantasies, in which water-rats pack sumptuous picnic hampers, and toads steal motor-cars and escape from prison by dressing up as laundresses.

At the same time, they are set in a recognisable social world, and characters can flit between the realm of the fantastical and the realm of the real within the same stretch of pages. Given all this, it is even more remarkable that the stories contain another kind of fantastical experience. One of the central chapters is entitled 'The Piper at the Gates of Dawn', and centres around the otter's young child going missing. The animals split up into groups and search desperately for the lost child, and in the process Ratty and Mole find themselves deep amongst the islands in the river The book's description of the natural world becomes more and more intense, until they find an unexpected figure in the heart of the countryside, who has been keeping the lost child safe:

> 'This is the place of my song-dream, the place the music played to me,' whispered the Rat, as if in a trance. 'Here, in this holy place, here if anywhere, surely we shall find Him!'
>
> Then suddenly the Mole felt a great Awe fall upon him, an awe that turned his muscles to water, bowed his head, and rooted his feet to the ground. It was no panic terror—indeed he felt wonderfully at peace and happy—but it was an awe that smote and held him and, without seeing, he knew it could only mean that some august Presence was very, very near. With difficulty he turned to look for his friend, and saw him at his side, cowed, stricken, and trembling violently. And still there was utter silence in the populous bird-haunted branches around them; and still the light grew and grew.
>
> Perhaps he would never have dared to raise his eyes, but that, though the piping was now hushed, the call and the summons seemed still dominant and imperious. He might not refuse, were Death himself waiting to strike him instantly, once he had looked with mortal eye on things rightly kept hidden. Trembling he obeyed, and raised his humble head; and then, in that utter clearness of the imminent dawn, while Nature,

flushed with fulness of incredible colour, seemed to hold her breath for the event, he looked in the very eyes of the Friend and Helper; saw the backward sweep of the curved horns, gleaming in the growing daylight; saw the stern, hooked nose between the kindly eyes that were looking down on them humorously, while the bearded mouth broke into a half-smile at the corners; saw the rippling muscles on the arm that lay across the broad chest, the long supple hand still holding the pan pipes only just fallen away from the parted lips; saw the splendid curves of the shaggy limbs disposed in majestic ease on the sward; saw, last of all, nestling between his very hooves, sleeping soundly in entire peace and contentment, the little, round, podgy, childish form of the baby otter. All this he saw, for one moment breathless and intense, vivid on the morning sky; and still, as he looked, he lived; and still, as he lived, he wondered.[29]

This is, to say the least, an unexpected passage in a children's story about talking animals. (It may be doubly unexpected for those who know *The Wind in the Willows* well: a number of modern editions, especially those printed in the US, simply leave out this chapter.) Beatrix Potter's Peter Rabbit never looked up from stealing lettuces to find himself gazing into the face of an ancient deity. For that is what Ratty and Mole have encountered in this scene. Though he is never named explicitly, this is clearly a depiction of the god Pan. He has the elements attributed to that deity by classical myth: the horns on his head, the hairy animal legs ending in hooves, the beard and the instrument known as the 'pan pipes'. The narrator comes very close to giving him a name, when he insists that the 'great Awe' which Mole felt 'was no panic terror'. The modern word 'panic' originates in the idea of a fear felt in wild and natural places, literally the 'fear of Pan' or 'panic fear'. I suspect there is a quibble lurking in Grahame's description here: it may not be a 'panic terror' that Mole experiences, but it may be a Pan-ic awe. This is not an entirely isolated appearance of Pan in the fiction of this era. As the scholars Ronald Hutton and Paul Robichaud have revealed, Pan had something of a literary renaissance in English-speaking literary culture in the nineteenth and twentieth centuries.[30] The stories of the satirist Hector Hugh Munro, better known by his pen-name Saki, include more than one narrative of Pan manifesting himself in Edwardian England, and D. H. Lawrence was deeply interested in the god, to take only two famous examples. Nonetheless, even if other writers of the time were interested in the figure of this woodland god from the myths of ancient Greece, it comes as a shock to many readers when they encounter him in the centre of *The Wind in the Willows*. The sensation is more remarkable because of the mystical and reverent language use to describe the animals' feelings when they see Pan's face. It might be suggested that Grahame's novel does not technically show the existence of Pan in Edwardian England, since it might be read as part of the fantasy side of the book, akin to talking animals. Still, the book accords a weight and a power to the episode which makes it the symbolic centre of the stories.

Turning back to Lantern Waste after these events on the Riverbank, we can see distinct parallels between the figures of Pan and Mr Tumnus. Lucy's companion also has horns, a tail, shaggy feet and a beard. When they have had tea in his cave, Mr Tumnus even brings out some pipes to play. (He is described as a 'faun', but this mythological creature is more or less identical in appearance to Pan in its combination of human and goat characteristics.) The parallels are even more striking when we note the fictional situations the two characters are in: Ratty and Mole discover Pan looking after the lost otter child, whilst Mr Tumnus befriends Lucy when he finds her wandering alone in the woods. Though the very precision of the echoes between these figures may direct our attention to the differences as well. Pan is presented as a (literally) awe-inspiring divinity whose presence brings the animals to the edge of their reality, and whose care for the young lost creature gives them an insight into the spirit of the woods. Tumnus, on the other hand, is a domestic and rather comic figure. He is first seen with his tail looped up over the arm carrying his umbrella, and he drops his parcels on seeing Lucy. Rather than providing a mystical vision, he invites her back for tea, and seems to be a creature of the fireside and the comfy armchair rather than the wilderness. Admittedly his playing of the pan pipes brings a more mysterious and visionary element into their meeting, and Lucy sees images of the way Narnia used to be. This sequence, though, only serves to underline the differences once again. Pan rescued and cared for the lost otter child, but Tumnus eventually admits that he has accepted service with the White Witch, and his duty is not to tend to Lucy, but to kidnap her for a murderous sorceress.

Lewis's Mr Tumnus echoes and evokes the Piper at the Gates of Dawn, but does so to produce a figure which a rather different emotional impact and moral character. We might see it as appropriate that Grahame's Pan inspired the visionary first album by Pink Floyd, entitled 'The Piper at the Gates of Dawn' containing Syd Barrett's psychedelic songwriting, whilst Mr Tumnus tends to inspire tea-parties. The similarity, and yet difference, of the characters prompts us to think about why Lewis chose to present this echo, and what the figure of Mr Tumnus means when read in the aftermath of Grahame's Pan. One solution is that Lewis put a Pan-like figure into his magical woodland simply in order to belittle a pagan god. We might suggest that the nineteenth-century revival of interest in this particular deity had been so widespread that some readers at the time would be unsurprised to see a horned, goat-legged figure with pipes in an enchanted English woodland. From this point of view, Lewis would be poking fun at the dabblings in paganism which contemporary authors had indulged in. His Mr Tumnus would be a joke about what Pan might actually look like if he was encountered in England: not a panic-inducing deity, but a fussy, domestic little creature with a cowardly streak. Given the strain of religious allegory in the Narnia novels, we might even speculate that Mr Tumnus is intended to denigrate paganism in favour of the Christian faith which the books present as true. In this reading, Mr Tumnus is to Pan what Aslan is to Jesus. Having just outlined it, I must admit that I do not find this theory persuasive. There were a number of references to Pan in the literature of the time but surely not so many that readers would actively expect to see the goat-god in any given woodland (especially in a children's book). Moreover, Mr Tumnus may be less than divine, but he is not simply a fussy little traitor. He is overcome with conscience at the realisation of what he has agreed to do, and does not hand Lucy over to the Witch. Instead, he helps her to escape, and ends up paying the heavy (albeit temporary) price for choosing his moral principles over his dread of the secret police. The idea of Tumnus as a proxy to ridicule Pan does not quite cover all the facts, nor does it do justice to the emotional charge which the character provides.

A more persuasive reading of Mr Tumnus would take into account a very peculiar fact about the history of the god Pan: that he was sometimes seen as interchangeable with Christ. As Paul Robichaud relates, some renaissance writers and thinkers were struck by the similarities between Pan and Christ. They were both gods who died, they were both shepherds, and Pan's name could be interpreted as meaning 'all' in Greek, reflecting Christ's role as universal wisdom and saviour. It may seem ludicrous to modern sensibilities, and unpleasant to modern faith, to associate the shaggy lascivious goat-god with the Jesus of the gospels. Nonetheless, the great reconciling of the pagan and Christian past, which some Renaissance intellectuals undertook, brought together these two figures. The English poet Edmund Spenser makes this allegorical connection in a poem between two shepherds:

> And wonned [lived] not the great God Pan
> Upon Mount Olivet;
> Feeding the blessed Flock of Dan,
> Which did himself beget?

> O blessed Sheep! O Shepherd great!
> That bought his flock so dear:
> And them did save with bloody Sweat,
> From Wolves that would them tear.[31]

The great 'Shepherd', who tends his sheep and sacrifices himself to save them, fuses the images of Pan and Christ. Or perhaps it would be better to say that a knowing reader can see Christ through the symbols and language which claim to refer to Pan. The deeply devout poet John Milton, who wrote *Paradise Lost* as an attempt to 'justify the ways of God to man', included Pan in his poem 'On the Morning of Christ's Nativity'. The birth of Jesus is imagined in this work as cleansing the world of paganism and its power, but Milton then includes this passage about a group who will be told about the birth of the Messiah:

> The Shepherds on the Lawn,
> Or ere the point of Dawn,
> Sat simply chatting in a rustic row;
> Full little thought they then,
> That the mighty Pan
> Was kindly come to live with them below;
> Perhaps their loves, or else their sheep,
> Was all that did their silly thoughts so busy keep.[32]

WHAT LUCY FOUND THERE

We can interpret this as suggesting that ancient shepherds would initially have understood Jesus as like the god Pan, but it is a powerful example of a resolutely Christian poet (who classed all other pagan gods as demons in *Paradise Lost*) using the language of Pan to celebrate the birth of Christ.

This association between Pan and Christ suggests to me that something rather complex is going on in Lewis's depiction of Mr Tumnus. Lewis had a great affection for the literature and culture of pagan Europe, including both the Viking and Scandinavian culture of the North and the Classical culture of the South. I do not think Mr Tumnus is intended to deride that rich heritage of myths. After all, in a later novel in the Narnia sequence, *Prince Caspian*, the Classical demigods Bacchus and Silenus appear, with their wild entourage, as part of a procession led by Aslan. Instead, I think Lewis's version of a goat-legged forest creature is writing back to, and modifying, the revival of interest in Pan. It feels significant that the Pan of *The Wind in the Willows* appears in an episode in the middle of the book, providing the story with its mysterious and transcendent centre. In contrast, Mr Tumnus meets Lucy at the beginning of the adventures in Narnia, as soon as she steps through the wardrobe, and guides her into the fantastical world. Lewis has displaced the Pan-like figure from the central space of his magical woodland, and put him at the edge of Narnia. Aslan occupies that defining role in *The Lion, the Witch and the Wardrobe*, whilst Tumnus is instrumental in the Pevensies' eventual encounter with the lion himself. I see Lewis's novel as presenting its characters with an exciting and enchanted woodland, with pagan-looking creatures, but a woodland which they must move through in order to meet Aslan. The lion may be King of the Wood, but he is not contained or defined by it. This rewrites the kind of stories which featured Pan in the English literary tradition of previous decades, in which a return to the depths of the rural world revealed the ancient god, waiting from before the time of Christianity. In Narnia, the Pan-like figure is not the end of the quest, but merely the beginning of it. Tumnus, with his hairy legs and his buttered toast, may be a creature of the woods, but is not nearly so truly wild as Aslan. This reading would fit with what we know of Lewis's own spiritual experiences. To paint with broad strokes, he was an atheist with a love for mythology, who eventually came to see myth as the fragments which reflected the original truth. The notion of shepherds tending their sheep whilst 'Pan' was born in Bethlehem, or of the intelligence which set the universe in order being contemplated under the name of 'Pan', might well have pleased Lewis, who believed that Christ was the true Good Shepherd and the true Logos. We can read Tumnus as a figure who emphasises the attractions and the possibilities of the woods and the fields, who evokes the magic and inspiration of the English countryside, but who suggests that they are not an end in themselves. He is not the divinity himself, but rather the piper at the gates of Narnia.

CHAPTER THREE

EDMUND AND THE WARDROBE

SLEIGH BELLS

n this chapter, Edmund follows Lucy into Narnia, and has his own encounter with a magical person. The White Witch is the novel's major antagonist, but I am mostly not going to discuss her in this chapter. (Or in the next, for that matter, where the focus will be firmly upon Turkish Delight.) In the following pages I will mostly be considering the figure of Father Christmas.

I may appear to be getting ahead of myself by mentioning Father Christmas in this chapter, when he does not enter the story until some time later. However, I think there is a minor fictional trick being played on the reader by Lewis at the first appearance of the White Witch. Since this is a book about rereading *The Lion, the Witch and the Wardrobe*, we are probably all expecting the appearance of the self-styled Queen at this point. We're thinking of Turkish Delight and its consequences. We may be noticing on a second (or twenty-second) rereading the psychological acuteness with which Lewis depicts Edmund's attempt to deal with his own bad conscience towards Lucy. He calls out for her, whether to apologise or to reassure himself that he's not entirely alone, and as soon as she doesn't reply, he decided she has rejected his intended apology because she's a girl and they don't understand honour and decency like chaps do. Suddenly Edmund has persuaded himself that not only is he in the right, but that Lucy has in fact wronged him rather than the other way around. If we can ignore some of our pre-existing knowledge about what is going to happen next, I think the White Witch's arrival comes as rather a shock in this part of the novel.

We are told that '[e]verything was perfectly still, as if he were the only living creature in that country', and that after his attempt to call Lucy back, Edmund heard 'very far off in the wood, a sound of bells'.[33] This is followed by a sledge drawn by two reindeer, whose white hair and gilded antlers are described, then their scarlet harness with its silver bells. The novel is presenting us with Edmund's perspective at this point. We only see and hear what he sees and hears, and we only know what he knows. So, to state the obvious, we know that Lucy is somewhere else in Narnia, and we know that they have both got in via the wardrobe. But we do not know what Lucy is doing, or who is arriving in the sledge. Even more precisely, we are presented with Edmund's perceptions as well. When the sound of bells enters the scene, we are told he can hear them, and as the sledge moves into view, it is described in the order in which Edmund sees it. The passage is quite specific about this: we are given a description of each element, as if we are walking from the front of the sledge to the back. Or rather (as is actually happening), as if we are standing still next to Edmund and we notice each detail from front to back as it moves into view. I've stressed this point because taking this fictional approach builds up suspense, as we know someone is arriving in the story, but we can only deduce who it is via the incremental appearance of the details of the sledge. After the reindeer at the front of the vehicle comes the person sitting behind them, driving it. This is a 'fat dwarf' with a red hood and gold tassel and a long beard. We're also told that his clothes are made from polar bear fur. Then 'behind him, on a much higher seat in the middle of the sledge, sat a very different person'.[34] Lewis has spun out the gradual arrival of the White Witch here, with each incremental detail. Other characters aren't described as if someone was looking at their shoes, then tracking up past their trousers, noticing the buttons on their shirt and the badge on their blazer, then finally arriving at their face. It feels as if there is some fictional purpose to this slow, even suspenseful, description. I think Lewis intends us to guess who is about to enter the adventures of the Pevensie children, and to guess wrongly.

After all, we are in a snowy landscape, in a novel which has already demonstrated that fantastical and magical people can appear. The most famous sledge in all literature and folklore is surely that of Father Christmas. (Or Santa Claus, or St Nicholas, depending on which region you meet him in.) The mention of the general hush followed by the sound of bells and the arrival of a sledge pulled by reindeer reminds me of the opening of the nineteenth-century poem 'A Visit from St Nicholas':

> 'Twas the night before Christmas, when all thro' the house
> Not a creature was stirring, not even a mouse;[35]

The reindeer are being driven by a diminutive figure in a tasselled hood, who is dressed in polar bear furs which he could only have acquired in the Arctic Circle, the region where the North Pole can be found. When the White Witch arrives in Edmund's (and the reader's) line of sight, she is described in terms of red and white: 'her face was white – not merely pale, but white like snow or paper or icing-sugar, except for her very red mouth'. The narrator calls it 'a beautiful face in other respects, but proud and cold and stern'.[36] The traditional picture of Father Christmas, as laid out in 'A Visit From St Nicholas' uses similar colours to a very different effect:

> His eyes—how they twinkled! his dimples, how merry!
> His cheeks were like roses, his nose like a cherry!
> His droll little mouth was drawn up like a bow,
> And the beard on his chin was as white as the snow;
> The stump of a pipe he held tight in his teeth,

And the smoke, it encircled his head like a wreath;
He had a broad face and a little round belly
That shook when he laugh'd, like a bowl full of jelly:
He was chubby and plump, a right jolly old elf,
And I laugh'd when I saw him, in spite of myself;
A wink of his eye and a twist of his head
Soon gave me to know I had nothing to dread;

Indeed, the witch almost appears as an inverted image, or a photographic negative of Father Christmas. His red face and white beard against her white face and red lips. Her pride and sternness against his warmth and cheer. She is the symbolic antithesis of the generosity and goodwill the children associate with him. In fact, I should modify the suggestion, made above, that the reader is exactly aligned with Edmund's perspective in this passage. We are certainly only given information as he perceives it in the scene, and we follow his gaze as he takes in the new arrivals. However, readers also have access to what previously happened to Lucy in the earlier chapter, and there is a line she heard which should prevent them from falling into Lewis's mild fictional trap. 'Always winter and never Christmas'. Lucy is told by the faun Tumnus that the White Witch has kept Narnia under this spell. Probably not every reader will have this fact at the forefront of their minds during the description of the sledge and its occupants, but Lewis has given them the information. Edmund has just met the embodiment of 'always winter and never Christmas'.

When Father Christmas does appear, some chapters later, I believe the same fictional trick is played in reverse. The Pevensies have got into Narnia all together, met the beavers and had supper with them. Edmund has slipped away unnoticed, and the other characters have realised they are being betrayed. Fearing that they will be treated the same way as Mr Tumnus, they have gathered provisions (though not the sewing-machine) and left the dam. They have taken refuge in a hole beneath the snow, which Mr Beaver mentions is a traditional hiding place in bad times. They have deliberately taken a route which would be difficult for the Witch to follow, because as Mr Beaver says 'she'd have to keep to the top, for you couldn't bring a sledge down here'.[37] When the beavers and Pevensies wake up the next morning, they are horrified by a noise from outside the cave:

> they were all sitting up with their mouths and eyes wide open listening to a sound which was the very sound they'd all been thinking of (and sometimes imagining they heard) during the walk last night. It was the sound of jingling bells.[38]

Of course, it is not the White Witch, but Father Christmas. The reader has not seen the way he looks in Narnia before, so when I suggested the White Witch was an inverse image of him, I had to assume the reader had the traditional image of him in mind. When we do see Father Christmas, he is described in the same colour scheme which stresses him as the Witch's counterpart. He has 'a bright red robe (bright as hollyberries)' a fur hood and 'a great white beard that fell like a foamy waterfall over his chest'[39] All is well, for the moment at least. The children have met the figure of kindness and generosity, not the danger who was chasing them. More than that, Father Christmas' appearance is a sign of something more than himself: 'I've come at last', he declares, 'She has kept me out for a long time but I have got in at last'. His arrival is a suggestion that the White Witch no longer has complete control over Narnia, and that 'Aslan is on the move'.[40] His arrival is presaged by a moment which is similar to the Witch's arrival, though rather more brief: we are told about the characters listening to the noise of bells in the cave. Just as with Edmund seeing the sledge and its inhabitants moving into view, the reader is aware that there is someone present but they can only see or hear through the characters' perceptions. There is another similarity: Lewis has once more left a clue in the text which should enable the reader to deduce correctly. The previous chapter ended with the Witch ordering the dwarf to '[make] ready our sledge ... and use the harness without bells'.[41] The readers have technically been given the information which should let them identify the sound of bells as harmless, but many of them may make the same assumption as the characters, making Father Christmas' arrival an extra surprise.

Having argued (perhaps tendentiously) that Father Christmas's presence, and even some of his physical attributes, are invoked by the story long before he actually appears in Narnia, it is worth asking what this figure brings with him into the fantasy world. From one point of view, he brings an additional level of chaos and incoherence. This was certainly the view taken by J. R. R. Tolkien, in his famous comment on the eclecticism of Narnia: 'It really won't do you know!'[42] With a faun from Classical myth, talking animals from either Aesop or Beatrix Potter, some sort of ice witch, and now Father Christmas from British folklore and modern popular culture, Lewis seems to be drawing in a constellation of inconsistent fantastical creatures. We cannot tell, but I would speculate that it was Father Christmas' part in twentieth-century culture which most marked him out as jarring for Tolkien. A figure who appeared on wrapping paper, advertising posters and the shop windows in London must have seemed entirely discordant next to the pipe-playing faun of Arcadia. However, Lewis (or Lewis's narrator) insists that what the children see is something rather different to their previous images of Father Christmas: 'Some of the pictures ... in our world make him look only funny and jolly', but 'he was so big, and so glad and so real ... They felt very glad, but also solemn'.[43] For me, this comment is key to what Father Christmas is doing in this story. He is not just a cheery man who gives out presents, but possesses the deeper history of that figure. One strand of the traditions surrounding Father Christmas are bound with the image of Santa Claus (or Sinterklaas), who derives from the medieval St Nicholas. The stories surrounding this bishop of the early church stressed (amongst other attributes) his generosity, and he became associated with gift-giving. This became specifically tied to buying small gifts for children at fairs named after him, and the figure of 'St Nicholas' or 'Sinterklaas' became 'Santa Claus'. (St Nicholas was also renowned for his strong theological views: one persistent but apocryphal story describes him attending the church council of Nicaea, and punching the priest Arius over his denial of the doctrine of the Trinity.) Another strand of the popular image of Father Christmas comes from a folkloric personification of the festival, sometimes known as 'Sir Christmas' and sometimes as 'Father Christmas'. He is associated with feasting, drinking and celebration, rather than specifically with gift-giving. The opening of one medieval carol mentions him thus:

> Nowell, Nowell, Nowell, Nowell,
> 'Who is there that singeth so?'
> 'I am here, Sir Christëmas.'
> 'Welcome, my lord Christëmas,
> Welcome to us all, both more and less
> Come near, Nowell!'

From the arrangement of the lines, it is clear that this is intended to be sung between two groups, with at least one person singing 'Nowell!' boisterously, and others asking who is singing, and then a reply coming from 'Sir Christemas'. The poem goes on with Sir Christmas declaring that the Christ child has been born, and encouraging everyone to drink and celebrate: 'Buvez bien par toute la campagnie,/ Make good cheer and be right merry.' Father Christmas appearing in a novel may immediately spark associations with wrapping paper, seasonal jingles and children's parties. The way he is described by Lewis, however, gestures towards the deeper connections of this figure: to medieval feasting, to debates over the natures of Christ, to the winter festivals across Europe. Lewis does not present his young readers with a new character who will tell them all about the coming of Aslan. Instead he shows them a figure they already know, but suggests that there is more to know about him than they thought. As ever with *The Lion, the Witch and the Wardrobe*, I find myself thinking of terms of depth, of the way the bright surface of the fiction brings in old and strange associations to disturb the readers' apprehension of the world around them.

This discussion of Father Christmas raises another question: why he is apparently being paired with the White Witch, or she with him. Having found this textual pattern which sets them in opposition to each other, I think there are a couple of meanings which emerge from it. Firstly, it presents the White Witch as the anti-Christmas. That phrase 'always winter but never Christmas', familiar to readers of Narnia, is embodied in this presentation of her. She is the photographic negative of Father Christmas, down to the inverted colours of their faces, the opposite of everything he stands for. When he finds his way in, she is symbolically undermined. Secondly, it seems important for the novel's theology that the White Witch is the antithesis of Father Christmas, rather than the antithesis of Aslan. This may appear rather illogical, since she is the novel's major antagonist. She is cold, violent and spiteful, in contrast to Aslan's warmth, healing and loving. She carries out the death, he rises again. Nonetheless, I think the novel is careful not to equate them too fully. As we will see in a later chapter, Aslan is not another magical creature who happens to be more powerful than the Witch. He is not a creature at all, in one sense, since he was there before the world was created. To set them up as opposites, equal enemies who battle for control of Narnia, would be to imply a Manichean or dualistic world-view. This image of the cosmos, in which balanced and opposed forces of good and evil struggle with each other, is one which orthodox Christianity has disclaimed over the centuries. Christian thinkers have repeatedly asserted that the forces of evil are not another metaphysical power, equivalent to God, but are kinds of absence, degradation and void. Particularly when writing a fantasy novel, in which theological metaphors can take on lively shape, and particularly when writing it in the form of a quest narrative, there would be a risk of setting up this dualistic vision of the universe. Pairing the White Witch with Father Christmas offers a pattern in which she is already lesser than Aslan, because she is the opposite of a splendid but lesser figure. It may not be evident at this point in the story, but the intellectual framework for the 'deeper magic from before the dawn of time' is being quietly set up.

CHAPTER FOUR
TURKISH DELIGHT

The Turkish Delight which the White Witch offers Edmund, and which gives this chapter is title, is one of the most memorable images of the entire novel. When I first started a C. S. Lewis reading group at the university where I work, one of the new members brought us some Turkish Delight to share. Many people who have only a vague memory of the book's details crack a joke about enjoying Turkish Delight when I mention that I write about Narnia. It is clearly a potent symbol, and worth pausing on, so I am devoting an entire chapter to exploring its meanings and connections. I will compare the box of sweets to the apple of the Tree of the Knowledge of Good and Evil in the biblical book of Genesis, examining how Lewis reshapes the notion of temptation and fall for his young audience. I will consider the particular meaning which this Turkish Delight might have had for those young readers at the time, which might have become less obvious to us in the early twenty-first century. In order to draw out this aspect, I will place a non-fictional text alongside Edmund and the Witch: the legislation which instituted rationing in wartime Britain. This might not be an immediately compelling work to spend time with, but these laws shed a great deal of light on how Lewis's first readers would have felt about someone appearing with a box of Turkish Delight. Finally, I will ponder why it was that particular kind of sweet, and suggest that the stuff's appearance at the denouement of Dorothy L. Sayers' detective novel *Strong Poison* prompted Lewis to write it into his own book.

In one sense it is a modern substitute for the temptation scene in Genesis. In the King James Bible (or Authorised

Version, as it would have been called in Lewis's time), the passage runs thus:

> Now the serpent was more subtil than any beast of the field which the Lord God had made. And he said unto the woman, Yea, hath God said, Ye shall not eat of every tree of the garden?
>
> And the woman said unto the serpent, We may eat of the fruit of the trees of the garden: But of the fruit of the tree which is in the midst of the garden, God hath said, Ye shall not eat of it, neither shall ye touch it, lest ye die.
>
> And the serpent said unto the woman, Ye shall not surely die: For God doth know that in the day ye eat thereof, then your eyes shall be opened, and ye shall be as gods, knowing good and evil.
>
> And when the woman saw that the tree was good for food, and that it was pleasant to the eyes, and a tree to be desired to make one wise, she took of the fruit thereof, and did eat, and gave also unto her husband with her; and he did eat.
>
> And the eyes of them both were opened, and they knew that they were naked; and they sewed fig leaves together, and made themselves aprons.
>
> And they heard the voice of the Lord God walking in the garden in the cool of the day: and Adam and his wife hid themselves from the presence of the Lord God amongst the trees of the garden.
>
> And the Lord God called unto Adam, and said unto him, Where art thou?
>
> And he said, I heard thy voice in the garden, and I was afraid, because I was naked; and I hid myself.
>
> And he said, Who told thee that thou wast naked? Hast thou eaten of the tree, whereof I commanded thee that thou shouldest not eat?

TURKISH DELIGHT

And the man said, The woman whom thou gavest to be with me, she gave me of the tree, and I did eat.

And the Lord God said unto the woman, What is this that thou hast done? And the woman said, The serpent beguiled me, and I did eat.

(Genesis 3:1-13)

Though much of the incidental details are different, the eating of something forbidden is a crucial moral moment in the story. Edmund meets a supernatural-seeming figure who offers him a tasty treat. The resultant eating seems to turn him selfish and greedy, and he afterwards commits more serious infractions such as lying and betrayal of those closest to him. This fits with the temptation of Eve in the Bible: as commentators over the centuries have pointed out, the eating of the apple seems to cause a chain reaction of sin and unhappiness in the story. As soon as they have both eaten, Adam and Eve become estranged from their bodies by shame, gathering leaves to cover themselves. They then become separated from God, as they hide from him when they know he is walking in the garden. When they are asked if they have eaten from the forbidden tree, Adam turns on Eve, blaming her for tempting him, and even implicitly blaming God for creating Eve in the first place. Eve, in her turn, blames the serpent. The narrative shows a set of ripples developing from the initial transgression of the commandment, leaving distrust and blame within the closest of relationships. We are not told specifically in the Narnian story that Edmund eating the Turkish Delight, and drinking from the magic cup, causes him to become meaner. Nonetheless, the events soon afterwards show a similar fracturing of relationships. He will become embarrassed about having been in Narnia, then lie to Peter and Susan about it, in the process betraying Lucy. When the two narratives are compared like this, it is striking that

Lewis has bracketed out what many modern interpretations of this story focus on: the question of physical shame. The combination of the forbidden fruit and the realisation of nakedness has often centred attention on the apple story as a 'loss of innocence' in a physical way, and a specifically sexual one. It obviously makes sense to avoid this element in a children's book, which is presumably why Lewis did so, though it is worth pointing out that one of his most famous successors in fantasy literature deliberately emphasised it. Philip Pullman's *Northern Lights* trilogy, the Young Adult series which seems to rewrite the Narnia novels themselves with the intention of replacing them in the fictional canon, contains a crucial sequence near the end in which a pastoral scene, fruit, and sexual knowledge are all connected for the young heroine. The very insistence with which Pullman stresses the association between Lyra Belacqua's moral and sexual coming of age, highlights the way Lewis has avoided this association in *The Lion, the Witch and the Wardrobe*.

Whilst doing so, he has apparently chosen to highlight the effects of the eating of the apple rather than the act itself. If we read Turkish Delight as a substitute for the fruit of the forbidden tree, then Lewis seems much less interested in disobedience and breaking rules than in the consequent betrayal and breaking down of trusting relationships. Perhaps this might be explained again by his intended audience: children's literature is full of worthy and often dull stories about children breaking parental rules and finding out the rules were for their own good. Rowan Williams interprets the Narnian stories as an attempt to dramatise the experience of meeting the divine, removed from the existing associations readers have with religion and churches.[44] We could read Lewis's Turkish Delight in this way, as a means of exploring sin and its tragic effects without framing the spiritual life as a matter of knowing the rules and following them to the letter. Edmund has, after all, not been taught by his parents never to eat Turkish Delight offered to him by a magical queen on a sledge drawn by white reindeer.

Though, in another sense, he has been warned against doing exactly that. Edmund may not have been told to beware Anatolian delicacies distributed by unnervingly tall sorceresses, but he might have been warned about accepting sweets from strangers. The story mentions that when the Witch (or the Queen as it calls her at this point) invites Edmund to sit beside her on the sledge he is not very comfortable with the idea, and a few pages later it remarks that he had been afraid at first that the sledge might drive off with him still on it, but that this fear had disappeared from his mind with the eating of the Turkish Delight. This is the kind of awareness of 'stranger danger' which is muted but nonetheless present in the children's fiction of the era, and is familiar to modern readers. However, the prospect of luxurious sweets should have been even more suspicious to a schoolboy during the 1940s, when *The Lion, the Witch and the Wardrobe* is set, and at the beginning of the 1950s, when it was first published. Any schoolboy, or anyone else, living in Britain at the time would have daily experience of food rationing.

Rationing was introduced in Britain in the early years of the Second World War, after it had been a reasonably successful policy in the previous war. An announcement from the Ministry of Food, released in late 1939, encapsulates the public explanation for the scheme:

RATIONING BEGINS ON JANUARY 8TH

Bacon and ham, butter and sugar will be rationed as from 8th January. Meat will be rationed at a later date.

WHY WE ARE BEING RATIONED

The rationing scheme has been prepared to provide an

orderly system of distribution of essential foodstuffs down to the consumer. It assures to every member of the community an equal share, everyone being treated alike.

For the foods to be rationed we are dependent to a large extent on overseas sources of supply. The amounts are based on the present import programmes determined in the light of available resources in foreign exchange and shipping space. The requirements of other imported commodities such as armaments and industrial raw materials make large demands on these resources. Economy in the use of foodstuffs practised carefully and without detriment to efficiency sets free our resources for the needs of the Services. Every consumer will thus make his or her contribution to the national war effort.[45]

The clipped, official phrasing of 'overseas sources of supply' and 'available resources' gestures towards Britain's desperate situation as a set of islands surrounded by seas which had become battlefields in their own right. In order to feed its population and supply its military forces, Britain needed to import materials which came by ship. The 'Battle of the Atlantic', as it was known, pitched the German navy (and other Axis forces) against the navies of Britain, Canada and the United States, as convoys of merchant shipping travelled from North America to Britain. As resources became scarcer, and some ships were destroyed, supplies were carefully managed in Britain. Foodstuffs like eggs, cooking fat, cheese, milk and tea were also rationed at various points in the war. Petrol was strictly controlled, and clothing was increasingly rationed as the war continued. The Ministry of Food notice I quoted gives the main justifications for rationing which were outlined to the public. Firstly, that it ensured resources were not being squandered which could be used in helping fight the war, so 'every consumer will thus make his or her contribution to the national war effort'. Secondly, that the supplies which were available could be shared out equally amongst everyone in the population', that rationing 'assures to every member of the community an equal share, everyone being treated alike'. This principle was often summed up in the phrase 'fair shares' which appeared frequently in newspapers and public discussion. This was the principle, though in practice it did not always work out so equitably. A 'black market' appeared, in which rationed goods could be obtained illegally by those willing to pay higher prices and risk the sanction of the law if they were discovered.

The same announcement, in its later paragraphs, gives a flavour of the way restrictions affected everyday life. Every member of the public might be able to congratulate themselves that their frugal habits were contributing to the effort to defeat Nazism, but the practicalities were unappealingly petty and drab:

> Butter may be served in a restaurant without a coupon but if you wish to obtain a cooked meal of bacon in a hotel or restaurant you must take your ration book and allow the person who serves the meal to detach one half coupon.
>
> If you live in a hotel or boarding house or hostel you must hand your ration book to the proprietor or manager who will detach the appropriate coupons and who must return the ration book to you when you leave.

This scarcity, and the system put in place to manage it, forms a backdrop to much of literature in English from the era. In Kingsley Amis' novel *Lucky Jim*, the hero is a university lecturer, but he still discusses rations with the landlady of the boarding house where he lives (having presumably handed over his ration book to her). Rationing produced social stereotypes and recognisable characters, most notably the 'spiv'. Originally a slang term for a small-time crook or thief, 'spiv' came to designate a stereotypical black marketeer. Joe Walker in the TV show *Dad's Army* and Flash Harry in the original *St Trinian's* films are typical representatives: lively, shifty, dressed in a long wide-shouldered coat and a soft hat pulled down over the forehead, with a Cockney accent and a thin moustache. Cecil Day-Lewis's children's novel *The Otterbury Incident*, published in 1948, presents the same figure in a much less charming light, in the character of Johnny Sharp. He is a spiv who counterfeits money alongside trading in rationed goods, and slashes people with a cut-throat razor.

The effects of rationing can be seen as well in the records of Lewis's own life, and that of the group called the Inklings which formed around him at Oxford. At the end of the 1940s, the meetings of this group occasionally involved 'ham suppers', which were the result 'of lavish food parcels from one of Lewis's American admirers, Dr Warfield M. Firor of Maryland' (109). The group's biographer, Humphrey Carpenter, notes that 'these parcels were most welcome, and they invariably included something that could scarcely be bought in England then, a large ham'.[46] After 'a number of further hams [from America] had been consumed with due ceremony, Lewis wrote to the donor Dr Firor: "To all my set you are by now an almost mythical figure – Firor-of-the-hams, a sort of Fertility god".'[47] From the early twenty-first century there is something remarkable about the sheer excitement produced in Lewis, Tolkien and their other friends, by these food parcels. But this is the context through which we should read the scenes of eating and drinking in *The Lion, the Witch and the Wardrobe*: years during which a Fellow of Magdalen College, Oxford would invite the Merton Professor of English Literature over to dinner with great ceremony, because there was the chance of eating as much ham as they liked without anyone stopping them.

All of this would be a significant factor in our understanding of the author of the Narnia novels, but would be largely irrelevant for his child readers, if rationing had ended with the Second World War. After all, *The Lion, the Witch and the Wardrobe* was published in 1950, at a time when most of its young readers would have only the dimmest memories of a war which had been waged from 1939 to 1945. However, in Britain rationing continued throughout the late 1940s and into the 1950s. Indeed, some forms of rationing became severer during this period, with bread and potatoes being rationed for the first time during the post-war years. The rationing of sweets and chocolate, which had begun in 1942, lasted until early 1953, and was therefore still going on when the novel was published. The Turkish Delight that the Witch offered Edmund would have been especially tempting to a generation of children who had lived with rationing for ten years, many of whom would not be able to remember a time when you could simply buy as many sweets as you could afford with your pocket money. It is telling that when Edmund has finished eating the contents of the box, he looks pointedly at it, hoping that his new friend will offer him more. The narrator explains this via magic, since it is enchanted Turkish Delight which will always tempt you to eat more, but young readers in 1950 would instinctively understand Edmund's feelings. The attraction of the Witch is not only that she gives him delicious confectionery, but that she promises she has access to an unlimited supply of it which he can eat in the future. This, of course, makes her a dubious character as well as an attractive one, since anyone who could offer a huge supply of sweets would be dealing on the black market and involved with various forms of criminality.[48]

In fact, examining the historical record more closely calls into question my sweeping statement that children reading *The Lion, the Witch and the Wardrobe* would not have been able to remember a time when sweets were not rationed.

Although they did not permanently come off the ration until 1953, there was a remarkable episode in 1949 when the British government attempted to remove sweets from rationing. Newspapers ran stories in the preceding months, declaring to the public that '[r]ationing of sweets is to end completely on April 24', after a 'surprise statement was made in the House of Commons ... by Mr Strachey Minister of Food'[49] They also reported the words of 'Mr C. G. Monk, secretary of the Cocoa, Chocolate, and confectionery Alliance' who said:

> The Minister's decision to de-ration all chocolate and sugar confectionary has been taken after consultation with all branches of the industry – manufacturers, wholesalers and retailers. We fully agree with what he has done, and have assured him of our help in making de-rationing a success.
>
> ...
>
> If the public – especially the grown-ups – will go easy at the beginning there should be enough to go round at the new level of supply. We believe all concerned, consumers, distributors and manufacturers, will be glad to co-operate in showing that there can be fair distribution without the necessity of coupons.[50]

This remarkable blend of industrial policy, political administration, and sweet-guzzling provided one of the big news stories of the year. When the day of de-rationing came, the papers were full of anecdotes about the scenes on British high streets. The *Gloucester Citizen* ran the headline SHOP SELLS ¾ TON OF SWEETS AS CITY RUSH STARTS, continuing that:

> Soon after one City shop opened at 7.30 yesterday morning a queue began to form, and the staff were kept busy non-stop throughout the day. THEY ESTIMATE THAT THEY SOLD

TURKISH DELIGHT

OVER THREE QUARTERS OF A TON OF SWEETS. They continued selling until they had run out of supplies.

As at some other sweet shops in the City however, it is expected that stocks will soon be restored as some manufacturing firms have still to make deliveries for the last ration period.

It was a great day for the children for many of whom it was the first time they could buy as many sweets as they had money for.

'The Citizen' was told that as the hour approached for the morning service at one City church, choirboys had failed to put in an appearance.

The organist and choirmaster went in search of them, and found them in a sweet shop.

At another shop there were scenes resembling a spring or summer sale. At times the queue was of such dimensions that the shop door was closed, and customers were served in relays.

...

At one store, a small boy his face beaming with smiles, bought 10/- worth of sweets, and lost no time in beginning to eat them.

'Half Gloucester will be ill to-morrow!' prophesied one member of the staff.

The sweet counter was surrounded by 60 or 70 people.

The sum of money mentioned, 10/-, is ten shillings, or half a pound sterling in British currency before decimalisation. A very rough calculation of the equivalent in modern purchasing power suggests that the small boy in question had just bought about twenty pounds' (or twenty-five dollars') worth of assorted sweets. These scenes of unrationed joy, however, did not signal the end of restrictions in the long term. Even after the short-term rush, the supply of sweets was apparently not able to keep up with the demand. Anecdotes suggest that shops sold out quickly, and that restocking from manufacturers could not provide them with enough of what the public demanded. In early July of 1949, a group of Members of Parliament tabled a motion which called for sweets to be rationed again, which read 'This House, having watched the way in which derationing of sweets has prevented large numbers of the population obtaining any sweets at all, calls upon the Government to re-introduce rationing at once as the only way to ensure fair shares for all.' Measures to ration sweets were reimposed in August of that year.

That familiar wartime phrase, 'fair shares', was a crucial element in the public debate over the issue. Some shops found it necessary to impose their own improvised forms of rationing, such as Bradford Bros, Ltd, in Derby, who were reported to have established a 'children-only' queue in July of 1949. Only children were served that day, since an assistant explained 'We feel that it is only fair to let the children, while they are on holiday, have a share of the sweets'. The newspaper in which this was reported noted that '[t]hey were each allowed to purchase up to a quarter of a pound', adding without any apparent irony that '[f]or many it was the first time they had had a chance to buy unrationed sweets for themselves'.[51]

An exchange of letters in the *Evening Telegraph* suggested that tempers and attitudes could become distinctly frayed on the subject of the shortage. A reader of the paper signing himself 'Sweet-Hungry Male' declared that

[s]weets are going back on the ration – and none too soon either. We may now expect an outbreak of moaning from those women who caused this.

I say women, because it only needs a casual look round the queues to discover the cause of all the unrest and grumbling amongst decent customers and shopkeepers alike. Women have had a complete monopoly since rationing was lifted.

Men have long since given up trying to sweeten their weary way for the simple reason that they will not descend to the methods used by greedy women. The unfortunate Government will now come in for a lot of abuse – and from whom? From the women, of course.

Repeatedly they brushed aside warnings that if consumption did not drop, rationing would have to be reimposed. Well, they've learnt the hard way.

This generalisation suggests that there was something peculiarly apt in Lewis choosing sweets to replace the apple in the Garden of Eden in his novel; the writer's conviction that everyone will now have to suffer because the women could not restrain their greed has something of Adam's denunciation of Eve. This letter was answered by an equally anonymous woman in the columns of the same newspaper:

'Sweet-Hungry Male' has my sympathy, although I am of the sex he blames for the present shortage. Personally, I welcome the return to sweet rationing which gave everyone a fair share and their own choice of confectionery on display instead of having to accept any sticky mess in a paper bag.

I haven't seen a bar of chocolate or a decent brand of assorted chocolate since sweets came off the ration. Where have they gone? Your guess is as good as mine, sweet-hungry one, but I opine they've gone under the counter for the specially favoured, and these are not always of the female species.

Queueing has grown to be like a bad habit [:] hard to get rid of when once acquired, but it doesn't necessarily follow that those in line are the lucky ones.[52]

Amidst her defence of women against the charge of greed and chicanery, this writer repeats the principle of fair share[s]', and even hints that de-rationing may have resulted in sharp practices. Her suggestion that packets of sweets are kept 'under the counter', and that some sort of black market or favouritism is taking place, was apparently widespread enough for the charge to be denied in the letters page of a different newspaper. An acerbic letter to the *Dundee Courier* in August 1949, by a correspondent who signed themselves 'Weary Confectioner', disclaimed that any such practice was going on, and set a few other things straight:

> Those people who glare into the windows of confectioners, and remark that there is now plenty of sweets, seem to forget the sweets are there because people can only buy their ration. During derationing, my sweets never had the chance to be put into the window, for whenever a van stopped at my door, in came the mob, and the first thing they said was, 'How much can I have?' Consequently sweets were sold off the counter in record time – not under the counter.
>
> It's those greedy people who have spoiled the efforts of the confectionery trade to give us some freedom which we would have enjoyed by Christmas.[53]

All this controversy, with sweets being taken off the rationing system, and put back on it six months later, took place in the year before *The Lion, the Witch and the Wardrobe* was published. I am not suggesting that the derationing episode caused Lewis to write the Turkish Delight into his story, but that any British child reading the book when it first came out would have strong feelings about sweets and their availability. It would have made Edmund's temptation even more understandable, when sweets had so recently been de-restricted, subject to mass buying and scarcity, and then brought under regulations again.

At the same time, it would have framed the Turkish Delight more strongly as a moral issue. The language of 'fair shares' which surrounded rationing, and the discussion of underhand (or under-the-counter) selling meant that consuming sweets had been framed (to put it rather grandly) as a question of social ethics rather than personal enjoyment. For Edmund to want another box of Turkish Delight, and to be attracted by promises of whole rooms full of sweets for himself, was not simply a matter of wanting more delicacies than was good for him. Eating lots of sweets in this situation could be seen as almost literally taking them away from other people. Edmund's acceptance of the box, and the prospect of more, could be understood as depriving other children of their fair share. The ongoing rationing, and the recent uproar about derationing, would have made the Turkish Delight a resonant symbol for children, as well as for many adult readers. Thus Edmund is not breaking any specific rule or commandment. He has never been taught 'thou shalt not gorge upon Turkish Delight' as an ethical principle or a religious maxim. Nonetheless, the historical situation in which Edmund and the novel's first readers found themselves in would have given this sweetmeat a particular moral charge. The moral queasiness which surrounds it has less to do with disobeying a grown-up and more to do with ideas of fairness and decency towards other children.

DUSTED WITH WHITE POWDER

Reading this episode through the lens of rationing, especially the months before the book's publication, shows Edmund's transgression as both more understandable and more serious than breaking a rule. I'd also like to think about why Lewis chose this particular foodstuff as his alternative to the apple of Eden. The appearance of Turkish Delight may have been suggested by a novel published by Dorothy

L. Sayers in 1930. She had a remarkable career as a writer, moving from relatively minor poetry to detective novels which changed the genre in the 1930s, before becoming a playwright and Christian apologist in later decades, and finishing as a translator of Dante. Lewis was not fond of detective novels, but he admired Sayers and a personal friendship and correspondence between the two developed. Her novel *Strong Poison* involves her sleuth, the aristocratic Lord Peter Wimsey, attempting to prove the innocence of a young woman who has been arrested for murder. Harriet Vane, the woman in question, is a detective novelist whom the police accuse of giving her lover a cup of coffee laced with arsenic. The book follows Wimsey as he explores the Bohemian literary world of the 1920s, which both Harriet and her alleged victim (another novelist, called Philip Boyes) inhabited. He goes to a studio run by a pair of lesbian artists, and a party at which modernist poetry is declaimed over atonal music. The novel makes much of the disapproval which traditional society has for young people who live a ramshackle artistic life, and sleep with each other outside marriage. One of the typically paradoxical details in *Strong Poison* is the reason Harriet and Philip broke up before his death. He believed in free love and opposed marriage as a bourgeois shackle of oppression, and Harriet (despite her religious upbringing) had agreed to live with him without marrying. Some time later he decided they should get married after all, and she was furious that his principles, for which she had sacrificed her own moral scruples, were so fickle. As she puts it, she was offered marriage after proving that 'my devotion was abject enough', as a sort of 'bad-conduct prize'.[54] Despite the disapproval of the judge, and some for the jury, for arty youngsters with no apparent morals, the plot reveals that Harriet is not the murderer. That role was taken by the impeccably respectable solicitor Norman

Urquhart, a cousin of Boyes' who was in need of money after embezzling his clients' funds and speculating with them on the stock exchange. Sayers' satire takes another turn when it is shown that the family money which would have come to Boyes (but which Urquhart would inherit instead) was originally made not by respectable Victorian trade, but by a Victorian actress and demi-mondaine, Cremorna Garden. The administering of the poison was managed by Urquhart by slipping arsenic into an egg through a crack in the shell, after which both men ate an omelette made with the egg. Only Boyes died, however, since Urquhart had built up a resilience to arsenic by taking tiny quantities of it over time, increasing the dose until he was essentially immune to the poison.

Thus, in Sayers' exciting and ironic novel of Bohemian London, the killer was not any of the louche, randy young artists, but a respectable lawyer who habitually ingested white powder whilst stealing money from his clients. Urquhart has a particular fondness for sweets, which Wimsey eventually uses to unmask him as the killer, and one of his particular favourites links him to Edmund. Here is a letter from Miss Murchison, a clerk whom Wimsey has placed in Urquhart's office to investigate him:

> 'I've only been here a couple of days, so there isn't very much I can tell you about my employer, personally, except that he has a sweet tooth and keeps secret stores of chocolate cream and Turkish Delight in his desk, which he surreptitiously munches while he is dictating. He seems pleasant enough.'[55]

Urquhart's habit of munching sweets in the office is emphasised as a private and slightly embarrassing vice. When Wimsey invites him to dinner to discuss his cousin's murder, the difference between their forms of connoisseurship is stressed:

Bunter [Wimsey's valet] thanked him gravely for his good opinion, and proffered a box of that equally nauseating mess called Turkish Delight which not only gluts the palate and glues the teeth, but also smothers the consumer in a floury cloud of white sugar. Mr Urquhart immediately plugged his mouth with a large lump of it, murmuring indistinctly that it was the genuine Eastern variety. Wimsey, with an austere smile, took a few sips of strong black coffee without sugar or milk, and poured himself out a glass of old brandy.

During their conversation Wimsey accuses Urquhart of the murder, and the solicitor denies it, pointing out that he would have died from eating the poisoned omelette as well. Then the detective springs his trap:

'Then how is it,' asked Wimsey, coolly, but with something menacing in his rigidly controlled voice, 'how is it that you have this evening consumed, without apparent effect, a dose of arsenic sufficient to kill two or three ordinary people? That disgusting sweetmeat on which you have been gorging yourself in, I may say, a manner wholly unsuited to your age and position, is smothered in white arsenic. You ate it, God forgive you, an hour and a half ago. If arsenic can harm you, you should have been rolling about in agonies for the last hour.'[56]

In fact the Turkish Delight had nothing more lethal than powdered sugar dusted over it, but Wimsey's bluff is enough to make Urquhart believe he has been caught out. His resulting fury involves him confessing and the case being proved. This parallel in the two novels may be sheer coincidence, but I suspect the image of the sweet-eating solicitor lodged somewhere in Lewis's imagination, and provided him with the symbol he wanted when he came to arrange Edmund's meeting with the White Witch. In Sayers' novel it represents

Urquhart's secret, selfish vice, and is associated with his betrayal of Boyes, a member of his family, just as Edmund's greed causes him to betray the other Pevensies. Wimsey commenting disparagingly on how unsuitable it is for a grown man to gorge himself on sweets has an echo in Edmund's touchy insistence that he is older than Lucy and no longer as childish as her. My facetious remark above about respectable lawyers who have a stash of white powder in their drawers for a little self-indulgence after dinner comes into sharper relief when put next to Lewis's description of the magic sweets:

> ... for she knew, though Edmund did not, that this was enchanted Turkish Delight and that anyone who had once tasted it would want more and more of it, and would even, if they were allowed, go on eating it till they killed themselves.[57]

Though this doesn't become much of an influence on the plot, the Turkish Delight is enchanted in a way which makes it work like a drug. The image of Urquhart obsessively eating sweets, and also taking regular doses of poisonous white powder has the same symbolic associations in *Strong Poison*. This highlights the function of the Witch's gift for Edmund: it is tempting, consuming, and corrosive to his relationships with those he loves most. Chillingly, she gives him the first box freely, and then explains what he'll have to do to earn the next one.

CHAPTER FIVE

BACK
THIS SIDE OF
THE DOOR

LUCY AMONG THE PHILOSOPHERS

The fantastical explorations of the last few chapters are put on hold in this chapter, as the Pevensies deal in different ways with the discovery of Narnia. As Lucy, Edmund, and their two older siblings take various approaches to the new world opening up before them, Lewis's narrative becomes more philosophical. In this chapter, we see him weaving various strands of mid-century intellectual culture into the plot of the novel.

When Lucy returns from Narnia, she is made very unhappy by the fact that none of her siblings believe her story. They go so far as to investigate the back of the wardrobe but, when they find nothing, they conclude she is either lying or joking. Peter, in a telling moment, attempts to laugh it off by deciding Lucy was hoaxing them, and inviting her to triumph over their gullibility. Recognising his role as temporary head of the family, Peter attempts to keep everyone together by reframing what has happened as a prank. (This prefigures the responsibilities he will take on when they enter Narnia, of eventually becoming High King, and blaming himself that he contributed to Edmund's betrayal of the other Pevensies.) However, Lucy will not sacrifice speaking the truth for an easy life, and the whole affair makes her very unhappy. This becomes acute when she and Edmund both wander into Narnia, and when they return he pretends that they were only playing a game. (Another prefiguring of more weighty issues here: Lewis only calls it 'letting her down' but Edmund has betrayed his sister.) Peter and Susan become so concerned about Lucy that they ask the advice of the Professor. From their point of view, Lucy has either developed a surprising moral aberration, deciding to continually lie for no reason to her siblings, or she is suffering a form of mental breakdown. In response to their worries, the Professor assures them that she is not 'mad', and elicits from them the information that Lucy is more usually truthful than Edmund. In this conversation, we can see the novel setting up an argumentative technique which has become known as 'Lewis's trilemma'. In fact C. S. Lewis did not invent this argument, but he made it popular in his public writing and speaking about Christianity and it has become associated with his name. The classic formulation of it appears in *Mere Christianity*, a book based on his radio talks:

> I am trying here to prevent anyone saying the really foolish thing that people often say about Him: I'm ready to accept Jesus as a great moral teacher, but I don't accept his claim to be God. That is the one thing we must not say. A man who was merely a man and said the sort of things Jesus said would not be a great moral teacher. He would either be a lunatic — on the level with the man who says he is a poached egg — or else he would be the Devil of Hell. You must make your choice. Either this man was, and is, the Son of God, or else a madman or something worse. You can shut him up for a fool, you can spit at him and kill him as a demon or you can fall at his feet and call him Lord and God, but let us not come with any patronizing nonsense about his being a great human teacher. He has not left that open to us. He did not intend to. ... Now it seems to me obvious that He was neither a lunatic nor a fiend: and consequently, however strange or terrifying or unlikely it may seem, I have to accept the view that He was and is God.[58]

As a purely logical and theological argument, there are various potential weaknesses in the Lewis trilemma. As people have pointed out, Jesus might have been mistaken about the messianic element in his teaching, but a generally wise and benevolent leader who simply couched his timeless moral insights within the metaphysical framework of his time. More commonly, it is objected that the Gospels do not report exactly and accurately what Jesus said and did, so it is possible that Jesus of Nazareth never actually claimed to be God, but his later followers included that idea when they came to retell the story of his life. Whatever the quality of the theological argument, something similar is clearly being lined up in this chapter of *The Lion, the Witch and the Wardrobe*. It is obviously the form of the trilemma, rather than its content or conclusions, being sketched out: Lucy is not making claims about herself, and none of the Pevensies have yet met Aslan. In a sense, the dice are stacked, since the reader has followed both Lucy and Edmund into Narnia and they know it to exist. (Insofar as the reader has decided to trust not only Lucy and Edmund's perceptions, but also those of an apparently neutral narratorial voice.) However, the Professor's words (or Lewis's smuggling in of the argument) seem unfair only if we read them as logical argumentation intended to convince the reader of a proposition. We could see them instead as the embedding of a logical form in a world which the reader already knows to be fantastical. They playfully demonstrate that logical arguments may support the experience of something beyond our world, but that they only provide a skeletal outline. The excitement of the story is focused around the world which Lucy has discovered. This brief scene has an edge of typically Lewisian provocation: it uses one of his favourite argumentative weapons, by suggesting that in a truly logical world, only openness to the possibility of the mysterious could make strictly logical sense of all possible phenomena. (This attitude turns up frequently in his more combative public essays and articles, where he is fond of positioning himself as the only open-minded and empirical participant in a conversation with materialist atheists who have ruled out the possibility of anything supernatural beforehand, committing themselves to a sort of religious belief in atheism.) Here it provides a less pugnacious account of the intellectual space within which belief can operate. It also dramatises another of Lewis's favourite themes: that modern culture is too obsessed with the idea that it has 'grown up' and that the culture and religion of previous centuries are 'childish' and 'immature'. He expressed this at length in *An Experiment in Criticism*, when discussing literary judgements

> ... if we are to use the words childish or infantile as terms of disapproval, we must make sure that they refer only to those characteristics of childhood which we become better and happier by out-growing; not to those which every sane man would keep if he could and which some are fortunate for keeping. On the bodily level this is sufficiently obvious. We are glad to have outgrown the muscular weakness of childhood; but we envy those who retain its energy, its well-thatched scalp, its easily won sleeps, and its power of rapid recuperation. But surely the same is true on another level? The sooner we cease to be as fickle, as boastful, as jealous, as cruel, as ignorant, and as easily frightened as most children are, the better for us and for our neighbours. But who in his senses would not keep, if he could, that tireless curiosity, that intensity of imagination, that facility of suspending disbelief, that unspoiled appetite, that readiness to wonder, to pity, and to admire? The process of growing up is to be valued for what we gain, not for what we lose.[59]

On the next page of the same book he points out an irony of hurrying to label things 'childish':

> Nothing is more characteristically juvenile than contempt for juvenility. The eight-year-old despises the six-year-old and

rejoices to be getting such a big boy; the schoolboy is very determined not to be a child, and the freshman not to be a schoolboy. If we are resolved to eradicate, without examining them on their merits, all the traits of our youth, we might begin with this – with youth's characteristic chronological snobbery.[60]

Here, in a less than subtle move, he attributes the assumption that the world consists only of our immediate material circumstances to Peter and Susan, who are literally children, but who are not the youngest in the family. We might note that Edmund's spiteful teasing of Lucy earlier harps on the idea that he is older than her, and attempts to co-opt his elder siblings against the stupidities of 'these young kids'. People either side of Peter and Susan's age are apparently capable of believing in other worlds. Their younger sister Lucy entertains the idea, and so does the elderly Professor. The sense of wonder and possibility which Peter and Susan find themselves unable to exercise is evident in those who are earlier and later in development, suggesting that their materialism is not the final state of maturity, but something like a stage they will (hopefully) grow out of in time.

The suggestion that a man as learned as the Professor might be open to believing in multiple worlds is brought into relief by a particular detail which he notices about Lucy's story. Peter and Susan mention the fact that Lucy's trips to Narnia apparently took no time at all, as part of the indications that what she is describing is impossible, and so she must be either lying or mentally unbalanced. The Professor takes this fact to point in exactly the opposite direction:

'That is the very thing that makes her story so likely to be true,' said the Professor. 'If there really is a door in this house that leads to some other world (and I should warn you that this is a very strange house, and even I know very little about it) – if, I say, she had got into another world, I should not be at all surprised to find that the other world had a separate time of its own; so that however long you stayed there it would never take up any of our time. On the other hand, I don't think many girls of her age would invent that idea for themselves. If she had been pretending, she would have hidden for a reasonable time before coming out and telling her story.'[61]

This is another pure twist of logic, of the kind Lewis has been indulging in throughout this scene. The suggestion that one should believe Lucy because her claims are completely impossible – rather than merely fanciful or unlikely – is one of those ideas which seems absurd on first view, but which contains a certain internal logic. The very strangeness of Lucy's accounts of Narnia acts as their own warrant. There is also an added significance to this particular aspect of Narnia, which might well attract the attention of an erudite person like the Professor in the 1940s. The idea that time might be fluid and non-linear was an extremely popular one in the British public culture of the mid-twentieth century. It might not only be that Lucy's ideas about Narnia seem impossible, but also that they sound similar to the theories of some very educated adults of the time.

The central text in this cluster of ideas is J. W. Dunne's *An Experiment With Time*. This book was published in the late 1920s, after Dunne (an engineer) had become increasingly interested in the relationship between thoughts, memories, dreams and our perceptions of the world. He made experiments in recording his own dreams and seeing when and where they appeared to relate to future events as well as to past memories, and persuaded some friends to do likewise. The theory of 'serialism' which Dunne came up with, and published in *An Experiment With Time*, involves the idea that there are multiple regressing timelines. We move along one 'line' of time at which events are 'spaced out', but as humans our attention to the present moment does not prevent us from being aware of the existence of other parts of the timeline. In its normal form, this involves remembering the past and speculating about the future. Thus Dunne argues that we also inhabit a kind of time further back from the single timeline, and from which we can survey and reflect upon our own movement along that line. This activity constitutes our consciousness as humans. However, we are also aware of our own consciousness and our exertion of it, suggesting that there are other timelines behind this one. In this way, Dunne's theories suggest that humans are both moving in time, and able to experience forms of time outside the normally-accepted sequence.

Amidst Dunne's own explanations of his theories, in the third edition (published in the 1930s), there are two elements which make for interesting comparisons with *The Lion, the Witch and the Wardrobe*. Firstly, Dunne roots his experiment in an intuition which he says goes back to childhood:

> But the glaring regress in the notion of 'time' was a thing which had intrigued me since I was a child of nine (I had asked my nurse about it). The problem had recurred to me at intervals as I grew older. I had troubles enough without this one, and I wanted it out of the way. Finally, I set to work to discover what were the contradictions and where were the obscurities. I spent two years hunting for the supposed fallacy. None, I think, can have subjected this regress to a fiercer, more varied or more persistent attack. These assaults, to my great surprise, failed. Slowly and reluctantly I acknowledged defeat. And, at the end, I found myself confronted with the astonishing facts that the regressions of 'consciousness', 'will' and 'time' were perfectly logical, perfectly valid, and the true foundations of all epistemology.[62]

Here is a very similar situation to that depicted in Lewis's novel: a child becomes aware of the non-linear qualities of time because of their peculiar personal experiences, and consults an adult about them. (I assume Dunne mentions the nurse because she told him the 'official' explanation of how time works, or perhaps to explain how he knows at what exact age he started to examine the problem.) In the middle years, the issue is ignored, but when a sufficiently erudite and philosophical point is arrived in his thinking, Dunne addresses and solves the problem. Though perhaps 'solves' is not the right word, since this turns out not to be an isolated issue with time perception. As in *The Lion, the Witch and the Wardrobe*, an anomaly with time is a clue to a whole other dimension of reality which calls into question many of the assumptions in which we live in our world. The other element which parallels Lewis's novel, and which flows from this one, is the metaphysical and existential implications which Dunne believes arise from his discovery:

> As soon as I realised this I sat down and wrote the book. It contains the first analysis of the Time Regress ever completed. Incidentally, it contains the first scientific argument for human immortality. This, I may say, was entirely unexpected. Indeed, for a large part of the time that I was working, I believed that I was taking away man's last hope of survival in a greater world.[63]

These kinds of ideas about time became unusually popular across various forms of literature in the mid-twentieth century. The playwright J. B. Priestley, for example, wrote a cluster of plays in which unusual arrangements of time are both part of the plot mechanism and a theme of the narrative. Probably the most famous of these is *An Inspector Calls*, which is widely taught in British schools. The play shows a comfortable middle-class family sitting down to dinner, whose pleasant evening is interrupted by the arrival of a police inspector. He is investigating the death of a young woman, and as he questions various members of the family it becomes clear that they all wronged her in some way. She was sacked from the factory owned by the father for leading a strike, she was fired from another job in a dress shop after the daughter complained about her, the daughter's fiancée kept her as his mistress briefly before abandoning her, the mother refused her charity because she was pregnant outside marriage, and the son of the house sexually assaulted her on a drunken night out. The family come to realise that they are all implicated in the woman's suicide. The play ends with several dramatic twists: firstly a speech by the inspector directed to the family (and implicitly to the audience), which declares how inter-connected people's lives are, and threatens that if everyone will not learn this lesson, then it will be taught in fire and blood. Next, after he leaves, some phone calls to the local police and hospital reveal that no such policeman exists and no such suicide has taken place. Thirdly, the family receive a phone call to say that the police have just discovered the suicide of a young woman, and are sending an officer to speak to the family about her. Either the previous inspector was a more mysterious figure than they had thought, or time is looping around on itself. *An Inspector Calls* tends to be taught to students in terms of its socially-conscious message about the unknowing damage that the lives of the privileged enact on the less fortunate, and its themes of social change around the two world wars. However, the unusual stage-craft which allows those issues to surface is more than a writerly trick to drive home a message: Priestley is experimenting with the ideas of time around in contemporary intellectual culture. *Dangerous Corner*, another of Priestley's plays, stages a similar sequence in which a group of people are listening to the end of a radio play after dinner. The ensuing scenes reveal a series of awful secrets under the surface of their respectable lives, and the play ends with time looping round in a way which avoids the revelations, and their lives continuing onwards. In this play, there is more of a sense of hope offered by the feeling that time's fluidity may offer a way out or an opportunity to learn. The most explicit example of time theories by Priestley comes in the play *Time and the Conways*. The first act shows another middle-class family, full of hopes for the future. The second act shows the same people years later, and dramatises the way those hopes have ended in one character dead, another in an abusive marriage, another's talent wasted, and the family money dwindled away. One of the family, named Alan, seems surprisingly able to bear these disasters, and he refers to J. W. Dunne's theories as his consolation in a dialogue:

> Kay: Oh no, Alan, it's hideous and unbearable. Remember what we once were and what we thought we'd be. And now this. And it's all we have, Alan, it's us. Every step we've taken – every tick of the clock – making everything worse. If this is all life is, what's the use? Better to die, like Carol, before you find out, before Time gets to work on you. I've felt it before, Alan, but never as I've done to-night. There's a great devil in the universe and we call it Time.
>
> …
>
> Alan: No, Time's only a kind of dream, Kay. If it wasn't, it would have to destroy everything – the whole universe – and then remake it again every tenth of a second. But Time doesn't destroy anything. It merely moves us on – in this life – from one peep-hole to the next.
>
> Kay: But the happy young Conways, who used to play charades here, they've gone, and gone for-ever.
>
> Alan: No, they're real and existing, just as we, here now, are

real and existing. We're seeing another bit of the view – a bad bit, if you like – but the whole landscape's still there ... it's hard to explain ... suddenly like this ... there's a book I'll lend you – read it in the train. But the point is, now, at this moment, or at any moment, we're only a cross-section of our real selves. What we really are is the whole stretch of ourselves, all our time, and when we come to the end of this life, all those selves, all our time, will be us – the real you, the real me. And then perhaps we'll find ourselves in another time, which is only another kind of dream.[64]

Alan suggests that a lot of the world's troubles are caused by people thinking that they have to snatch and grab at their chances against the flow of time, causing Kay to ask if he thinks they should live as if they were 'immortal beings'. Alan agrees, adding 'Yes, and in for a tremendous adventure'.

Priestley was not the only writer of the time whose imagination was caught by the possibilities of Dunne's theories, and the other ideas about time floating around. References pop up in a number of novels, across strikingly disparate genres. Agatha Christie's *Sleeping Murder*, written in the 1940s, begins with a young woman arriving in England from New Zealand and buying a house in the West Country. She begins to renovate the house, and odd coincidences occur. She asks the builder to put a connecting door between two rooms, and he finds there is one already underneath the plaster. She asks the gardener to clear some bushes to put some steps down to the lawn, and he uncovers some old steps in exactly that place. She has been imagining a wallpaper patterned with flowers on one wall, and opens a cupboard to find exactly that pattern used to be on it:

Gwenda stood there staring a long time, then she went shakily over to the bed and sat down on it. Here she was in a house she had never been in before, in a country she had never visited – and only two days ago she had lain in bed imagining a paper for this very room – and the paper she had imagined corresponded exactly with the paper that had once hung on the walls.

Wild fragments of explanation whirled round in her head. Dunne, Experiment with Time – seeing forward instead of back ... She could explain the garden path and the connecting door as coincidence – but there couldn't be coincidence about this. You couldn't conceivably imagine a wallpaper of such a distinctive design and then find one exactly as you had imagined it ... No, there was some explanation that eluded her and that – yes, frightened her. Every now and then she was seeing, not forward, but back – back to some former state of the house. Any moment she might see something more – something she didn't want to see ... The house frightened her ... But was it the house or herself? She didn't want to be one of those people who saw things ...[65]

Christie's gifts for the Gothic are put to full use in these opening chapters, as Gwenda seems to be in a form of haunted house, or to be developing paranormal powers herself. There is a rational explanation for Gwenda's unsettling experiences, but *Sleeping Murder* indulges for some pages the apparent possibility that something stranger is going on. The plot eventually reveals that she stayed in the house when she was a very young child, and so has forgotten memories of it. It is noticeable that Christie not only mentions Dunne's *Experiment with Time* by name, as if contemporary readers would be familiar with it, but structures her opening chapter around the idea of time becoming non-linear. Here it is threatening, rather than consoling or hopeful, as it is in the Priestley plays.

Theories about time also made their way beyond fiction

for adults into children's books. Philippa Pearce's *Tom's Midnight Garden* tells the story of a young boy sent away to live with family because his brother has measles. He is bored by the town flat they live in, and the lack of anywhere to play, but discovers that there is something remarkable about the grandfather clock in the hall. Sometimes, in the middle of the night, it strikes thirteen, and he finds that the door out to the back yard and the dustbins leads instead to a garden. In it he meets a young girl called Hattie, who used to live there in the past, before the house was made into flats and the garden built on. He visits Hattie on a number of occasions, and she begins to get older. Tom realises he is visiting her at different points in her childhood, and eventually she seems to be losing interest in him as she meets a young man who courts her. On Tom's unsuccessful last attempt to get into the garden, he calls out Hattie's name, waking an old lady who lives in the top flat. She is the girl who used to play in the garden, and she spends many of her nights dreaming about the past. It is these dreams which Tom has been walking into through the garden door. A brief summary of the plot cannot quite convey the enchantment of this novel, nor the powerful pathos and even melancholy of its meditation upon time and change. A similar comment could be made about the 'Green Knowe' novels by Lucy M. Boston, which are more explicitly fantastical, but equally plangent. In the first of these, a young boy called Toseland goes to live with his grandmother in a mysterious old house. Playing alone in the house and grounds, he gradually becomes aware of the presence of other children just beyond his view. They are the presences of children who lived in the house in the seventeenth century, and the novel relates both the dramatic moments of their childhood and his own magical experiences at Green Knowe. Boston does not shy away from the realisation which Toseland comes to at one point: that these children have died. The general contemplation of a lost past is sharpened as well as personalised by the individual characters of the children. The later novels also centre on Greene Knowe and explore ideas of time, place and enchantment. The last one, *The Stones of Green Knowe*, involves a Norman boy who discovers that two stone seats on a hill near the house allow him to travel through time. After exploring the different centuries of Green Knowe, and meeting other children from earlier novels in the series, he finds that the stones are gone in the modern world. The novel ends with a kind of fierce consolation which recognisably parallels the other time narratives I have been discussing:

> The quiet hill was streaked with shadows from the setting sun, but no shadows marked the presence of the Stones. Where they had been were two small gaping holes that would soon be grown over. Roger looked with tears running down his face.
>
> 'They were so old,' he said, 'and in their own places. Where have they been taken?'
>
> 'To the local Museum, where old things are kept.'
>
> 'But they were in their own place,' Roger repeated. 'Out of it they will be dead. It's a dreadful thing to do. As bad as sacking a church. And those men behaved like ruffians, the sort that drag people away to be killed' … He turned melancholy eyes upon Tolly.
>
> 'Do you take that sort of thing for granted?' he asked.
>
> 'It happens,' Tolly answered … 'But my grandmother and I do all we can to prevent it. She fights for Green Knowe every day of her life. We didn't know about this.' Then he added sadly, 'Now I shall never be able to come to you again. I shall never see your house as it was.'
>
> 'As it is,' said Roger, finding his wits again. 'And that means I can see you again because in my time the Stones are still there.'
>
> He was alone, and the Stones were standing in their place, throwing long shadows before them.[66]

There is one final author worth mentioning, who includes an explicit reference to J. W. Dunne in their writings: C. S. Lewis. In *Reflections on the Psalms*, Lewis discusses the kinds of vision and image which appear in the Hebrew Scriptures, as part of the poetic and prophetic genres. At one point he remarks 'Our ancestors would have thought that Isaiah consciously foresaw the sufferings of Christ as people see the future in the sort of dreams recorded by Mr Dunne.'[67]

As with other works whose echoes we have heard in Narnia, it is worth considering what it means that *An Experiment in Time* has left traces in *The Lion, the Witch and the Wardrobe*. For many readers, it may have no effect in particular, especially if they are not aware of the feverish cultural and literary interest in time in mid-century Britain. The question of Narnian time might simply be a quirk of this particular fantasy novel, analogous to the fact that Alice enters Wonderland through a rabbit-hole. It serves a plot function, especially at this point, by rendering Lucy's stories less believable, and also by ensuring that the children's adventures in Narnia do not involve them being absent for days, weeks, and years at a time. If we recognise the echo, though, we can see another example of Lewis employing the images and concepts of contemporary culture to produce his vision of faith.

This begins from the typically Lewisian idea, as I mentioned above, that a lot of intellectual and spiritual muddle is caused by people and societies who are desperate to appear 'grown-up'. The anxious elder Pevensies are worried, with some reason, that their younger sister's sudden outbreak of marvellous stories is a sign of either mendacity or mental problems. It is only the much older Professor who takes the elementary, but correct, logical step of considering that Lucy may be telling the truth. The oddness of Lucy's description of Narnian time persuades the Professor by the very improbability that a small girl would invent that aspect of the metaphysics of her imaginary land, but also because it chimes with a number of theories about time which were around in contemporary culture. Lucy is even more unlikely to have come up with an oddity of Narnian life which lines up with the ideas which her adult contemporaries were poring over in *An Experiment with Time*. Once we have noticed the potentially larger importance of Narnian time, we might notice other mentions of it around the novel's climax. When Aslan returns after his death at the hands of the White Witch, his explanation mentions his own relationship to time:

> 'though the Witch knew the Deep Magic, there is a magic deeper still which she did not know. Her knowledge goes back only to the dawn of time. But if she could have looked a little further back, into the stillness and the darkness before Time dawned, she would have read there a different incantation. She would have known that when a willing victim who had committed no treachery was killed in a traitor's stead, the Table would crack and Death itself would start working backwards.[68]

I will discuss in another chapter the metaphysical implications of this plot-point, and why 'actually there was another magic a bit earlier' is not as flimsy a piece of fantastical hand-waving as it may at first appear. At the moment, though, it is interesting that time has such a central place in Aslan's account of the resurrection. The White Witch's inability to get outside time and look behind it is the cause of her ignorance, and thus her defeat. Not only that, but Aslan describes the resurrection as Death 'working backwards', as if the time sequence of the universe has been disrupted. biblical and theological metaphors surrounding the atonement and resurrection do not tend to describe it as a rolling back of events: more common are images of Christ's triumph, of Death's defeat, of a ransom paid, or of a sickness healed. Lewis's choice of image recalls the fluidity and non-linear quality of time in the theories and fictions of the mid-century.

We can read *The Lion, the Witch and the Wardrobe* as inhabiting some of those ideas, and reframing them in a Christian mode. The brief descriptions I gave of works like *Sleeping Murder, An Inspector Calls, Tom's Midnight Garden* and *The Children of Greene Knowe* showed the similarities of emotional tone between them. Time-slips, and time's non-linearity could be threatening as in *Sleeping Murder*, or nostalgic and melancholy whilst also offering consolation as in *Tom's Midnight Garden* and *Time and the Conways*, or a sign of crisis and a call to action, as in *An Inspector Calls*. Lewis, however, takes on the idea of time's fluidity and changes the emotional atmosphere. It is no longer a means of contemplating a vanished world to which we can never return, nor a suggestion that human action might avert future horror. It is a triumphant assertion of humanity's salvation. The possibilities of time, its tragedies and pleasures, its risks and hopes, are centred on the Christian narrative of the incarnation and redemption.

CHAPTER SIX

INTO THE FOREST

YOU CAN TELL A LOT FROM A HANDSHAKE

In this chapter, I would like to consider shaking hands, and what it might tell us about Lewis's attitude to the Bible, as well as his fictional project in creating Narnia. An apparently casual moment, which I would like to explore in more depth, takes place when the Pevensies realise that Lucy was right about Narnia. Peter asks her pardon:

> Peter turned at once to Lucy.
> 'I apologise for not believing you' he said, 'I'm sorry. Will you shake hands?'
> 'Of course,' said Lucy, and did.[69]

This is not a very dramatic incident. Indeed, part of its meaning resides in how unobtrusively it happens. On seeing the magical wood, Peter immediately realises not only that Narnia is real, but that he has wronged Lucy. He offers his apology, asks for a sign of her forgiveness, and she provides it as a matter of course. (We might contrast this with Edmund's half-hearted apology when he first entered the wood, partly motivated by a desire for Lucy to come and help him, which soon turned to condemning her.) This might seem a typical moment of English emotional inarticulacy, or English restraint and understatement if one wanted to put it more positively. Rather than pouring out a flood of self-recrimination and hopes for mercy, Peter asks for a handshake. Rather than throwing her arms around his neck, Lucy gives him a handshake. Nonetheless, this exchange is a significant moment in the Pevensies' story. Peter, the eldest, has admitted he is wrong and asked forgiveness from the youngest. This is one of the lessons he has to learn before he is suited to becoming High King of Narnia, and be crowned at the other end of their adventures. In fact, Peter then makes a crucial, if understandable, mistake. When Edmund mentions the lamp-post, and thus betrays the fact that he has already been in Narnia, Peter is furious at the implication. This means Edmund has been bullying Lucy whilst knowing all along that she was telling the truth and he was lying himself. Peter also realises that he has complicit in calling her a liar, and enabling his younger brother's nasty behaviour, by continuing to insist that Lucy must be making it all up. (Perhaps his anger is increased even further by the worries he had gone through about Lucy's mental balance.) He is so incensed that he cannot bring himself to do more than point out Edmund's actions and call him a 'poisonous little beast'. The narrative mentions that he then stops speaking and shrugs. This is the crucial moment when Edmund might potentially have been brought back, but Peter condemns him in public and does not continue the conversation. Having been forgiven by Lucy, he does not extend his own forgiveness, nor give Lucy an opportunity to do so. Edmund, instead of having a chance to apologise himself (however unlikely that might seem), is thrown back upon silently insulting his siblings and vowing vengeance. When Edmund does express regret, after he has been saved from the White Witch and has talked privately with Aslan, the same action accompanies forgiveness:

'Here is your brother,' he said, 'and – there is no need to talk to him about what is past.'

Edmund shook hands with each of the others and said to each of them in turn, 'I'm sorry,' and everyone said, 'That's all right.' And then everyone wanted very hard to say something which would make it quite clear that they were all friends with him again – something ordinary and natural – and of course no one could think of anything in the world to say.[70]

Indeed, the combination of apology and handshake has already happened in Narnia, a few chapters earlier, when Lucy last saw Mr Tumnus. When he admitted he was intending to kidnap her and deliver her to the Witch, and then decided to help her escape instead, the following dialogue appears:

'Then be off home as quick as you can,' said the Faun, 'and – c-can you ever forgive me for what I meant to do?' 'Why, of course I can,' said Lucy, shaking him heartily by the hand. 'And I do hope you won't get into dreadful trouble on my account.'[71]

This is clearly more than a coincidence. The handshake after asking for forgiveness appears three times in the novel. I believe it has a particular resonance for Lewis, because of the way it echoes the Epistles in the New Testament. For example, the last chapter of the Epistle to the Romans contains these strenuous encouragements to handshaking:

I want this letter to introduce to you Phoebe, our sister, a deaconess of the Church at Cenchrea. Please give her a Christian welcome, and any assistance with her work that she may need. She has herself been of great assistance to many, not excluding myself.

Shake hands for me with Priscilla and Aquila. They have not only worked with me for Christ, but they have faced death for my sake. Not only I, but all the Gentile churches, owe them a great debt. Give my love to the little church that meets in their house.

Shake the hand of dear Epaenetus, Achaia's first man to be won for Christ, and of course greet Mary who has worked so hard for you. A handshake too for Andronicus and Junias my kinsmen and fellow-prisoners; they are outstanding men among the messengers and were Christians before I was. Another warm greeting for Amplias, dear Christian that he is, and also for Urbanus, who has worked with me, and dear old Stachys, too.

...

Shake the hand of Rufus for me—that splendid Christian and greet his mother, who has been a mother to me too. Greetings to Asyncritus, Phlegon, Hermes, Patrobas, Hermas and their Christian group: also to Philologus and Julia, Nereus and his sister, and Olympas and the Christians who are with them.

Give each other a hearty handshake all round for my sake. The greetings of all the churches I am in touch with come to you with this letter.[72]

This is, of course, not the version of Romans that most English-speaking readers are familiar with. In the King James Version, the passage contains an injunction to 'salute' or 'greet' the people named, and 'give each other a hearty handshake all round' appears as '[s]alute one another with an holy kiss' (16:16). The version I just quoted is the passage as it appears in a volume entitled *Letters to Young Churches*, which was published in 1947 by an author and clergyman called J. B. Phillips. This book was apparently spurred by Phillips' experience as a clergyman in London, where he discovered that many of his congregation, especially the younger people, found it difficult to understand the language of the King James Bible. During the Second World War, he began to translate the Epistles of the New Testament into contemporary English, and brought out *Letters to Young Churches* just after it finished. He later continued the project, with *The Young Church in Action* (a translation of Acts) and a version of the Gospels, and eventually some of the prophets of the Hebrew

Scriptures. C. S. Lewis not only knew of this project, but also wrote an introduction to the 1947 *Letters to Young Churches*, clearly thinking this was a worthwhile project. In order to understand the significance of Lewis potentially echoing this version of the New Testament, particularly in the matter of handshakes, it is worth examining Phillip's project, how his version sounded, and what it was intended to accomplish.

Phillips' preface explained that he had set five rules or guidelines for himself when translating the Epistles:

1. As far as possible the language must be such as is commonly spoken, written and understood at the present time.
2. When necessary the translator should feel free to expand or explain, while preserving the original meaning as nearly as ascertained.
3. The Letters should read like letters, not theological treatises. Where the Greek is informal and colloquial, the English should be the same.
4. The translation (or in some cases, the paraphrase) should 'flow' and be easy to read. Artificial 'verses' are to be discarded, though cross-headings can be introduced to divide the letters into what seem to be their natural sections.
5. Though care must be taken to make the version accurate, the projected value of this version should be in its 'easy-to-read' quality. For close meticulous study, existing modern versions should be consulted.[73]

Phillips commented that he did not believe that he had managed to achieve everything he had intended but did hope that 'in the following pages there will at any rate be times when the reader will completely forget that the words are a translation and will feel their sense as if they were 'written for today'.[74] To give a sample of the way Phillips handled the text, we can look at the famous passages about love in the first Epistle to the Corinthians. In the King James Bible it runs thus:

> Though I speak with the tongues of men and of angels, and have not charity, I am become as sounding brass, or a tinkling cymbal. And though I have the gift of prophecy, and understand all mysteries, and all knowledge; and though I have all faith, so that I could remove mountains, and have not charity, I am nothing. And though I bestow all my goods to feed the poor, and though I give my body to be burned, and have not charity, it profiteth me nothing.
>
> Charity suffereth long, and is kind; charity envieth not; charity vaunteth not itself, is not puffed up, Doth not behave itself unseemly, seeketh not her own, is not easily provoked, thinketh no evil; Rejoiceth not in iniquity, but rejoiceth in the truth; Beareth all things, believeth all things, hopeth all things, endureth all things.
>
> (I Cor, 13: 1-6)

Phillips renders it like this, in *Letters to Young Churches*:

> If I were to speak with the combined eloquence of men and angels I should stir men like a fanfare of trumpets or the clashing of cymbals, but unless I had love, I should do nothing more. If I had the gift of foretelling the future and had in my mind not only all human knowledge but the secrets of God, and if, in addition, I had that absolute faith which can move mountains, but had no love, I tell you I should amount to nothing at all. If I were to sell all my possessions to feed the hungry and, for my convictions, allowed my body to be burned, and yet had no love, I should achieve precisely nothing.
>
> This love of which I speak is slow to lose patience – it

looks for a way of being constructive. It is not possessive; it is neither anxious to impress not does it cherish inflated ideas of its own importance.

Love has good manners and does not pursue selfish advantage. It is not touchy. It does not compile statistics of evil or gloat over the wickedness of other people. On the contrary, it is glad with all good men when Truth prevails.

Love knows no limit to its endurance, no end to its trust, no fading of its hope: it can outlast anything. It is, in fact, the one thing that still stands when all else has fallen.[75]

The comparison illuminates some of the most striking features of Phillips' translation (or, as the rules note, paraphrase). The most obvious and immediate difference is that the King James Bible talks about 'charity' and the *Letters to Young Churches* about 'love'. Changes in the usage of the English language meant that, by the 1940s, 'charity' had moved from a large range of meanings which included Christian love, general benevolence, warm affection and moral generosity, to a narrower and more specific meaning of institutional acts of generosity to the less fortunate. At that point, making 'charity' a central value of Christian ethics sounded as if the apostle intended everyone to form charitable trusts and sit on the committees of groups sending shoes to underprivileged children. The word had shifted from the religious and emotional state to the practical outworkings of that state. Phillips' change from 'charity' to 'love' was fairly straightforward, and can be seen in other modern English Bibles. By contrast, he retains the word 'men' in the phrase 'of men and of angels', where other modern versions have 'mortals' or 'humans'. 'Men' in the older vocabulary was understood to refer to humanity or mankind, 'men' as opposed to animals or gods. The same word could also be used to distinguish between two groups within humanity: 'men' as opposed to 'women'. In this context it is clear that Paul means 'humanity', since 'men' appears immediately distinguished from 'angels'. However, a lot of scholarship, especially in feminist and linguistic fields, has pointed out that there is a risk in using the same words for 'humans' and 'male humans'. Men can seem to be the default state of humanity, and women seen only as an additional variation or even a flawed version of the archetype. From this point of view, the double use of the word 'men' is not a quirk of language history, it is an ongoing way in which women are marginalised. It both reflects and reproduces a mindset which sees women as lesser. For this reason, amongst others, many modern translations are wary of using 'men' in this double sense, but this was clearly not something which struck Phillips as anachronistic.

On a broader level than that of individual words, Phillips' version has a deliberate alteration in the tone of the passage. There are phrases such as 'on the contrary', 'compile statistics' and 'look for a way of being constructive', which sound both modern and practical. A reader who disliked this tone might suggest that Phillips has made the apostle sound rather like someone addressing the board of a company rather than a visionary writing to a Christian community. Phillips might be rather pleased by this imputation. His preface celebrates the fact that 'these human, un-selfconscious letters of the very early days of Christianity should have been preserved' and declares that only Romans (and possibly Hebrews) was written 'deliberately as a religious treatise and not merely in the ordinary way of correspondence'.[76] He clearly sees great value in the fact that the Epistles not only inform modern Christians about the doctrines and ethics of Christianity, they also allow them to eavesdrop on the first generations of Christian leaders making arrangements to spread the Gospel throughout the known world. As its title suggests, *Letters to Young Churches* was aiming more for a Christian movement's internal correspondence than the tone of a reading at a church service. That touch of administrative language is even employed for literary effect in the sentence which runs 'If I were to sell all my possessions to feed the hungry and, for my convictions, allowed my body to be burned, and yet had no love, I should achieve precisely nothing'. The slight bathos or anticlimax of the modern phrase 'achieve precisely nothing' after the grand images of 'sell all my possessions' and 'allow my body to be burned' highlights the passage's meaning. The last clause shows up how empty those gestures would be without the essential quality of love, and Phillips' translation dryly uses its modern tone to emphasise the point.

The translation is strongly of its time: it is unlikely that many modern translators would produce phrases such as 'I have made a fool of myself in this "boasting" business, but you forced me to do it' (2 Cor 12) or 'he is not behaving honourably towards the woman he loves, especially as she is beginning to lose her first youth, and the emotional strain is considerable' (1 Cor 7). Noticing this, however, simply emphasises Phillips' purpose, since he was not intending to produce another 'timeless' version to rival the King James Bible. His project naturally had a relatively short shelf life, if it was intended to sound natural and immediate to a few generations of people in the twentieth century. A more searching critique might ask who in that generation spoke and wrote like *Letters to Young Churches*. A modern reader might find it translated into a particular class vernacular, as if it sounds like an officer or a manager giving instructions. There is a definite 'Now then, you chaps ...' flavour to the apostle's words, and even a touch of 'See here, my good man man ...' at times. The notion of clear contemporary English which guides Phillips' translation is the dialect of a particular group in that society, the voice of the upper middle-class and educated, implicitly white and male. This is not to disqualify the version somehow, but to emphasise the way translating the Bible always involves choices of tone and dialect, as well as simply considering whether archaic or modern words should be used.

Lewis's preface approved this approach strongly. It begins on the assumption that the King James Bible is so much the standard version of the text in English that a reader may need persuading that a new translation will be valuable. Against this attitude, Lewis urges that translation has been a necessity throughout Christian history, and that '[d]ozens of sincerely pious people in the sixteenth century shuddered at the idea of turning the time-honoured Latin of the Vulgate into our common and (as they thought) "barbarous" English.'[77] Thus the process which led (in the early seventeenth century) to the King James Bible was regarded by many with the same discomfort which modern people might regard a new and more colloquial English Bible: 'sacred truth seemed to them to have lost its sanctity when stripped of the polysyllabic Latin, long heard at Mass and at Hours, and put into "such language as men do use" – language steeped in all the commonplace associations of the nursery, the inn, the stable and the street'.[78] We can surely detect a whiff of a joke when Lewis picks those particular spaces to associate with commonplace language, since any Christian imagination which shrinks from associating the glories of the faith with a nursery, an inn, a stable and a street is going to have a hard time with the Gospels' depictions of Jesus' Nativity. He continues, going on to insist that the 'only kind of sanctity' which can be lost from the New Testament by this kind of translation 'is an accidental kind which it never had for its writers or its earliest readers' because in the original Greek text it 'is not a work of literary art: it is not written in a solemn ecclesiastical language' but in 'a sort of "basic" Greek; a language without roots in the soil, a utilitarian, commercial and administrative language'.[79]

Does that shock us? It ought not to, except as the Incarnation itself ought to shock us. The same divine humility which decreed that God should become a baby at a peasant-woman's breast, and later an arrested field-preacher in the hands of the Roman police, decreed also that He should be preached in a vulgar, prosaic and unliterary language. If you can stomach the one, you can stomach the other. The Incarnation is in that sense an irreverent doctrine. Christianity, in that sense, an irreverent religion.[80]

Lewis states, in a phrase which will prick up the ears of many readers of the Narnia novels, that '[t]he real sanctity, the real beauty and sublimity of the New Testament (as of Christ's life) are of a different sort: miles deeper or *further in*'.[81] Having connected the 'unliterary' Greek of the New Testament to the condition of the Incarnation, Lewis suggests that the familiar and beautiful phrases of the King James Bible may even impede religious faith at times:

And finally – though it may seem a sour paradox – we must sometimes get away from the Authorised Version, if for no other reason, simply because it is so beautiful and so solemn. Beauty exalts, but beauty also lulls. Early associations endure but they also confuse. Through that beautiful solemnity the transporting or horrifying realities of which the Book tells may come to us blurred or disarmed and we may only sigh with tranquil veneration when we ought to be burning with shame or struck dumb with terror or carried out of ourselves by ravishing hopes and adorations. Does the word 'scourged' really come home to us like 'flogged'? Does 'mocked him' sting like 'jeered at him'?[82]

The fact that 'flogged' and 'jeered' probably have a rather old-fashioned ring to them for twenty-first century readers, and that they have moved closer towards 'scourged' and 'mocked' on the spectrum of contemporary to archaic language, simply underlines Lewis's (and Phillips') point. Language continues to change, and translations which wish to sound as if the Bible was being written by a contemporary of the reader need to be renewed regularly. Phillips was not the only person to think the Epistles, in particular, needed to be rendered in vigorous and comprehensible language. In the mid-1940s, J. W. C. Wand, the Bishop of London, produced a 'paraphrase' of them entitled *The New Testament Letters*. The cover blurb of this volume stated that:

> Letters to friends run, as a rule, straight on from opening to signature, and it would be a great advantage if we could read these letters of the New Testament in the same way. That we cannot is mainly due to the archaic and pedantic style in which they have been mostly presented to us. The Bishop of London's paraphrase attempts to overcome this difficulty. Dr. Wand has put the letters into the sort of English which might have been used by a modern bishop writing a monthly letter in his diocesan magazine.[83]

Aside from risking potentially unkind jokes about whether writing in the style of a modern bishop in the diocesan magazine will necessarily eradicate all pedantry and archaism, this advert displays a similar attitude to the Epistles. The reference to reading letters from a friend 'straight on from opening to signature' implies that devotional reading of the Epistles – whether in church services or in set passages for private Bible study – has tended to chop them up into individual chapters and verses and prevented them from reaching the reader as a continuous document addressed directly to them. *The New Testament Letters* offer a different and more immediate experience, where the reader can imagine that they are part of the Christian communities to whom the letters were written. This cluster of ideas around Bible reading – what we might call an ideology of scripture – is probably familiar to many modern Christians. It is a commonplace of Bible notes and sermons that the Bible (especially the Epistles) should be approached as if it speaks directly to the listener. Moments when the believer experiences the scriptures addressing them personally are highly valued, especially in Evangelical Protestant circles, and a whole sector of the publishing industry caters to this hope. This is why booksellers carry volumes like *The NIV Bible for Teen Guys*, *Mom's Bible: God's Wisdom for Mothers*, the *Outdoorsman Bible (Lost Camo Edition with Field-Ready Cover)*, *The Sports Devotional Bible* or for steampunk fans, *The Aetherlight Bible (New Living Translation): Chronicles of the Resistance*. Underpinning this array of niche Bibles is the assumption which Phillips and Lewis articulated: that the Bible is best read as a message intended for the reader. (An idea attested by the title of probably the most famous modern paraphrase, Eugene Peterson's *The Message*.)

The move from bestowing a holy kiss of peace to giving a hearty handshake all round is a practical implication of this theory of scripture. I chose the passage from Romans to illustrate Phillips' substitution of the one for the other, but there are a series of other examples in the *Letters to Young Churches*. 1 Peter has an injunction to '[give] each other a handshake all round as a sign of love. Peace be to all true Christians', 1 Thessalonians has 'a handshake all round among the brotherhood' and 2 Corinthians has the slightly crisper 'A handshake all round, please!'. The end of 1 Corinthians has a superbly characteristic declaration that the apostle is glad that Stephanas, Fortunatus and Achaicus have arrived, '[t]hey are a tonic to me and you. You should appreciate having men like that!' alongside 'I should like you to shake hands all round as a sign of Christian love'. This was clearly not an isolated translation choice, but a deliberate part of Phillips' approach to the biblical text. In translation terminology, it involves a 'dynamic equivalence' rather than a 'formal equivalence', since it attempts not simply to reproduce the meaning of the original text in a new language, but to express the significance behind that meaning in terms of the new language's culture and world-view.[84] Translating the Greek word for 'kiss' into English (as the King James Version and more modern Bibles do) keeps the word and the action it referred to in ancient culture, but it is at risk of being misunderstood in modern culture. Kissing is no longer something done casually between friends in most English-speaking cultures, and usually has a greater and more exclusive emotional significance, whether between family members or romantic partners. The kind of general kissing which the Epistles encourage might seem awkward or embarrassing to an Englishman like me, implying that here was a church which either had rather different sexual ethics to those I expected, or was a family cult, or was part of a denomination entirely made up of French people, actors and Valley girls. This would, of course, entirely miss the point. It is to avoid confusions like this that some translators adopt a 'dynamic equivalence' approach, rather than a 'formal equivalence' one. The handshakes in The Lion, the Witch and the Wardrobe and Letters to Young Churches seem to epitomise this approach, trying to present the text in terms which will be emotionally and culturally meaningful for the reader. This might give us a useful way of reading Narnia itself, as a world in which we should not expect to see a series of literal representations of biblical ideas or Christian doctrines. Rather, we should look for moments of drama which show something of what the biblical text means, rendered in the emotions and experiences of a later world.

CHAPTER SEVEN

A DAY WITH THE BEAVERS

AS GOOD AS A FEAST

This chapter, with its depiction of the domestic atmosphere of the Beavers' home, and its idealised meal, has been described by some scholars of fantasy as 'a little outpost of jollity' and a collection of 'unexpected domestic moments'.[85] It certainly stands out against the scenes of high fantasy and snowy questing. It is, after all, a cosy interior world in which a tasty meal is eaten amidst an atmosphere of good companionship and cheerful family life. (Even if some of the members of this family are, strictly speaking, different species.) This may lead to some readers finding it too comfy and snug, or even twee and smug. At the same time, this chapter introduces the name of Aslan to the Pevensies, beginning the quest which they are apparently destined to follow. In keeping with Lewis's eclectic style of fantasy, my exploration of these topics will include reference to the Epistle to the Philippians, *The Wind in the Willows,* St Augustine and *Harry Potter.*

When looking at the question of food, rather than connect this scene with a single specific text or two, I will range across depictions of meals within English pastoral and fantasy writing in the twentieth century. I'm going to suggest that 'A Day with the Beavers' can be understood best if we set it within a century-long history of eating and drinking in the English (and Scottish) countryside, as well as the particular conditions under which eating and drinking happened in Lewis's own generation.

The first pastoral meal which springs to mind is Kenneth Grahame's *The Wind in the Willows,* which shows Mole and Ratty indulging in a picnic on the first occasion they meet:

135

'Hold hard a minute, then!' said the Rat. He looped the painter through a ring in his landing stage, climbed up into his hole above, and after a short interval reappeared staggering under a fat wicker luncheon basket.

'Shove that under your feet,' he observed to the Mole, as he passed it down into the boat. Then he untied the painter and took the sculls again.

'What's inside it?' asked the Mole, wriggling with curiosity.

'There's cold chicken inside it,' replied the Rat briefly: 'coldtonguecoldhamcoldbeefpickledgherkinssalad frenchrollscresssandwichespottedmeatgingerbeerlemonade sodawater—'

'O stop, stop!' cried the Mole in ecstasies. 'This is too much!'

'Do you really think so?' enquired the Rat seriously. 'It's only what I always take on these little excursions; and the other animals are always telling me that I'm a mean beast and cut it very fine!'[86]

This excursion is the beginning of Mole's discovery of the wider world of the riverbank and the other animals, beyond the confines of his small burrow. During the meal the two animals will meet Otter and Badger, and catch sight of Toad. The food marks good fellowship and the opening out of the fantastical landscape in which animals talk and behave like humans. Both the Mole and the reader discover something about the way this world works, via Ratty's generosity and the picnic. I think the meal with the Beavers owes something to the hospitality of another talking animal in the English countryside in Spring.

We might consider the meal in its historical, as well as its literary context. During the chapter on Turkish Delight I discussed the conditions of rationing in Britain during the 1940s and 50s, and how this would have affected the way sweets were viewed by the first readers of the novel. The shadow of rationing also hangs over the homely meal by the dam, most notably in the emphasis that there was a big lump of butter in the middle of the table, from which everyone could take as much as they needed. In the abstract this is a symbol of the generosity and fellowship of the meal: since everyone can take what they need, no one takes too much and there is enough for all. Edmund's greed has already undermined this kind of table-companionship, and he rejects it by slipping away to betray his family to the Witch. In the early 1950s, this would also strike readers as an image of wholesome plenty. The idea of unlimited butter taken from a lump, rather than carefully scraped out to make sure the ration lasted the week, would have seemed delightfully luxurious. Fresh fish would also have appealed to many readers as an unusual treat. Despite the fact that fish was not included in the rationing system, it was in decidedly short supply in Britain during the Second World War and the period afterwards. Britain's extensive coastline as a collection of islands, which made supply lines so vulnerable to enemy shipping, might have offered opportunities for fishing. However, that same situation meant that boats were in high demand for commandeering by the navy, and the smaller vessels still operating were at risk from enemy action.

In the post-war period, Britain even went as far as importing canned fish, notably snoek from South Africa, which proved notably unpopular with the population. Discontent, visible in the newspapers, often focused on the fact that the government was apparently foisting this food on the public as part of its import and export policy during post-war scarcity. One northern shopkeeper complained to a public meeting that it was not even fit for pets:

> Mr C. E. Baggs, a Beverley grocer, has a cat which cannot be accused of political leanings. But it does not approve of

Mr Strachey's [the Minister for Food] latest South African delicacy, canned snoek ... 'Snoek', said Mr Baggs, 'is about equal to third-grade salmon, with the toughness of crayfish. I opened a tin the other day and our cat wouldn't eat it'[87]

A Mrs. J. Gray, evidently also in the food trade, wrote to the *Nottingham Evening Post*, to complain of the fish:

> After reading of the millions of tins of Snoek, which the British housewives will soon be seeing in the shops, I would like to say that I have had this so-called fish now for months on my shop shelves. After 'pushing' a couple of tins for my customers to try, 24 people came back and remarked 'What rubbish.' We have had to put up with so many inferior products that the British people are fighting shy of all this strange tinned food we are getting in the shops. Instead of the Government spending all that hard-earned money on this crazy stuff, why don't they buy something more substantial for us to eat?[88]

Whale meat was also controversial, when the government imported it in shiploads to attempt to ease both the fish and meat shortages. Some newspapers ran articles encouraging consumers to try this unusual foodstuff. The regular column 'As Mrs Hubbard Sees It' (in the *Aberdeen Journal*) remarked that a schoolfriend of the pseudonymous Mrs Hubbard 'lives in a northern outpost of Empire where whalemeat is one of the more succulent items on their menu', so that the sensible housewife has 'been spared the shudders that many folk seem to experience at the idea of eating whalemeat'.[89] If this seemed a little double-edged as an endorsement, the *Cheltenham Chronicle*'s Cookery Corner praised the 'appetising and satisfying meals' which could be made from the meat, which it mentioned temptingly was 'unrationed and free from points'. It went on to offer recipes for whale meat for breakfast with grilled tomatoes and fried potatoes, mashed whale meat and tomato sandwiches, whale meat Toad-in-the-hole and escalops of whale meat.[90]

However, the papers also testify to a widespread rejection of this comestible, and an insistence that it was not at all as palatable as official sources claimed. Official recognition of public opinion can be gleaned from the newspaper article in 1949 which reported that 'the Food ministry is banning whale meat in pies which contain other meat ... [p]reviously a loophole in the regulations allowed pie makers to mix a proportion of whale meat in their pies. Butchers, too, were able to eke out their supplies of sausages by adding some whale meat, although it had the disadvantage of making the sausages too dark'. Henceforth, the paper noted with a touch of scepticism, '[p]ie makers who think there is a market for them can sell whale-meat pies, but they must not contain any other meat and must be labelled'.[91]

The narrator's comment about how delightful fish taste when they have only just come out of the pan, and have not long been out of the river, reads in the modern era as a touch of nostalgic yearning for a simpler and more natural way of eating. In the early 1950s it would have contrasted starkly with the canned lumps of dubious origin, which constituted people's main experience of fish suppers. Perhaps the anecdote which sums up best the contrast between the food landscape of Lewis's readers, and the Beavers' table laden with fresh fish and butter, is provided by a bet in Oxford in 1949. Dr Edith Summerskill, who held the post of Parliamentary Secretary in the Ministry of Food, was addressing the Oxford Labour Club on the subject of food, when she is reported to have said, 'People are acclimatised to the new food – snoek, whale-meat and marge. They can't tell the difference between marge and butter'. When there were shouts of denial from the group listening, Summerskill continued, 'I challenge anyone to tell the difference blindfold'. One undergraduate student, the 22 year-old Colin Prestige, immediately stepped up to accept, and the *Daily Mail* sent a reporter down to Oxford to investigate. The paper interviewed Prestige in his college rooms in Oriel and ran an article with the headline 'Butter or margarine man is in training', reporting that he had successfully told the two substances apart whilst wearing a blindfold during a trial run. The stakes of the wager were put up by Dr Summerskill, with a touch of irony: if Prestige successfully told real butter from margarine she would owe him one can of snoek.

This exploration of how the meal with the Beavers would have looked to the book's first audience is based on historical judgement and speculation. Lewis did not write anything about the meaning of food in his books, though (as mentioned in a previous chapter) the gifts of ham from America prompted him to a florid letter of thanks. Another novelist of the time did record the effect which food supplies had on his fiction, though. Evelyn Waugh's *Brideshead Revisited*, written during the 1940s, tells the story of an aristocratic Catholic family in decline. The protagonist, Charles Ryder, meets the younger son of the family, Sebastian Marchmain, at Oxford, and becomes drawn into the family's orbit. The book contains a number of sumptuous meals, and the first comes near to nudging the two young men into fantasy literature:

> On a sheep-cropped knoll under a clump of elms we ate the strawberries and drank the wine – as Sebastian promised, they were delicious together – and we lit fat, Turkish cigarettes and lay on our backs, Sebastian's eyes on the leaves above him, mine on his profile, while the blue-grey smoke rose, untroubled by any wind, to the blue-green shadows of foliage, and the sweet scent of the tobacco merged with the sweet summer scents around us and the fumes of the sweet, golden

wine seemed to lift us a finger's breadth above the turf and hold us suspended.

> 'Just the place to bury a crock of gold,' said Sebastian. 'I should like to bury something precious in every place where I've been happy and then, when I was old and ugly and miserable, I could come back and dig it up and remember.'[92]

This near-magical experience of Sebastian's company in the countryside contrasts with another meal, which takes place when Charles' cousin visits his rooms when he first goes to Oxford:

> he was in his fourth year and, the term before, had come within appreciable distance of getting his rowing blue; he was secretary of the Canning and president of the J.C.R.; a considerable person in college. He called on me formally during my first week and stayed to tea; he ate a very heavy meal of honey-buns, anchovy toast, and Fuller's walnut cake, then he lit his pipe and, lying back in the basket-chair, laid down the rules of conduct which I should follow; he covered most subjects; even today I could repeat much of what he said, word for word.

Waugh's narration, even when discussing a meeting between two grown men, lingers on the delights of 'honey-buns, anchovy toast, and Fuller's walnut cake', before continuing on to detail the pompous life advice which Jasper offered to his young cousin. (This included going to a London tailor because they offered longer to pay the bills, how to address the college dons, and avoiding Anglo-Catholics.) There are several other depictions of lavish eating in the book, but I chose this example because of its similarity to the scene in *The Lion, the Witch and the Wardrobe*, even down to the leaning back and filling a pipe before getting on to discuss serious matters.

When *Brideshead Revisited* was republished in the 1960s, it included a slightly apologetic preface by Waugh himself, in which he described the writing of the book.

> Its theme – the operation of divine grace on a group of diverse but closely connected characters – was perhaps presumptuously large, but I make no apology for it. I am less happy about its form, whose more glaring defects may be blamed on the circumstances in which it was written. In December 1943 I had the good fortune when parachuting to incur a minor injury which afforded me a rest from military service. This was extended by a sympathetic commanding officer, who let me remain unemployed until June 1944 when the book was finished. I wrote with a zest that was quite strange to me and also with impatience to get back to the war. It was a bleak period of present privation and threatening disaster – the period of soya beans and Basic English – and in consequence the book is infused with a kind of gluttony, for food and wine, for the splendours of the recent past, and for rhetorical and ornamental language, which now with a full stomach I find distasteful. I have modified the grosser passages but have not obliterated them because they are an essential part of the book.

Waugh also commented that the drastic social upheaval in mid-century British society, which had inspired the book, did not in fact obliterate the aristocracy as he had expected, His novel, therefore, had the air of nostalgia for a world which had not yet disappeared. The 'gluttony' which he identified later in his own writing included both a hankering for the 'splendours of the recent past' and literal greed for food and drink which was not available in the era when he was writing. The meals in Mr Tumnus' cave and at the Beavers' dam do not exactly qualify as 'gluttony', but they do suggest that Lewis's imagination was similarly shaped by the privations of the time. Having recognised this, we can then look further into the twentieth century, and notice that lavish spreads of food were still part of the language of fantasy literature, even when living standards had risen considerably. A classic example is provided by the feasts in the Hall at Hogwarts, in J. K. Rowling's *Harry Potter* novels. In the first account of a meal at the School of Witchcraft and Wizardry, Harry is astounded by both the magical arrival of the food, and by its abundance:

Harry looked down at his empty gold plate. He had only just realised how hungry he was. The pumpkin pasties seemed ages ago.

'Potatoes, Harry?' Harry's mouth fell open. The dishes in front of him were now piled with food. He had never seen so many things he liked to eat on one table: roast beef, roast chicken, pork chops and lamb chops, sausages, bacon and steak, boiled potatoes, roast potatoes, chips, Yorkshire pudding, peas, carrots, gravy, ketchup and, for some strange reason, mint humbugs. The Dursleys had never exactly starved Harry, but he'd never been allowed to eat as much as he liked. Dudley had always taken anything that Harry really wanted, even if it made him sick. Harry piled his plate with a bit of everything except the humbugs and began to eat. It was all delicious.

'That does look good,' said the ghost in the ruff sadly, watching Harry cut up his steak.

'Can't you –?'

'I haven't eaten for nearly five hundred years,' said the ghost. 'I don't need to, of course, but one does miss it'.

When everyone had eaten as much as they could, the remains of the food faded from the plates, leaving them sparkling clean as before. A moment later the puddings appeared. Blocks of ice-cream in every flavour you could think of, apple

> pies, treacle tarts, chocolate éclairs and jam doughnuts, trifle, strawberries, jelly, rice pudding ... As Harry helped himself to a treacle tart, the talk turned to their families.[93]

It is striking that this magical feasting is highlighted by reference to the scarcity of food or eating. Nearly Headless Nick is unable to partake of the delicious meals which are served regularly below him in the hall, and Harry has grown up not being allowed to have all the food he wanted. It is almost as if the cultural memory of rationing has lodged in this strand of magical children's literature and required a hero whose culinary life accidentally resembles that of the Pevensies and their generation. Certainly this tour through a hundred years of meals has suggested a connection between lavish meals and comradeship in the fantastical tradition, which came into sharper relief during the British mid-century. Readers of Brian Jacques' 'Redwall' novels will know the lengths to which this theme can be taken, but the domestic details of the meal with the Beavers must have been particularly significant for Lewis's first readers.

AT THE NAME ...

As well as containing of the novel's important meals, this chapter is when the children first hear about Aslan. This happens before the fish are caught and cooked, and the butter laid on the table, but since they are about to discuss Aslan further as the meal ends, it makes sense to consider the topic here. When Mr Beaver mentions him, it has a remarkable effect on each of the children:

> At the name of Aslan each one of the children felt something jump in its inside. Edmund felt a sensation of mysterious horror. Peter felt suddenly brave and adventurous. Susan felt as if some delicious smell or some delightful strain of music

had just floated by her. And Lucy got the feeling you have when you wake up in the morning and realise that it is the beginning of the holidays or the beginning of summer.[94]

The narrator also compares the impression to hearing something in a dream which has an effect on you all your life, and you wish to get back into the dream. On one level, this is a pretty effective way of letting the reader know that they will have to pay attention to a character named Aslan. This is something of a plot necessity, since he is one of the most important figures in the novel, but does not appear until the twelfth chapter of seventeen, comfortably more than halfway through the book. However, the passage clearly does more than that. It brings a feeling of transcendence, of the mysterious, into *The Lion, the Witch and the Wardrobe*. That might seem a rather fatuous thing to say. After all, the characters have wandered through a portal into another world, met a faun, a witch and a talking beaver, and become caught up into a magical eternal winter. This is hardly the moment when the first strange or inexplicable thing has happened to them. Still, there is something qualitatively different about Tumnus, the White Witch and Mr Beaver on one side, and Aslan on the other. We might call it the distinction between the fantastical and the mystical.

The effect of Aslan's name on the Pevensies begins to bring his significance into focus, through a small textual detail. The phrase 'At the name of Aslan ...' echoes an especially famous passage of the New Testament, in the second chapter of the Epistle to the Philippians:

That at the name of Jesus every knee should bow, of things in heaven, and things in earth, and things under the earth; And that every tongue should confess that Jesus Christ is Lord, to the glory of God the Father.

(Phil 2: 10-11)

In textual terms this puts Aslan in a parallel position to Jesus. 'At the name of ...' both remarkable things happen. (Those familiar with hymns of a certain vintage may already be humming the opening of a well-known one: 'At the name of Jesus/ Ev'ry knee shall bow,/ Ev'ry tongue confess Him/ King of Glory now ...') Neither Mr Beaver not the children have 'confessed' that Aslan is Lord, but the children have experienced feelings which suggest the name is having an effect on them. Peter's sense of courage, Susan's sense of beauty, Edmund's sense of fear, and Lucy's sense of a wonderful experience just beginning. We might go further and suggest that these equate to particular themes in the Bible: the mighty deeds of God, the beauty of Creation, the impending judgement, and the possibility of unlimited joy in unlimited time. (The beginning of the holidays or the first day of summer is not a bad image for the closest feeling a youngster might have experienced which equates in some way to the notion of an eternal, and blessed, life.) It would be too simple to state that this passage means that Aslan equals Jesus. As I have been arguing in this book so far, Lewis's method seems uninterested in alluding outside the story in a way which simply dissolves one meaning into another. This is emphasised by the particular passage which he chooses to use in introducing the name of Aslan. It is one which stresses the power of merely using that name, and the fact that it is the name of a Lord and sovereign. In modern English-speaking culture we are probably so used to hearing the phrase 'Lord Jesus' or 'Jesus is Lord' (whether in affirmation or denial), that the two words are close to synonymous. But here Lewis chooses to give Aslan a particular aspect which is associated with Jesus in the Epistle. It is also worth noticing the context of the biblical passage, especially the lines which precede it:

> Let this mind be in you, which was also in Christ Jesus: Who, being in the form of God, thought it not robbery to be equal

with God: But made himself of no reputation, and took upon him the form of a servant, and was made in the likeness of men: And being found in fashion as a man, he humbled himself, and became obedient unto death, even the death of the cross. Wherefore God also hath highly exalted him, and given him a name which is above every name: That at the name of Jesus every knee should bow, of things in heaven, and things in earth, and things under the earth; And that every tongue should confess that Jesus Christ is Lord, to the glory of God the Father.

(Phil 2:5-11)

This is a crucial passage for Lewis to invoke with the mention of Aslan's name. It identifies the lion with Jesus' sending as the Messiah and atoning death. This, again, may seem too obvious to a Christian (or post-Christian) society. Particularly amongst Evangelical Christians, the notions of sovereignty and redemptive death are essentially synonymous with the name 'Jesus'. but Aslan is being connected with specific aspects of Christ. He is, for example, not being associated with biblical passages about Jesus' moral teachings, or his status as the Good Shepherd, or his miracles of healing. It is specifically Christ as Incarnation and Christ as redeemer which this passage places alongside the name of Aslan.

A number of questions are asked in the next chapter: Who is Aslan? Is Aslan a man? Could the White Witch turn him into stone? How will we feel if we meet him? These questions could be interpreted as the children groping their way towards a 'correct' identification of Aslan as Jesus with furry ears and a tail. Any reader who has guessed (or already knows) the 'real' meaning of the lion in the book's title is a few steps ahead of them. However, the questions provide a problem for any such simple identification. After all, they point up that this Christ-figure is not human. Jesus' humanity is one of the most fundamental issues of theological reflection on the Bible. Christianity itself has ended up in schism and hostility over different answers to the question 'was Christ a man?' Orthodox Christian thought has held that he was genuinely a human and genuinely divine. The phrase of Gregory of Nazianzus, the early Church bishop, is sometimes quoted on this subject: 'that which is not assumed is not saved'. In other words, Christ needed to enter fully into human nature in order to redeem humanity. The phrase comes from a letter critiquing the theology of Apollinarius, one of his contemporaries, and comes in a longer sentence:

> For that which He has not assumed He has not healed; but that which is united to His Godhead is also saved. If only half Adam fell, then that which Christ assumes and saves may be half also; but if the whole of his nature fell, it must be united to the whole nature of Him that was begotten, and so be saved as a whole.[95]

I have paused on this point, since it highlights the difficulty of simply saying that when Aslan appears in the story, Lewis means Jesus. Aslan is specifically stated not to be a man. Christian theology, as Lewis was very well aware, has never regarded Jesus' human identity as a matter of indifference or triviality. Whichever side of the theological disputes in the early Church one came down on, it certainly mattered. Lewis was particularly aware of these kinds of early Christian debates, since he wrote a preface to a translation of Athanasius' treatise *On the Incarnation*. That work includes the following passage, when discussing the need for Christ to be incarnated as a human in order to carry out the redemption of humanity:

> Next, this must also be known, that the corruption which had occurred was not outside the body, but attached to it, and it was necessary that instead of corruption, life should cleave to

it, so that as death had come to be in the body, so too might life come to be in it ... if death was interwoven with the body, and dominated it as if united to it, it was necessary for life to be interwoven with the body, so that the body putting on life should cast off corruption ... For this reason, the Saviour rightly put on a body, in order that the body, being interwoven with life, might no longer remain as mortal in death, but, as having put on immortality, henceforth it might, when arising, remain immortal. [96]

So I would suggest that the invocation of Philippians does something rather more interesting than giving a broad wink to those 'in the know' that they should replace the name Aslan with that of Jesus. Instead, it brings into the story the aspects of the Christian understanding of Jesus which that passage declares: the sovereignty, the humility, the atoning death, the glorification. It sets questions in motion about the way these themes may be played out in the story to come. For readers noticing the allusion (most likely on a rereading) it probes what they understand by those themes, by attaching them to a figure not called Jesus. It is striking that this kind of theological musing, and the children's own questions about Aslan's identity, occur after the name of Aslan has been mentioned. It is only after the Pevensies experience the different effects which that name has upon them that they come to ask about him, and Mr Beaver attempts to explain. Asking about Aslan in Narnia is not a matter of demanding information, but of looking for the meaning of a mystery. It is the theological process which Augustine phrased as 'fides quaerens intellectum', or 'faith seeking understanding'. In the structure of this chapter, it is the name of Aslan which has brought them to the table.

CHAPTER EIGHT

WHAT
HAPPENED
AFTER
SUPPER

ALWAYS WINTER AND NEVER CAROLS

As a literary critic, writing a book about the textual connections to be traced across *The Lion, the Witch and the Wardrobe*, I was inevitably interested by the moment at which one of the talking animals starts reciting Narnian poetry.

The rhymes which Mr Beaver recites have a deliberately old-fashioned sound to them. Their vocabulary and grammar seem to be not only literary, especially when compared to the homely language of the beavers, but archaic. Mr Tumnus was a much more genteel character, with his 'upon my word' and invitations to tea, and he may have addressed Lucy as 'daughter of Eve', but even he did not talk about 'Adam's bone'. This poem – or scrap of poetry – seems to have survived from an earlier era of Narnia's history. I mentioned in the introduction that Lewis is much less concerned than Tolkien to build a coherent fantasy universe, and that Narnia has less of the trappings of prehistory or geography than Middle-Earth. (He is also less likely to fill pages with verse after verse of songs and poetry declaimed by his characters, which may be more or less to the taste of particular readers.) Narnia does have flashes of a past when Lewis needs it to, though, and this poetic prophecy is an example. The deliberately archaic style of it recalls another text which concerns itself with Adam's lineage and their salvation. This is a medieval carol entitled 'Adam lay i-bowndyn', usually modernised as 'Adam lay ybounden' (which is only a step closer to modern English). It has a bearing on the situation which the Pevensies and the Narnians find themselves in:

PATHS IN THE SNOW

Adam lay i-bowndyn
Adam lay bound
bowyndyn in a bond
bound in a bond
Fowre thowsand wynter
Four thousand winters
thowt he not too long
Thought he not too long

And al was for an appil
And all was for an apple
An appil that he tok.
An apple that he took
As clekes fyndyn wretyn
As learned men will find written
In here book.
In their book

Ne hadde the appil take ben,
If the apple had not been taken
The appil taken ben,
The apple not been taken
Ne hadde never our lady
Then never would Our Lady
A ben hevene quen
Have been heaven's Queen

Blyssid be the tyme
Blessed be the time
That appil take was!
The apple was taken!
Therefore we mown syngyn
Therefore we sing
Deo gratias!
Thanks be to God![97]

154

As that translation shows, the song is about the Fall and humans' gratitude for salvation. Adam, who took the apple, is imagined as languishing in bonds for four thousand years until Christ came to free humanity from sin. The specificity of the image owes something to the tradition in Christian thought that Adam and other souls who lived before the time of Christ were caught in Purgatory until they had the opportunity to be saved by him when he descended into that realm after his crucifixion but before his resurrection. (It is an idea which we will encounter again, in connection with another medieval poem, near the end of *The Lion, the Witch and the Wardrobe*.) The first verse depicts Adam chained, the second reveals the cause by mentioning the forbidden apple, and refers listeners to 'the book' in which learned clerks can read, which is probably the Bible. The third verse connects Adam's sin with the coming of Christ, though it describes this obliquely. It does not mention Jesus himself, but talks about Mary becoming Queen of Heaven, which took place via her acceptance of Gabriel's message at the Annunciation, and her bearing of Christ. The fourth verse expounds another Christian idea more familiar to medieval people: that of the *felix culpa* or 'happy fault'. This is the idea in theology and poetry that there was something mysteriously glorious about the Fall since it called forth God's mercy and love in the Incarnation. Christianity's adoration of Jesus, and gratitude for his sacrifice, led some thinkers to call Adam's sin a *felix culpa*, since it resulted in the arrival of Christ amongst us.

The carol is often used as a hymn or anthem in Advent, as the church year approaches Christmas. It is unusually suitable for the weeks before the celebration of Christ's birth because of its oblique rhetoric. It vividly imagines Adam's sin, and the consequences of salvation, and praises God, but never actually mentions or depicts Christ himself. It certainly does not depict the stable at Bethlehem, with the Holy Family clustered with angels, shepherds or magi. The song manages to evoke the idea of the Incarnation behind its lines, without ever showing it to the singer or the listener. I think it's also very apt for Advent because it begins with an image of cold and wintry weather, the sort of conditions which carollers have always been surrounded by when singing in Britain, and ends in a peal of thankfulness. I wonder whether the people who sang and heard it in the fourteenth century had an even more physical sense than we do of this carol's imagery. People whose wooden pattens had sunk into the mud on the way to church, or whose horse had stumbled on the frozen cart-ruts. People who looked out at the fields beyond the glebe, and knew they would be trying to break open that close, chilly soil with a plough-share in a few months.

If they worked the land, and winter meant hard ground and unyielding soil, then perhaps they would have been reminded of the fact that agricultural labour was one consequence of the Fall about which the carol sings. The creation story in Genesis includes a detail which might have stuck in the memory of people earning their living from the fields of Britain:

> And every plant of the field before it was in the earth, and every herb of the field before it grew: for the Lord God had not caused it to rain upon the earth, and there was not a man to till the ground. But there went up a mist from the earth, and watered the whole face of the ground.
>
> (Gen 2:5-6)

In this picture of the Garden of Eden, the ground contained everything needed for the plants to flourish, and effectively took care of itself without rain even having to fall or anyone to dig it. When Adam and Eve take the apple, later on in the same narrative, however, God explains to them the consequences of their disobedience. Eve is told that women will suffer pain in childbirth and the rulership of their husbands, and Adam is told that the ground has become cursed because of him. It will no longer bring up good food in the same untroubled way as before, and he will have to labour and sweat to get enough to eat:

> And unto Adam he said, Because thou hast hearkened unto the voice of thy wife, and hast eaten of the tree, of which I commanded thee, saying, Thou shalt not eat of it: cursed is the ground for thy sake; in sorrow shalt thou eat of it all the days of thy life; Thorns also and thistles shall it bring forth to thee; and thou shalt eat the herb of the field; In the sweat of thy face shalt thou eat bread, till thou return unto the ground; for out of it wast thou taken: for dust thou art, and unto dust shalt thou return.

(Gen 3:17-19)

In the carol 'four thousand winters' might simply be a poetic way of indicating four thousand years, but it connects the song with the time it is mostly likely to be sung, with the world around the singers and their way of life.

It is this detail which finds such a parallel in the world of Narnia as Lewis depicts it. The evocative idea of Adam being bound for 'four thousand winters', before the arrival of Christ, is literalised in the fantastical world where Lucy finds herself. Narnia has lived through the equivalent of winter after winter whilst the land lay under the witch's spell. The seasonal detail which 'Adam lay y-bowndyn' uses to summon up the idea of suffering, endurance and the curse which Adam caused upon the ground, becomes a physical state of affairs. There is even, perhaps, a hint of the last verse as well in Narnia. The carol rejoices that Our Lady (Mary) has become the queen of heaven, whilst the White Witch has assumed the title of Queen of Narnia under false pretences. It is so much part of her image of herself, and of her control over Narnia, that one of the very first things she says to Edmund is a rebuke that he has not addressed her as 'your Majesty'. In a sense, the permanent winter which the Witch has established in Narnia traps the inhabitants in the occasion on which 'Adam Lay Y-Boywndyn' would have been sung. 'Always winter and never Christmas', as Mr Tumnus expresses it, may appear to be a fairly clunky way of emphasising to child readers that this is not a good thing. Imagine winter, but without snow days off school, without sledging, or roasted chestnuts or the prospect of Christmas. Winter, but without what you like about winter, it might seem to indicate. However, it is also quite a precise description of Advent, the season of the Church's year leading up to Christmas. 'Always winter, but never Christmas' gets over the sense of waiting which this period involves. It puts the characters in the first verse of 'Adam Lay Y-Bowndyn' and keeps them there.

Having looked in a little detail at the carol, we can compare it in depth to the verses which the Pevensies hear after dinner. Mr Beaver's rhymes are somewhat less odd and oblique. After all, it is difficult for any fantasy novelist to invent anything as genuinely weird and surprising as actual medieval literature. Nonetheless, we can see the same themes appearing in his snatches of prophetic verse.

> When Adam's flesh and Adam's bone
> Sits in Cair Paravel in throne
> The evil time will be over and done.[98]

This three-line piece shares three elements seen in 'Adam Lay Y-Bowyndyn'. It concerns Adam, it talks about the crowning of royalty, and it discusses the end of a time of trial and suffering. Similar themes are there in the other verse too:

WHAT HAPPENED AFTER SUPPER

Wrong will be right, when Aslan comes in sight
At the sound of his roar, sorrows will be no more
When he bares his teeth, winter meets its death
And when he shakes his mane, we shall have spring again.[99]

Winter appears explicitly here, just like the 'four thousand winters' of the old carol, though of course in Narnia it is an actual everlasting winter. This verse also conveys more vividly the sense of expectation, of waiting for release, which is shared between Narnia and the image of Adam 'bounden in a bond'.

There's also a technical poetic detail which connects Mr Beaver's verses with medieval verse: the use of half-rhyme. The first scrap of poetry rhymes 'bone' with 'throne' and 'done', whilst the second rhymes 'right' and 'sight', 'roar' and 'more', 'teeth' and 'death', and finally 'mane' and 'again'. In each poem there are rhymes which chime fully, such as 'roar' and 'more', but 'done' does not fully rhyme with 'throne', and 'teeth' does not fully rhyme with 'death'. The sounds are sufficiently similar for the reader to recognise a connection, especially when set amongst other rhymes which sound more securely paired, but the sounds don't have the near-identical quality which we expect in rhyme. This does not disqualify them from poetry, or mean that Mr Beaver's verse is inadequately poetic. Many poets deliberately use half-rhyme as one of their literary technique, as it produces a more subtle, less clanging form of echo between words. These half-chimes might be entirely intended by whichever Narnian folk-poets first spoke the verse. However, half-rhyme can happen accidentally in poems from a different historical period. Rhymes which were full-throated become less secure as language and pronunciation changes and one of the words acquires a slightly different sound. To take a famous example, Shakespeare's hundred and sixteenth sonnet:

PATHS IN THE SNOW

Let me not to the marriage of true minds
Admit impediments. Love is not love
Which alters when it alteration finds,
Or bends with the remover to remove.
O no! it is an ever-fixed mark
That looks on tempests and is never shaken;
It is the star to every wand'ring bark,
Whose worth's unknown, although his height be taken.
Love's not Time's fool, though rosy lips and cheeks
Within his bending sickle's compass come;
Love alters not with his brief hours and weeks,
But bears it out even to the edge of doom.
If this be error and upon me prov'd,
I never writ, nor no man ever lov'd[100]

This sonnet is so well-known that many people have probably never noticed that it rhymes very erratically in modern English. In the first four lines, 'minds' and 'finds' rhymes fully, but 'love' and 'remove' are less than full-throated. Later on 'come' and 'doom' are rhymed, and the final couplet (where we would expect a strong rhyme to clinch the poem's argument) has 'prov'd' and 'lov'd'. This may be Shakespearean artistry, but it may also be the shifts which have taken place in English pronunciation between Shakespeare's time and our own. (Not to mention the shifts in place as well as time: depending on where 'we' are as we read this sonnet, we are likely to vocalise some of the words differently.) It may be that all these words rhymed perfectly when the sonnet was written, but linguistic change has pushed them apart over the centuries. This is why the half-rhymes in Mr Beaver's verses caught my attention. The imperfect chime of 'death' and 'teeth', and of 'throne' and 'done' implies that this poetry adds another touch of archaism to the words he recites. It gives them a patina of antiquity, rather like the half-rhymes we find in Shakespeare or Chaucer.

WHAT HAPPENED AFTER SUPPER

It gives Narnia an implied depth of history, as if talking beavers and other animals have been quoting these lines for centuries, even whilst their own pronunciation has been changing. (The problems with the sociolinguistics of talking animals, though it did come up occasionally at Narnia Club, is a subject probably best left to another time.) The form of the poetry underlines one of the themes developing through this novel: that beneath the icy surface of the Witch's reign there are older, deeper and more powerful things waiting to be recalled.

So it appears that Mr Beaver's scraps of old Narnian poetry are influenced by older English poetry. I'm not sure we could prove that Lewis had exactly 'Adam Lay Y-Bowndyn' in mind when he wrote, and not any other carol or verse, but the coincidences between the themes and the imagery are strong enough for me. If 'Adam Lay Y-Bowndyn' isn't a precise source for Mr Beaver's poems, it points us towards broader insights into Narnia as a fantasy world. It shows Lewis drawing – whether consciously or otherwise – on the riches of the medieval Christian literary tradition. We can see him using images which are poetic in the original as literal and systematic parts of a fantasy world: there genuinely is a continuous winter whose end will coincide with the establishing of true sovereignty.

CHAPTER NINE

IN THE WITCH'S HOUSE

BATHED IN A FLOOD OF SILVER MOONLIGHT

As Edmund forges out towards the White Witch's house, Lewis gives us another sketch of his moral psychology. He describes how Edmund manages to persuade himself that he doesn't really believe the Witch is so very bad, even against his own moral intuition. This insight into Edmund's thoughts continues with a grimly amusing passage in which the boy is prompted by his painful progress across the landscape into making grand plans for the improvement of Narnia. These will involve roads, for a start, and expand into railways and palaces, and legislation against beavers and elder brothers. Lewis gives a comic depiction of Edmund's genuine potential to become a tyrant if the Witch ever did give him power, including his crucial inability to distinguish between the interests of Narnia and his own personal spite against people he believes have wronged him. The sequence is interrupted by a change in the weather, the brightness of the moonlight, and his eventual arrival at the Witch's house. When Edmund approaches the place, he notices its resemblance to a castle, the bright moonlight and shadow, and the statue of a lion apparently guarding the gate. I would like to pause on that image, because I think tracing its sources can provide us with some insight into Lewis's novel.

The image of a castle in the moonlight, with a lion at the gateway, was one which clearly had a place in Lewis's imagination. In his work of literary theory, *An Experiment in Criticism*, one chapter involves him describing why he thinks some people do not enjoy what he regards as 'good' writing. Indeed, to Lewis they seem to positively enjoy 'bad' writing. He develops a theory as to how this can be the case, which goes beyond suggesting that people simply like different kinds of literature:

> The hackneyed cliché, for every appearance or emotion ... is for him the best because it is immediately recognisable. 'My blood ran cold' is a hieroglyph for fear. Any attempt, such as a great writer might make, to render this fear concrete in its full particularity, is doubly a chokepear to the unliterary reader. For it offers him what he doesn't want, and offers it on condition of his giving to the words a kind and degree of attention which he does not intend to give. It is like trying to sell him something he has no use for at a price he does not wish to pay.
>
> Good writing may offend him by being either too spare for his purpose or too full. A woodland scene by D. H. Lawrence or a mountain valley by Ruskin gives him far more than he knows what to do with; on the other hand, he would be dissatisfied with Malory's 'he arrived afore a castle which was rich and fair and there was a postern opened towards the sea, and was open without any keeping, save two lions kept the entry, and the moon shone clear'. Nor would he be content with 'I was terribly afraid' instead of 'My blood ran cold.' To the good reader's imagination such statements of the bare facts are often the most evocative of all, but the moon shining clear is not enough for the unliterary. They would rather be told that the castle was 'bathed in a flood of silver moonlight'. [101]

Lewis's argument, in this particular passage, is that 'unliterary' reading of fiction depends on a kind of literary shorthand or set of 'hieroglyphs' which short-circuit genuine attention to the words being used by the writer. A reader enjoying a badly-written book cannot spend time in close consideration of clichés like 'my blood ran cold' or 'a towering inferno', because they are not vivid or specific descriptions of what is actually happening to the characters. But the same fictional shorthand requires that the familiar stock terms are used, because the reader's imagination is too lazy (or unengaged) to deal with a minimalist description either. They are not willing to build up from their own imagination the elements which the scene needs; they require them to be supplied ready-made. Many people would disagree with Lewis here, and accuse him of a literary and intellectual snobbery, implying that popular fiction is shoddy work read by stupid people. To be fair to him, I think he is trying to avoid that brand of snobbery quite energetically in *An Experiment in Criticism*. He states elsewhere in the book that many very moral and intelligent people have terrible taste in literature, and that it is not in self-consciously 'literary' circles that one finds the truest appreciation of books. For Lewis, it is not possible to decide whether a book will be good or bad by noticing that it is a science-fiction story, or that it has been well reviewed in the literary supplements.

Whatever one thinks of Lewis's literary theory here, it is worth noticing that when giving an example of spare writing which strikes activity from the imagination of the literary reader, he reaches for that line of Malory. For him, it obviously had precisely that effect, of not only providing a vivid image but also stimulating the imagination to work on the few details given. I would suggest that Edmund's arrival at the house of the White Witch is partly the result of that impact, of Lewis's imagination being so taken by the image that he ended up using it to tell a different story. It is worth tracing the line back to its place, in Thomas Malory's *Morte d'Arthur*, where it appears during an adventure when Sir Galahad and Sir Launcelot are on a quest to find the Holy Grail:

'Now, my son, Sir Galahad, sith we shall depart and neither of us see other more, I pray to that High Father, conserve me and you both.'

'Sir,' said Galahad, 'No prayer availeth so much as yours.'

And therewith Galahad entered into the forest; and the wind arose, and drove Sir Lancelot more than a month through the sea, where he slept but little, but prayed to God that he might see some tidings of the Sangrail.

So it befell on a night, at midnight he arrived before a castle, on the back side, which was rich and fair. And there was a postern opened towards the sea, and was open without any keeping, save two lions kept the entry; and the moon shone right clear. [102]

In the passage which follows, Lancelot attempts to enter the castle and draws his sword to attack the lions, but a dwarf appears and strikes him so that he drops his sword. A mysterious voice calls out to him asking why he trusts more in his armour than in his Maker, and Lancelot makes the sign of the cross on his forehead and passes by the lions without being hurt.

Lewis's imagination was apparently spurred by that image in Malory, and worked on it to produce a rather different narrative episode. The parallels are striking, but so are the differences. Edmund and Lancelot both arrive at a castle on a quest, though one is on a noble adventure and the other is coming to betray his family to a sorcerer. (We might notice that Edmund is looking for food, wanting more Turkish Delight, whilst Lancelot is hoping he may find the Sangrail or Holy Grail, the cup from which Jesus drank at the Last Supper.) They both encounter lions, and are initially defeated, but both discover that a greater power has rendered the creatures unable to harm them. Here the parallel nearly tips over into mockery, since the power which saves Lancelot is that of Christ, but Edmund is safe because the White Witch has already turned his lion into stone. As a final touch, Lancelot responds to the greater power by placing the sign of the cross on his face, whilst Edmund's equivalent action is to deface the stone lion (whom he thinks might be Aslan) by scribbling on its face.

The connection between these two passages, which becomes more precise the more they are compared, suggests that Lewis's creativity was particularly engaged by the Malory passage. His account of it as a passage with real literary power – or at least a passage which 'unliterary' reading could never appreciate properly – chimes with the use he made of it in his own fiction. He bears his own theory out, not in copying the passage from Malory or reproducing its effect, but in using it to produce a very different scene. The parallels also underline the seriousness of Edmund's moral situation on this adventure. Just as the echoes of Dante and *Sir Orfeo* which surrounded Lucy give some sense of the importance of her stumbling through the wardrobe, Edmund has apparently wandered into a story of enormous significance. His scribbling on the face of a statue has almost attained the status of blasphemy, when compared with Lancelot's signing himself with the cross. This strikes me as part of what we might call the moral seriousness of *The Lion, the Witch and the Wardrobe*. This does not manifest itself in a laboured tone, or long passages of moralising to the reader. Instead it shows characters acting on perfectly understandable, if not very praiseworthy, motives and who find themselves caught up in something much larger and more significant than they had realised.

THE PRIDE OF EDMUND

As Edmund has left the dinner table at the Beavers' lodge, he has gathered the symbolic sins of Adam and Judas. He has eaten something he knows he should not (in defiance of authority), and he has betrayed those closest to him. There is yet another sinful figure who I believe is associated with Edmund, however. At the risk of piling damnation on his shoulders, I think we should see Edmund as committing the sins of Lucifer. The rather ordinary schoolboy from London is increasingly behaving like Satan. By that I do not mean that he is quintessentially evil, or committing the more epic crimes, or that he is starring in a Hammer Horror movie (though in a couple of chapters I am about to mention the novels of Dennis Wheatley). Nonetheless, there is a specific moral flaw which Edmund increasingly displays in this sequence, and it becomes evident that he has been acting on its impulses since the novel began. The sin of Lucifer is one which Lewis saw as absolutely central to Christian morality, as he explains in one of the talks collected in *Mere Christianity*. He gives this flaw a remarkable rhetorical build-up, saying that '[t]here is one vice of which no man in the world is free; which every one in the world loathes when he sees it in someone else; and of which hardly any people, except Christians, ever imagine that they are guilty themselves'.[103] By contrast, he says, people admit comfortably that they have a weakness for girls or drink, or that they are a bit cowardly. This sin however, is one which no one is aware they possess, and one which everyone hates in everyone else.

Then Lewis explains the sin he is taking about, which might come as a surprise to many of his readers, since it seems rather peripheral to contemporary morality. Indeed, it often has a mildly positive sense in popular discussion:

> The vice I am talking of is Pride or Self-Conceit: and the virtue opposite to it, in Christian morals, is called Humility... According to Christian teachers, the essential vice, the utmost evil, is Pride. Unchastity, anger, greed, drunkenness, and all that, are mere fleabites in comparison: it was through Pride that the devil became the devil: Pride leads to every other vice: it is the complete anti-God state of mind.[104]

This drastic assessment of human pride, Lewis goes on to explain, is because pride is wholly competitive and destructive: '[p]ride gets no pleasure out of having something, only out of having more of it than the next man'. Pride, according to him, does not enjoy being wealthy or comfortable or loved, but being wealthier, more comfortable and more loved than other people. For this reason, it is insatiable, because it does not want things (or even people) for their own sake. I should point out that Lewis does not see himself as expounding a new moral principle or psychological insight here. As with so much of his writings, he is elaborating what he has found in the Christian tradition, as highlighted by his comment 'it was through Pride that the devil became the devil'.

This is a reference to the tradition that Satan led a rebellion in heaven, and was cast out after being defeated. Its major biblical source is the passage in revelation which describes a heavenly war:

> And there was war in heaven: Michael and his angels fought against the dragon; and the dragon fought and his angels, And prevailed not; neither was their place found any more in heaven. And the great dragon was cast out, that old serpent, called the Devil, and Satan, which deceiveth the whole world: he was cast out into the earth, and his angels were cast out with him.
>
> (Rev 12: 7-9)

In theological and literary tradition this is often connected to the passage of Isaiah in which the prophet castigates a Babylonian ruler:

> How art thou fallen from heaven, O Lucifer, son of the morning! how art thou cut down to the ground, which didst weaken the nations! For thou hast said in thine heart, I will ascend into heaven, I will exalt my throne above the stars of God: I will sit also upon the mount of the congregation, in the sides of the north: I will ascend above the heights of the

clouds; I will be like the most High. Yet thou shalt be brought down to hell, to the sides of the pit.

(Isa 14: 12-15)

These passages provided a source of inspiration for the development of imagery and narrative about Satan and his rebel angels. Most modern Christians probably think of the Fall of Adam and Eve as the defining episode illustrating sin's arrival in the world, and think of the fall of the angels as marginal (if they are aware of it at all). It loomed much larger in Christian consciousness for many centuries. The most famous example is Milton's *Paradise Lost*, which begins with Satan and his cohorts having fallen from heaven, and involves him working his way through the cosmos to Eden in order to tempt Adam and Eve. For Milton, Satan's fall was narratively prior to Eve's, and it is repeatedly associated with the word 'pride'. The narrator of the poem, having asked how he first humans were tempted, answers that:

> Th' infernal Serpent; he it was whose guile,
> Stirred up with envy and revenge, deceived
> The mother of mankind, what time his pride
> Had cast him out from Heaven, with all his host
> Of rebel Angels, by whose aid, aspiring
> To set himself in glory above his peers,
> He trusted to have equalled the Most High,
> If he opposed, and with ambitious aim
> Against the throne and monarchy of God,
> Raised impious war in Heaven and battle proud[105]

Anyone exploring *Paradise Lost* will find pride as a repeated motif, but these early lines show a cluster of connections. According to Milton, the temptation of Eve was the result of Satan's envy of her happy state, after his pride and desire to be above his peers had caused him to rebel against God.

Edmund's crimes may be on a much smaller scale, but they are recognisably similar if viewed through Lewis's insistence on pride as the major sin. Even before discovering Narnia for himself, he sneers at his sister for being younger and lesser than him, then cannot bear to lose face by admitting she was right. When the White Witch offers to make his siblings courtiers, he hurriedly tells her that there is nothing special about them. When struggling through the snow on his way to the Witch' house, he thinks up schemes to put Peter down. By the time he arrives at the castle, he is ready to become an anti-Lancelot, to deface the stone lion and jeer at the name of Aslan. To trace these echoes in the chapter is not to suggest that Lewis is picking on one of his own characters, or exaggerating totally comprehensible bad behaviour by a schoolboy. Rather, the text shows human moral actions taking place against a grander backdrop than we realise.

CHAPTER TEN

THE SPELL BEGINS TO BREAK

I n this chapter, the Pevensies flee from the White Witch's secret police, spend the night in an underground hide-out, think they have been tracked down, meet Father Christmas and receive a series of magical gifts and weapons from him. Then arrives the climactic moment of the episode: everyone has a cup of tea:

> and he brought out (I suppose from the big bag at his back, though nobody quite saw him do it) a large tray containing five cups and saucers, a bowl of lump sugar, a jug of cream, and a great big teapot all sizzling and piping hot [106]

In fact, this moment has been foreshadowed at the very beginning of the chapter. Whilst everyone is frantically preparing to leave the Beaver's dam, knowing that their location has almost certainly been betrayed to the Witch, Mrs Beaver makes a point of packing the necessary items: 'And here's a packet of tea, and there's sugar, and some matches'. At both ends of this fantastical episode Lewis includes the wherewithal to make tea, with the addition of some bread and butter. This is an aspect of the chapter which I would like to spend some time considering.

The first point to make about the tea, which will probably be obvious to anyone who has read my earlier chapters, is that this is a vision of domestic plenitude. Tea was a firmly-established part of British culture by the early twentieth century. This was not solely the case for the upper and middle classes. For some modern readers, the idea of 'taking tea' might summon up images of dainty cups and finger sandwiches, with a vista of lawns beyond the table. However, tea was a big part of the daily life of all classes. George Orwell's study of poverty in the nation, *The Road to Wigan Pier*, discusses it as one of the cheap treats which the working class use to brighten their day, along with scraps from the chip shop. Tea was duly rationed during and after the war, and little packets of tea, such as Mrs Beaver makes up, became a part of everyday life. They would be carried home from the grocer's shop to be added to the meagre pile in the caddy at home, or handed over to a landlady, or even taken to a friend's house when visiting for a meal. The latter custom is mentioned in passing in a detective novel by Cyril Hare, which was published the year before *The Lion, the Witch and the Wardrobe*. The main character, a rather precise little solicitor called Francis Pettigrew, is hosting the Chief Constable of the county to discuss a case they are involved in, and the policeman helps himself to a rather large drink:

> 'Thank you,' said the Chief Constable. He helped himself liberally from the decanter, added the minimum of soda water and half emptied his glass at a gulp. 'I've left a couple of bottles for you in the hall,' he added.
>
> 'You've—what?' asked Pettigrew faintly.
>
> 'I have never been able to understand,' said MacWilliam, looking meditatively at the glass in his hand, 'why, in these days of shortages and rationing, it should be considered perfectly proper for guests to bring with them morsels of tea and sugar and disgusting little packets of margarine for the benefit of their hosts, while it is taken for granted that they should be supplied ad libitum with substances far more precious and—if you will forgive my mentioning it—a great deal more expensive. Now I don't very much care for tea and hardly take any sugar, but I do—as you may conceivably have observed— drink an appreciable quantity of whisky of an evening. I repeat, therefore, I have left two bottles for you in the hall.'[107]

THE SPELL BEGINS TO BREAK

The point of the episode for 1940s readers was surely the Chief Constable's eccentric behaviour and unusual application of the customs and etiquette around food which had developed since the introduction of rationing. For us in the twenty-first century, though, the more interesting point is the way MacWilliam reveals those customs by breaking them and having to explain why. I will not go further into the details of tea rationing, but it seems significant that this chapter book-ends the meeting with Father Christmas and the giving of the gifts (which make clear the children are on a quest) with a cup of tea.

This blend of the domestic, the folkloric and the chivalric suggests a comparison with the work of John Bunyan, the seventeenth-century preacher and writer. His allegorical question narrative *The Pilgrim's Progress* depicts a character called Christian who sets out on an adventure and has to face figures such as the Giant Despair and Mr Worldlywiseman on his way to the Celestial City. It was a huge influence on subsequent British literature and culture, and became a foundational text for many fantasy novelists. The rhetoric and genre of *The Pilgrim's Progress* impressed Lewis deeply, and his writing about the book sounds at times as if he is describing his own fiction in the Narnia novels.

When Lewis discusses the particular form which *Pilgrim's Progress* took, he writes that

> My own guess is that the scheme of a journey with adventures suddenly reunited two things in Bunyan's mind which had hitherto lain far apart. One was his present and lifelong preoccupation with the spiritual life. The other, far further away and longer ago, left behind (he had supposed) in childhood, was his delight in old wives' tales and such last remnants of chivalric romance as he had found in chap-books. The one fitted the other like a glove. [108]

Lewis suggests that the form meant that the 'high theme had to be brought down and incarnated on the level of an adventure story of the most unsophisticated type', since it was phrased as 'a quest story, with lions, goblins, giants, dungeons and enchantments'. Having traced this combination of spiritual meaning with adventure quest, Lewis argues that there was a 'further descent', since the 'adventure story is not left in the world of high romance'. On the contrary 'it is all visualised in terms of the contemporary life which Bunyan knew', with details such as

> the bullying, foul-mouthed Justice; the field-path, seductive to footsore walkers; the sound of a dog barking as you stand knocking at a door; the fruit hanging over a wall which the children insist on eating though their mother admonishes them 'that Fruit is none of ours'[109]

This double 'descent', though Lewis clearly did not see it as making the work lesser, seems a useful way to look at the current chapter. The children's spiritual journey is represented as a quest, and here we have the trappings of chivalric romance such as the weapons and armour, the horn and the bottle of miraculous potion. At the same time, there are the details of 'contemporary life', such as the sewing machine and the packet of tea. The combination is neatly highlighted by the fact that the scene in which Peter is given his sword ends with Mrs Beaver being glad she brought the bread-knife. Enemies may need to be cleaved in two on the battlefield, but in the meantime blades are needed for another purpose.

The discussion of Bunyan should not lead us, however, to think of the Narnia novels as simply an 'encoding', even if twice encoded. Tracing the way a spiritual theme is developed by chivalric imagery and domestic detail might sound as if there is a pre-existing 'real story' which has simply been covered up with incidental touches. Lewis's own writing on Bunyan makes clear that this was not how he imagined *Pilgrim's Progress* worked. He complains that one critic read the story of Christian's adventures and thought the motives attributed to him were 'too low':

> But that is to misunderstand the very nature of all allegory or parable or even metaphor. The lowness is the whole point. Allegory gives you one thing in terms of another. All depends on respecting the rights of the vehicle, in refusing to allow the least confusion between the vehicle and its freight. The Foolish Virgins, within the parable, do not miss beatitude; they miss a wedding party. The Prodigal Son, when he comes home, is not given spiritual consolations; he is given new clothes and the best dinner his father can put up. It is extraordinary how often this principle is disregarded. [110]

Lewis goes on to castigate the illustrator of the edition of Bunyan which he read as a child. In one scene, a very old lady is called over a river to the other side at the end of her life, with acclamation and a fanfare of trumpets. The illustrator had drawn a sweetly sentimental Victorian death-bed image, accurately identifying the symbolism of the episode, but totally missing the point according to Lewis:

> This stupidity perhaps comes from the pernicious habit of reading allegory as if it were a cryptogram to be translated; as if, having grasped what an image (as we say) 'means', we threw the image away and thought of the ingredient in real life which it represents. But that method leads you continually out of the book back into the conception you started from and would have had without reading it. [111]

He insists that the correct way to read allegory is the exact opposite, and that 'We ought not to be thinking "This green

valley, where the shepherd boy is singing, represents humility";
we ought to be discovering, as we read, that humility is like
that green valley'. This form of reading, the correct one for
Lewis, means that we are 'moving always into the book, not
out of it'.[112]

This is not Lewis's only statement on the subject of
allegory. He wrote an entire book on the subject, entitled *The
Allegory of Love*, which is something of a classic in the field. This
discussion of Bunyan does, however, shed a remarkable light
on how the novelist thought and felt about these topics. There
is no particular textual echo or parallel between 'The Spell
Begins to Break' and a specific episode in *The Pilgrim's Progress*.
Nonetheless, the chapter demonstrates exactly the qualities
which Lewis found and admired in Bunyan's work. The high
spiritual meanings, the story framed as an adventurous quest
complete with fantastical figures, and the characters' actions
rooted in the mundane world which author and reader both
knew. They are all there, as if Lewis had been writing about his
own novelistic style rather than the work of a seventeenth-
century preacher.

CHAPTER ELEVEN

ASLAN
IS NEARER

This chapter is one I often forget or overlook when mapping out the action of the novel in my head. It feels rather an afterthought to the main drive of the narrative, summed up by the fact that its first sentence runs 'Edmund meanwhile had been having a most disappointing time' and it is entitled 'Aslan is Nearer'.[113] Both seem to indicate a chapter defined by what is not going on. Edmund is not having a magical encounter with Father Christmas (unlike his siblings) and Aslan has not yet arrived. This feeling is slightly modified, on reading through the chapter, by the fact that it contains a notably dramatic incident. The White Witch and her two companions meet a small group of Narnians, who are celebrating the warmer weather with a small party, and she turns them into stone out of rage and spite. This is the first time we see the Witch's baleful powers in action in front of us as readers. We have previously seen her produce food and drink from nowhere, heard Tumnus' fears of what she will do to him, and seen the courtyard of statues at her house. The readers know she is capable of horrific things. But this is the first time the reader – and Edmund – see her carry out the petrifying magic for which she is so notorious. Nonetheless, the chapter still feels expectant rather than dramatic to me. On closer scrutiny, the Witch's encounter with the feasting Narnians only occupies about a page and a half, in contrast with at least double that number of pages which are taken up with describing the weather and the environment surrounding the characters. Trees drip, birds sing, flowers appear through the snow, breezes carry scents around and waters splash. This is the main focus of the chapter, even if it does not involve a lot of activity by the characters. We might be used to thinking of descriptions of the natural surroundings as a prelude to action, as something which the novelist puts in to allow us to situate the characters and imagine them more vividly. Here, however, the prelude has become the main drama and the background has become foreground. The characters themselves even turn and notice the natural world around them, going so far as to disagree about it. Just as the chapter is ending, the dwarf suggesting that the thaw they are experiencing is in fact a much deeper and more profound change: it is Spring, and it is the work of Aslan. The Witch, who has recently shown her powers of destruction, threatens to kill either of her companions if they ever mention the lion's name again.

So in this chapter, I will begin by focusing on what seems so important to both the narrator and the Witch: the small details of the natural world. The elements which Lewis makes a point of mentioning are those we probably associate with the arrival of warmer weather in Spring: flowers, trees, the singing of birds, the sound of splashing water now ice has melted, the soft touch of a breeze and the scents of the plants. There are particular details about the multiple descriptions of the natural elements, which bring to mind two sources: the medieval poet Geoffrey Chaucer, and the biblical book known as the Song of Songs. Chaucer was a fourteenth-century poet, most famous today for his long poem *The Canterbury Tales*. Like many writers of the time, his work includes enthusiastic descriptions of Spring, a season associated with returning life and renewed hope. A notable example appears in his poem *The Parliament of Fowls*. (It is a 'dream' vision, a medieval genre in which a poet relates an allegorical scene which they claim they experienced in a dream. This allows a certain amount of fantastical imagery and narrative, given the generally-experienced weirdness of dreams in general. It also allows an allegorical style which may hint that the symbolic actions in the dream are connected with things in the real world. Medieval theories about dreams included the prosaic idea that people often dreamed about things which they did in their everyday life, but also included the possibility that dreams could reveal hidden insights or even predict the future. From this brief description of the genre, it is easy to see similarities between some elements of dream vision poems, and fantasy fiction. Indeed some of the earlier fantasy writers before the existence of Narnia used the dream form as a way of transporting their main character into a world full of impossibilities, and John Bunyan used it to frame his *Pilgrim's Progress*, which had huge influence on the fantasy genre. (I should note here that I am grateful to Sam Masters for his very striking insights into dream poetry and fantasy literature, which he shared during meetings of Narnia Club.)

In *The Parliament of Fowls*, the poet begins by complaining that life is short, whilst wisdom and skill take a long time to learn. He relates that he was reading *The Dream of Scipio*, a Latin work involving a dream journey, one night before he fell asleep. Then it seemed to him that the great Scipio himself was standing by his bed, and took him to a walled park with a gate in it, above which were lines of verse which seemed to promise both delight and torment. As the dreamer hesitated before the gate, Scipio pushed him through, and he found himself in a beautiful garden landscape. The poem describes it thus:

> A gardyn saw I, ful of blossomed bowis,
> *I saw a garden full of boughs of blossom*
> Upon a river, in a grene mede,
> *By a river, in a green meadow*
> Ther as swetnes ever mo ynow is,
> *Where sweetness is always in abundance*
> With floures white, blew, yelow, and rede;
> *With flowers white, blue, yellow and red,*

PATHS IN THE SNOW

And colde well stremes, no thing dede,
And cold streams of water from a well, lively in flowing
That swymmyn ful of smale fisshes lyght,
That was full of small quick fishes
With fynnes rede and scales sylver bryght.
With red fins, and silver-bright scales
On every bough the briddes herde I synge,
I heard the birds singing on every bough
With voys of aungel in her armonye,
With angelic voices in their harmony
Som besyed hem hir briddes forth to brynge;
Which were looking after their youngsters
The lytel conyes to hir pley gunnen hye.
The little rabbits rushed off to their playing
And further al aboute y gan espye
All I began to see, all around
The dredful roo, the buk, the hert and hynde,
The timid roe, the buck, and hart and hind,
Squerels, and bestis smale of gentil kynde.
Squirrels, and small creatures of noble kinds
Of instruments of strenges in acord
I heard the music of stringed instruments playing in harmony
Herde I so pleye a ravisshing swetnesse,
With such a ravishing sweetness
That God, that maker is of al and lord,
That God, who is the creator and Lord of everything
Ne herde never better, as I gesse;
Never heard anything better, I would think
Therwith a wind, unnethe it might be lesse,
And with that a wind, it hardly could have been softer
Made in the leves grene a noise softe
Made a soft sounds amongst the green leaves
Acordaunt to the foules songe on-lofte.[114]
Which harmonised with the songs of the birds above

This passage contains the same elements which appear in Lewis's rapturous descriptions of the Narnian landscape as it began to wake from the winter. A couple of touches especially recall Narnia. Firstly, the running water is called 'cold well stremes, no thing dede', which simply means 'lively and flowing', but has a more literal resonance in the landscape where the Witch's reign brings both winter and death. Secondly, Chaucer describes the garden containing 'squerels, and betes smale of gentil kinde', whilst Edmund and the Witch meet a family of squirrels amongst Narnians celebrating at the table. The adjective 'gentil' adds a further echo, since in Middle English (the version of the language in which Chaucer wrote), this word does not mean 'tender' or 'not rough'. It has the older meaning of 'noble or fine', derived from 'gentle' meaning 'aristocratic and of high birth'; this is the meaning which is preserved faintly (and often ironically) in the modern words 'gentleman' or 'genteel'. Lewis's own book *Studies in Words* details a lot of these kinds of changes in meaning across the centuries, as we will see in a later chapter. Here it is interesting that the squirrels are counted amongst small beasts of 'gentil kinde', given that they may seem cute and cuddly, but at least one of them acts resolutely and nobly. The smallest squirrel refuses to lie and say that Aslan has not visited them, even under threat of death from the queen, an act which a medieval poet would certainly consider 'gentil'. Chaucer's poem continues on to show the dreamer finding a temple of Venus, surrounded by allegorical figures such as 'Dame Patience', and painted with scenes depicting famous lovers of myth and legend. On leaving the temple and going back to the garden, the dreamer sees the goddess Nature and a group of birds. Nature explains that since it is St Valentine's day, it is time for the birds to choose their mates. Three male eagles want the hand in marriage of one female eagle, and they engage in an elaborate debate to win her favour (hence the 'parliament of fowls' in the title), which descends into a general loud squabble between other kinds of bird, until Nature allows the female eagle to postpone her choice until another year has passed. The poem ends with all the birds singing a song in praise of the end of winter and the coming summer, and the dreamer wakes up. This is the song:

> But first were chosen foules for to synge,
> *But first [before they left] birds were chosen to sing*
> As yere by yere was alwey hir usaunce
> *As year by year was their custom*
> To synge a roundel at her departynge,
> *To sing a roundel at their departing*
> To do Nature honour and plesaunce.
> *To give honour and enjoyment to Nature*
> The note, I trowe, maked was in Fraunce;
> *The music, I believe, was made in France*
> The wordes were suche as ye may here fynde,
> *The words were such as you may find here*
> The nexte vers, as I now have in mynde.
> *The next verse, as far as I can remember:*
> Now welcome somer, with thy sonne softe,
> *Now welcome summer, with your soft sun*
> That hast thes wintres weders over-shake,
> *That has dispelled these winter storms*
> And drevyn awey the longe nyghtes blake!
> *And driven away the long dark nights!*
> Seynt Valentyn, that art ful hye on-lofte; --
> *Saint Valentine, that is high above,*
> Thus syngen smale foules for thy sake[115]
> *The small birds sing this for you*

To modern literary tastes, this is a very odd poem. In its fourteenth-century context, however, it would have seemed less inexplicable: the dream vision, the allegorical characters and the birds talking amongst themselves appear in other works of the era. In *The Parliament of Fowls* these elements come together in a way which seems to produce echoes in the chapter entitled 'Aslan is Nearer'. It is noticeable that when the birds beginning to sing is brought up as evidence of Spring's arrival, the narrator mentions that it sounded as if one bird was replying to another, and then a 'chattering and chirruping' broke out as if they were responding to a signal. This is followed by 'a moment of full song' and then the wood is full of the birds 'chasing one another or having their little quarrels'.[116] These are commonplaces of the way people often write about animals and birds in more realistic fiction, projecting human-like attributes such as conversation and quarrels onto their activities.

If there are echoes of Chaucer's *Parliament of Fowls* here, then that anthropomorphising habit is more accurate than usual. In the medieval poem, of course, the birds literally are discussing things with each other, breaking out into quarrels and singing songs in honour of the warmer weather. Considering Chaucer's poem alongside this passage brings into sharper focus some of the characteristic themes of the Narnian novels: the secret life hidden within the landscape and the creatures which inhabit it. What seemed to be general description of the landscape and the local wildlife on a first reading of the chapter is in fact the location of the real 'action' of these pages. The birds are, in some inchoate sense, making a diplomatic declaration that the true king has returned to the land. The angry words between the Witch, the Narnians and Edmund are more obviously dramatic to us as human readers. But something far stronger and deeper is happening in this chapter, to which the descriptions of nature keep alerting us. Chaucer's poem also helps us with the mode of fiction going on here. It is not just that birds can speak in *The Parliament of Fowls*, but that the landscape is dotted with allegorical figures. I have mentioned Dame Patience, and the dreamer also notices characters like Delight, Flattery and Courtesy in the garden. The most significant of these is a figure whom we still sometimes refer to in modern English, though with less awareness that she is an allegorical symbol:

> ther sate a quene
> *there sat a queen*
> That, as of lyght the somer sonne shene
> *Who, as the summer son's shining is greater than the stars*
> Passeth the sterre – ryght so, over mesure
> *In the same surpassing measure*
> She fairer was than any creature.[117]
> *She was more beautiful than any creature*

This is the goddess 'Nature', whom we sometimes call 'Mother Nature', or just 'Nature' as if that is the name of some personality or presence whose attributes we see in the landscape. It is worth pointing out, in passing, that 'Nature' for a medieval poet is not the same 'Nature' that we mean when we refer to a 'nature trail' or 'nature ramble'. As Lewis himself stated in his *Studies in Words*, the term 'nature' has had a lot of meanings over the centuries. In Chaucer the figure of Nature seems to combine a personification of the 'natural order', the way the world works under God, with a tinge of the fertility goddess, since she calls the birds together to choose their partners, and they please her with a song about the end of winter. The allegorical element of Chaucer's work also highlights the sense that there is an almost palpable force making itself felt in the scattered things which Edmund notices. The dripping trees, the sound of a stream, the quarrelling birds, the colours of flowers, are all personally inimical to the Witch. They seem to be more than physical facts which she dislikes and would prefer to ignore, but actually aimed at her. Her assault on the Narnian party takes on the feeling of a tyrant trying to resist the appearance of the rightful sovereign.

There is one final element which this chapter has in common with Chaucer's poem, and which gives us more reason to suspect a connection between them. (Or at least to see value in putting them next to each other.) In both the main character is dreaming. Perhaps that is not literally accurate, since Edmund does a certain amount of walking and talking in the passage. However, earlier in the chapter the narrator comments that Edmund was so miserable that the only way to keep up his spirits was to pretend that he was in a bad dream, and might wake up at some point. 'And as they went on, hour after hour, it did come to seem like a dream.'[118] In fact, the other Pevensies are experiencing a similar, but more enjoyable sense of somnambulism at the same moment. The very next chapter begins with a statement that while all this was going on, the others 'were walking on hour after hour into what seemed a delicious dream'.[119] Dream imagery is clearly important to Narnia), as when Mr Beaver spoke Aslan's name first in front of the children, Lewis compares the effect to the moment in a dream when someone says something incredibly important to you, but you don't understand precisely what it means. When the Pevensies become kings and queens over Narnia, they reign for years, and only sometimes recall their lives in our world 'only as one remembers a dream', whilst when they find the lamp-post again (and are about to tumble out of Narnia', Edmund says 'It runs in my mind that I have seen the like before; as it were in a dream, or in the dream of a dream'.[120] These could be regarded as a casual comparison between odd things happening in a fantastical novel, and the unreality one feels in a dream. However, there is a precision in them which brings dreams into the imagery of Narnia. The 'dream vision' poetry of the Middle Ages seems to stand behind some of the Pevensies' adventures here. The children are going deeper into a world of symbol and significance, which they do not yet understand, but which they instinctively compare to dreaming, just as if they are entering the *Parliament of Fowls*.[121]

LO, THE WINTER IS PAST

The wealth of natural imagery, the feeling that Spring is an almost personal presence, and the sense of the mysterious, are equally insistent in another text which this chapter strongly brings to mind. A passage of the Song of Songs, also known as the Song of Solomon, resonates with the same feelings:

My beloved spake, and said unto me, Rise up, my love, my fair one, and come away.

For, lo, the winter is past, the rain is over and gone;

The flowers appear on the earth; the time of the singing of birds is come, and the voice of the turtle is heard in our land;

The fig tree putteth forth her green figs, and the vines with the tender grape give a good smell. Arise, my love, my fair one, and come away.

O my dove, that art in the clefts of the rock, in the secret places of the stairs, let me see thy countenance, let me hear thy voice; for sweet is thy voice, and thy countenance is comely.

Take us the foxes, the little foxes, that spoil the vines: for our vines have tender grapes.

My beloved is mine, and I am his: he feedeth among the lilies.
(Song of Solomon 2: 12-16)

ASLAN IS NEARER

This is a short excerpt from a much longer poem, of course, and one which does not immediately seem to be relevant to this chapter. The Song of Songs depicts the relationship between two unnamed lovers in rapturous verse and a range of imagery. The extravagant praise of physical beauty which the pair lavish on each other involves similes which cite towers, goats, lilies and trees, amongst other images. Nonetheless, this text can illuminate and deepen our reading of 'Aslan is Nearer'.

The passage was well-known in Lewis's time, both as a biblical text and in musical settings such as Purcell's famous version. In 1947, shortly before *The Lion, the Witch and the Wardrobe* was published, it appeared in the libretto of Benjamin Britten's opera *Albert Herring*. This comic work concerns the revival of a May festival in an English country village, at the instigation of a local aristocrat who wants to encourage virtue and clamp down on vice. The first scene involves her explaining her plan to a group of local worthies including the mayor, the school-teacher, the police superintendent and the vicar. The passions which run turbulently through the English landscape, and which the May festival is intended to replace, find unexpected expression in a brief duet between Miss Wordsworth the teacher and the vicar, when the weather comes up in conversation:

MISS WORDSWORTH
Oh I find it so refreshing to escape from school on a sunny day like this.

VICAR
Playing truant?

...

MISS WORDSWORTH
Free for a perfect hour or two of liberty.

PATHS IN THE SNOW

MAYOR
Wonderful weather for April, Mr Gedge!

…

MISS WORDSWORTH
Look! That hedge of rosemary is humming with bumblebees!

VICAR
Quite perfect, Mr Mayor. Promises a splendid May and June.

MAYOR
That it does.

SUPERINTENDENT
'In like a lion, out like a lamb!' That was true of March this year!

MAYOR
It was...

MISS WORDSWORTH
(radiant)
'And lo! the winter is past...

VICAR
(joining in)
'The rain is over and gone. The flowers appear on the earth...

(explaining)

Solomon's Song, you know![122]

Britten's music gives a plodding sing-song to the policeman's quoting of the proverb about March weather, but Miss Wordsworth's observations about her freedom and the natural world are set with a beautiful series of shimmering notes behind them. When she begins to quote the Song of Songs, the vocal line stretches out melodiously, bringing a different atmosphere into the room. The libretto notes that the vicar 'join[s] in', but the music has him repeating her words with a slight delay between them, interweaving the musical lines until they meet in a rising harmony through the exultant final phrase about flowers appearing on the earth. Then the musical accompaniment immediately breaks off and the vicar adds 'Solomon's song, you know' in lower notes, as if embarrassed by the lyrical and passionate moment.

In the walk through Narnia we see some of the same association between the natural world and a sense of something breaking through. It is one of the triumphs of Lewis's form of fantasy that he manages to depict spiritual matters as joyous and profound, in contrast to the rigidity and coldness of opposing forces. It is easy enough to say that the truest delights to be found in life flow from spiritual enlightenment rather than personal power and ownership, and many preachers and writers have advanced the proposition. But it is something else to make an audience genuinely feel that attraction intuitively, rather than as a logical conclusion.[123] The lines from the Song of Songs weave together the cycle of the seasons and the sense of life returning to the land with a personal call. The speaker's entreaty to his lover to 'rise up ... and come away' is immediately followed by 'For, lo, the winter is past, the rain is over and gone'. That conjunction 'for' is logically odd: why should there be a causal connection between the season changing and the beloved coming away with him? On the most rational level perhaps it implies that the weather is now good enough for them to go outside and enjoy the flowers and trees. But that unexplained 'for' makes a much stronger, because implicit, connection between spring and the lovers. The call of the lover to the beloved associates their feelings for each other with the quickening pulse of the natural world. Without explaining how, the poem interweaves the romantic love and sexual desire of the two characters with the life flowing through the landscape. The two sets of idea are so closely mingled that they become blurred into one another at times. Are the birds calling to each other because they are seeking a mate, or does the lover simply hear them that way? At one moment the speaker is calling the listener's attention to the sound of the birds, next minute she is being addressed as 'O my dove'. Are the grapevines in the later lines the plants under which they lie down together, or are they a metaphor for the limbs wrapped around each other, or is it impossible to distinguish between these meanings? One scholar has put this in terms of a poetic vision being put forward, in which the world is created and sustained by love:

> As the poem proceeds, the images, given an importance independent of their referents, combine to form a cohesive picture of a self-contained world: a peaceful, fruitful world, resplendent with the blessings of nature and the beauties of human art. That world blossoms in a perpetual spring. Doves hide shyly, sit near water channels, and bathe in milk. Spices give forth their fragrance. Springs flow with clear water. Fruits and winds offer their sweetness. ... [S]ince that world comes into being and is unified only through the lovers' perception of each other, the imagery reveals a new world—one created by love.[124]

This heady combination of sex and nature poetry is very far from the world of children's literature, but there are still aspects of it which infuse Lewis's Spring landscape. Most significantly, the Song of Songs has been read as a religious text by both Jewish and Christian communities, hence its presence in the Bible. It has been interpreted as a depiction of the love between God and the people of Israel, and between

Christ and the Church. The ancient theologian Origen read it in this way, and even used the imagery of the lover and beloved to explain his experiences of divine presence:

> The Bride then beholds the Bridegroom; and He, as soon as she has seen Him, goes away. He does this frequently throughout the Song; and that is something nobody can understand who has not suffered it himself. God is my witness that I have often perceived the Bridegroom drawing near me and being most intensely present with me; then suddenly He has withdrawn and I could not find Him, though I sought to do so. I long, therefore, for Him to come again, and sometimes He does so. Then, when He has appeared and I lay hold of Him, He slips away once more; and when He has so slipped away, my search for Him begins anew[125]

This tradition of reading the text mystically is an essential part of the Song of Song's history within Judaism and Christianity; indeed, it is the reason that it is in the Bible and has thus become part of the spiritual and literary heritage of those communities. It is also crucial for understanding the apparent resonances between the passage and the Narnian chapter. In common with Lewis's handling of other biblical echoes – as we will see in later chapter – here he has taken the atmosphere and details of a Bible passage, and reworked it for his young readers. The mystical blend of romantic love, spiritual yearning and natural imagery has been reshaped, to remove the romance and stress the power of Spring. The feeding among the lilies is no longer a double entendre, but a literal meal which Father Christmas has provided for the Narnian creatures. In a particularly remarkable parallel (whether deliberate on Lewis's part or not), the young foxes that steal away the tender grapes from the vineyard in the Song of Songs have become a dignified old fox who is holding a glass of wine when the Witch arrives, and is on the point of proposing a toast. The physical delight of the lovers in each other has been changed into the good fellowship and pleasures of a festival meal. Lewis has, though, kept the strong sense of a call within the passage. I described above how the Chaucerian echoes made the Spring seem more personal and more inimical to the Witch, making the scattered collection of details about flora and fauna into a more focused presence. This goes even further when the chapter is read in the light of the Song of Songs. The passage beginning 'My beloved spake, and said unto me' associates the Spring weather not only with the presence of the lover (and thus with Christ in the Christian tradition), but also with his call to the beloved. In fact these lines are technically the beloved reporting what he said to her, before she resumes her own statements in the line which states that he is hers and she is his. In arranging the poem this way, the reader is presented with a vivid set of images, and is also caught up in the exchange of words and affection between the two characters; they are overhearing her delighted description of what he said to her, and how he pointed her to the birds and plants, with the emotional undertow of their feelings for each other. He is not simply telling her about the doves, but is calling her to see them with him; she is not only explaining what he said, but also expressing her joy in him.

Origen writes about the presence of God as the 'Bridegroom drawing near me', and this fits rather well with the chapter's title: 'Aslan is Nearer'. The lion himself does not appear until the next chapter, and then he meets the other Pevensie children, but the natural phenomena described throughout the chapter signal that he is close. This even has an effect on Edmund personally; it is during this chapter that he finds himself morally changed, and makes the first steps towards the right path. So far I have been discussing the scene with the Narnians at the table as an episode which shows the Witch's cruelty, which opposes her magic's petrifying and deadening effects with the wakening of life all around them, and which illustrates her futile rage against what is happening. There is another vital action in that scene, and it comes just before the Witch turns the creatures to stone. Edmund shouts, 'Oh don't, don't, please don't', though this has no effect on her, only causing her to strike him after petrifying them, as a punishment for 'asking favours for spies and traitors'.[126] His reaction, which is invisible to her, is noted by the narrator: 'And Edmund for the first time in this story felt sorry for someone besides himself'.[127] This may seem a moral tribute about as backhanded as the Witch's blow across his face, but it marks a turning point in Edmund's character. He could easily have felt a flash of resentment against the Narnians, since speaking out on their behalf did no good and only earned him pain. We have seen a similar moral dynamic happen earlier in the novel, when Edmund first finds his way into the snowy wood and calls out to Lucy in order to apologise for not believing her. When she does not answer immediately, however (because she is not there), Edmund quickly decides that she is sulking somewhere, 'just like a girl'.[128] When his wish to make amends does not immediately make his guilt go away, a sort of moral embarrassment causes him to twist the situation to give himself the upper hand. He reinterprets the silence in the wood as Lucy's refusal to forgive him, and decides that this makes him the injured party, rather than her. This is the sort of light-touch psychological and moral drama which appears across Lewis's fiction, and is especially evident in *The Screwtape Letters*. In the present chapter, however, Edmund's moral impulse survives the Witch's punishment of him, and opens his sympathies outwards. This recognition of the suffering of others prepares the way for his conversation (which the reader never overhears) with Aslan, and the scene of forgiveness with the other Pevensies. I would argue that this movement of Edmund's heart is bound up, in this narrative, with the burgeoning of Spring all around them. The birds he hears, the flowers he notices and the wind he feels on his face, are all outward signs that 'Aslan is Nearer' in the landscape of Narnia. Aslan is nearer to Edmund personally as well. Just as the Song of Songs combines the quickening world with the call of the lover, and just as Origen interprets that call as the presence of Christ, Edmund's moral senses are enlivened by the nearness of Aslan. The mystical readings of the Song of Songs down the centuries of Judaism and Christianity point to the meaning I think we can discern in this chapter. The imagery of nature is where the 'action' of the chapter is really visible, and that quickening of birds, plants, water and wind calls forth a movement within Edmund which puts him on the way to his return. On closer reading, almost everything in the chapter underlines its title, that 'Aslan is Nearer'.

CHAPTER TWELVE

PETER'S FIRST BATTLE

MYSTERIOUS AND MONSTROUS STONES

I n this chapter the children see another of the novel's major symbols for the first time: the Stone Table. They walk up a hill, until Lucy is not certain if she can climb any further without a rest, and suddenly arrive at a flat place surrounded on three sides by forest, and on one by the sea. They see the table, which is described as 'a great grim slab of grey stone supported on four upright stones', which 'looked very old' and 'was cut all over with strange lines and figures that might be the letters of an unknown language'.[129] The narrator mentions that those markings 'gave you a curious feeling when you looked at them'.[130] This might suggest that the lines and figures could have something to do with Aslan, because it prompts a comparison with the Pevensies' experience of hearing the lion's name in conversation with the Beavers. Here again is the sense that a word or symbol which you don't understand can still impart some feeling or sense to you. However, in the narrative there is no time to ponder whether this feeling is connected to Aslan, or whether it is simply a Gothic shiver, because the children immediately pass on to see Aslan's camp, with its lavish pavilions and fantastical creatures. This chapter, however, is going to stay with the Stone Table, and explore its associations.

The physical description of the Stone Table, as a slab of stone supported on other stones, puts it in a familiar category as a feature of the British landscape. Ancient standing stones are not uncommon, with several hundred such monuments surviving across the British Isles. The Narnian version, however, recalls the most famous of them, both by its name and its appearance: Stonehenge. This collection of large stones seems to have originally formed part of a larger monument, and has provoked curiosity and speculation for centuries. Over the years it has been attributed to the Druids, the Romans, the Anglo-Saxons, and (most recently after the development of archaeological science) to the prehistoric people of the Neolithic era. As Ronald Hutton details in his work on paganism in British history, the massive and apparently carefully-designed monument has provided a mysterious image onto which many people have projected what they wished to believe about the ancient past.[131] Some have seen it as a place of horror and sacrificial slaughter, where sinister druids carried out horrible rites in front of a superstitious and bloodthirsty crowd. Others have interpreted it as a temple to the sun, where enlightenment and harmony with nature were preached. It also became a significant part of modern Druidry as a religious movement in Britain, both as a spur to the religious imagination and a site where meetings and rites cold take place. During the mid twentieth century, when Lewis's novel was released, the standing stones had become a source of some friction between the Ministry of Works, which had responsibility for the site, and various groups of druids who pressed rival claims to enact their rituals there. Particular controversy centred on the summer solstice, a crucial date for Druidry.

The first readers of *The Lion, the Witch and the Wardrobe* would not have known about the intricacies of intra-Druidical strife, but newspapers did carry articles about their activities at Stonehenge. The *Daily Mail*, one of the most popular papers in Britain, published a piece entitled 'Druids Wait for Their Dawn' in June 1948, a couple of years before Lewis's novel came out. It combined a series of themes associated with the Druids in public culture:

PETER'S FIRST BATTLE

Stonehenge, immemorial mystery in stone, will tomorrow see once more an assembly of 'sun-worshippers', who will end a whole night's vigil by acclaiming on Monday the dawn of the longest day ... Legend has it that the touch of that first finger of light was the signal, in Druidical days, for the knife to descend upon the human sacrifice to the Sun God. Tomorrow it will merely set the choir of the Druid Universal Bond singing their 'Song of Dawn' or 'Canticle to the Sun', which will be the start of a semi-religious, semi-philosophical service.[132]

After gathering together images of ancient slaughter with peaceful modern Druidry, the article went on to note that several druid groups had made peace with each other and were holding a united service this solstice. It gave some details of the rite and the significance of the vestments involved:

Some members of the order will be seen tomorrow wearing the Druids' red hood, which is a sign of wisdom, a purple robe symbolising the blending of wisdom and understanding, and a white surplice signifying purity and universal brotherhood.

The Chief Druid, whose role is that of an officiating priest, will be clothed all in white. When he administers the sacrament of bread and wine he will say: 'I blend my life with those who lived in service of the Noble Past', and with a hand outstretched to the rising sun he will invoke the quick and the dead to 'stand before the Shrine of Love's Illimitable Light'.

It ended with a practical note about the current arrangements for access to the stone circle:

Time was – before Stonehenge was taken over by the Office (now Ministry) of Works – when the summer solstice festival of the Druids was made the occasion for a sort of all-night picnic, and hundreds of people would camp out around the monstrous and mysterious stones.

Now the whole procedure has been regulated: the Ministry of Works has granted permission to the Druids to conduct their ancient rites in Stonehenge itself, but members of the ordinary public must pay the usual admittance fee of 6d. to enter the circle.

The Stone Table is thus connected with a feature of the English landscape which is both familiar and inexplicable. Just as the figures of Mr Tumnus and Father Christmas seem to be drawing the characters (and readers) into the depths of a mysterious Britain, situating the novel's climactic events at the Stone Table builds on its numinous associations whilst playing out a distinctively Christian narrative. Standing stones seem to have had a particular place in Lewis's imagination. He incorporated them into another fictional setting, in his science-fiction novel *Out of the Silent Planet*. The protagonist, Ransom, has been kidnapped and taken to a planet called Malacandra, which turns out to be Mars. After escaping from his captors, and living with a tribe of highly intelligent and poetic creatures which resemble giant talking otters or beavers, he is summoned by the mysterious intelligence or spirit which rules the planet. This encounter is due to take place on an island, which the novel describes thus:

> For the rest the island seemed desolate, and its smooth slopes empty up to the grove that crowned them, where, again, he saw stonework. But this appeared to be neither temple nor house in the human sense, but a broad avenue of monoliths—a much larger Stonehenge, stately, empty and vanishing over the crest of the hill into the pale shadow of the flower-trunks. All was solitude; but as he gazed upon it he seemed to hear, against the background of morning silence, a faint, continual agitation

of silvery sound—hardly a sound at all, if you attended to it, and yet impossible to ignore.[133]

The main character, from whose perspective we are looking, has to walk into this Stonehenge-like monument, and finds himself surrounded by the various creatures of the island. He is addressed by an invisible spirit, and believes he is there to be judged and even executed for the damage which he and the humans who kidnapped him have caused to this planet. In fact, he is projecting his own guilt and sense of sin onto a benign and forgiving spiritual power. It turns out that the Fall only happened on Earth, and so other planets like Malacandra have not experienced Original Sin. The theological and science-fictional complexities of this plot are fascinating, if a little too complex to explore at length here. It is worth noticing, though, that Lewis twice used a Stonehenge-like monument in order to stage scenes in which questions of original sin, expiation and sacrifice are dramatised.

WITH GOD'S OWN FINGER A-WRITTEN

The name this monument is given opens up another cluster of associations. At first glance, the Stone Table is simply a name reflecting the appearance of the slabs: it looks like a massive table made of stone. However, delving more deeply into the history of the word 'table' complicates the matter. As I will discuss in more depth in a later chapter, Lewis's scholarly works include a book called *Studies in Words*. In it, he traces the history of various words and considers how they have changed in their implications. Though he does not investigate the word 'table', it would provide an intriguing example. The Oxford English Dictionary, which usefully records the different meanings of each word, as well as when those meanings were prevalent, gives an early meaning of 'table' as 'a flat and comparatively thin piece of wood, stone, metal, or other solid material; a board, plate, slab, or tablet, *esp.* one forming a surface used for a particular purpose'. It gives examples of 'tables' in Anglo-Saxon and later medieval sources which are flat bits of wood or stone. The meaning of a table as a flat piece of wood raised on legs and used to sit at or rest things on, seems to be derived from the first. This reversed the assumption I first made when I read the book: it seems that the Stone Table's name does not come from the domestic table, but rather the other way around. Domestic tables are called that because they are made from big flat surfaces or 'tables' which have been put onto legs. The word 'board' provides an interesting parallel: we use it now to simply mean a piece of flat wood which has been sawn into shape for building purposes. In medieval English, however, it could also mean a table. This meaning still survives in deliberately archaic references in literature to a banqueting table as a 'festive board', when the phrase 'bed and board' is used to mean the charge for accommodation and meals, or indeed when an executive gets promoted to a seat at the table in the 'boardroom' of a big company. It seems that 'table' and 'board' both designated something rather similar, and eventually the two words became attached to particular senses, with 'board' coming to mean the flat piece of wood, and 'table' the piece of furniture made from it.

All this etymological history would be largely irrelevant (and could be 'tabled' indefinitely), if the word 'table' had not also developed a specialised sense in English translations of the Bible. The thin, flat pieces of stone which Moses was given on Mount Sinai, and on which were engraved the word of the Law, are referred to in many English Bibles as 'stone tables'. The King James Bible, or Authorised Version, uses this term:

And the Lord spake unto Moses, saying,
 Speak thou also unto the children of Israel, saying, Verily my sabbaths ye shall keep: for it is a sign between me and you

throughout your generations; that ye may know that I am the Lord that doth sanctify you.

Ye shall keep the sabbath therefore; for it is holy unto you: every one that defileth it shall surely be put to death: for whosoever doeth any work therein, that soul shall be cut off from among his people. Six days may work be done; but in the seventh is the sabbath of rest, holy to the Lord: whosoever doeth any work in the sabbath day, he shall surely be put to death. Wherefore the children of Israel shall keep the sabbath, to observe the sabbath throughout their generations, for a perpetual covenant.

It is a sign between me and the children of Israel for ever: for in six days the Lord made heaven and earth, and on the seventh day he rested, and was refreshed. And he gave unto Moses, when he had made an end of communing with him upon mount Sinai, two tables of testimony, tables of stone, written with the finger of God.

(Exo 31:13-18)

Later translations tend to use the term 'tablets of stone', but in the King James Bible, the dominant English version from the seventeenth century to the twentieth century, they are called 'tables of stone'. The Oxford English Dictionary records earlier usages of the phrase, from Old English and Middle English versions: 'Moyses ... hæfde him on handa twa stænene tabulan. Þa wæron mid Godes agenum fingre awritene', and 'Efter þan drihten him bi-tahte twa stanene tables breode on hwulche godalmihti heofde iwriten þa ten laȝ', and later 'And gaf to tabeles of ston, And .x. bodeword writen ðor-on'. From 'twa stænene tabulan', which were 'with God's own finger a-written', to the 'twa stanene tables' on which 'God Almighty had i-written the ten laws', to 'to tabeles of ston', with 'the X [ten] bode-words written thereon', we can see the 'stone tables' emerging from the centuries of Christian writings in English. In a story which invokes Christian imagery in a narrative of sin and atonement, the phrase 'stone table' is definitely significant. This use of the word 'table' in Exodus did not stay in the pages of the Bible. During the Reformation many churches installed painted wooden boards on the walls, which had the Lord's Prayer and the Ten Commandments written on them. This was part of the project which the Reformers cherished of encouraging a literate piety focused on the words of the Bible, to replace what they saw as a superstitious visual piety centred on statues and paintings. Given the etymological history traced here, it is no surprise that these boards were referred to as 'tables'. They were 'tables' in the sense of being thin pieces of wood, but they were also representations of those more famous 'stone tables' which Moses brought down from Sinai. Many churches still have their 'tables' on the wall. (The library of my college, which had been a church before it was a library, had a pair.) The 'tables' of the Bible had already become part of the architecture of Christianity before Lewis wrote his novel.

In creating the Stone Table, Lewis blended several images into a resonant fictional location. He took one of the defining images of ancient Britain, one which was particularly significant for modern paganism, and used it to stage the drama of the atonement. He gave it a name which evoked the laws given to Moses and the boards fixed to the walls of English churches. This association is strengthened during the discussion between Aslan and the Witch, when they refer to what is written on the Stone Table (which the children cannot read). During the next chapters it will gather more associations around itself: the Stone Table combines the imagery of the altar, the cross, the veil of the Temple and the tomb. It would be too simplistic to say that the Table 'is' one or other of these things, or that it is intended to be 'decoded' into one of them. Instead, it remains one of the most potent images in the novel, through which Lewis's imaginative vision could be expressed.

CHAPTER THIRTEEN

DEEP MAGIC FROM THE DAWN OF TIME

THE BINDING OF EDMUND

At the end of chapters eleven and twelve, two of the Pevensie boys face physical danger and narrowly escape with their lives. Edmund is nearly murdered by the White Witch and Peter faces the wolf in combat. In between these two moments, Aslan takes Peter to look out towards Cair Paravel, where he will hopefully reign as High King. In this chapter I am going to suggest that these events, which happen in different places and to different characters, are all reflections of a story in the book of Genesis, the Binding of Isaac. In fact, refraction might be a better term to use than reflection: elements of the original story are split apart and combined in new shapes, like light through a prism or a kaleidoscope. This is characteristic of Lewis's handling of the echoes of the Bible in *The Lion, the Witch and the Wardrobe*. In the next few chapters we will see him carrying out this refraction at greater length on passages from the Gospels. For the moment, though, I shall quote at some length the story known as the Binding of Isaac, before relating it to Lewis's narrative.

And it came to pass after these things, that God did tempt Abraham, and said unto him, Abraham: and he said, Behold, here I am. And he said, Take now thy son, thine only son Isaac, whom thou lovest, and get thee into the land of Moriah; and offer him there for a burnt offering upon one of the mountains which I will tell thee of.

And Abraham rose up early in the morning, and saddled his ass, and took two of his young men with him, and Isaac his

215

son, and clave the wood for the burnt offering, and rose up, and went unto the place of which God had told him. Then on the third day Abraham lifted up his eyes, and saw the place afar off. And Abraham said unto his young men, Abide ye here with the ass; and I and the lad will go yonder and worship, and come again to you.

And Abraham took the wood of the burnt offering, and laid it upon Isaac his son; and he took the fire in his hand, and a knife; and they went both of them together. And Isaac spake unto Abraham his father, and said, My father: and he said, Here am I, my son. And he said, Behold the fire and the wood: but where is the lamb for a burnt offering? And Abraham said, My son, God will provide himself a lamb for a burnt offering: so they went both of them together.

And they came to the place which God had told him of; and Abraham built an altar there, and laid the wood in order, and bound Isaac his son, and laid him on the altar upon the wood. And Abraham stretched forth his hand, and took the knife to slay his son.

And the angel of the Lord called unto him out of heaven, and said, Abraham, Abraham: and he said, Here am I. And he said, Lay not thine hand upon the lad, neither do thou any thing unto him: for now I know that thou fearest God, seeing thou hast not withheld thy son, thine only son from me. And Abraham lifted up his eyes, and looked, and behold behind him a ram caught in a thicket by his horns: and Abraham went and took the ram, and offered him up for a burnt offering in the stead of his son.

And Abraham called the name of that place Jehovahjireh: as it is said to this day, In the mount of the Lord it shall be seen. And the angel of the Lord called unto Abraham out of heaven the second time, And said, By myself have I sworn, saith the Lord, for because thou hast done this thing, and hast not withheld thy son, thine only son: That in blessing I will bless thee, and in multiplying I will multiply thy seed as the stars of the heaven, and as the sand which is upon the sea shore; and thy seed shall possess the gate of his enemies; And in thy seed shall all the nations of the earth be blessed; because thou hast obeyed my voice.

(Gen 22: 1-18)

This narrative has inspired artists, writers, philosophers and theologians to extraordinary works over the centuries. For example, it is the focus of Søren Kierkegaard's treatise *Fear and Trembling*. Thirty years before *The Lion, the Witch and the Wardrobe*, Wilfred Owen used it as the focus for his poem about the previous war, entitled 'The Parable of the Old Man and the Young':

> So Abram rose, and clave the wood, and went,
> And took the fire with him, and a knife.
> And as they sojourned both of them together,
> Isaac the first-born spake and said, My Father,
> Behold the preparations, fire and iron,
> But where the lamb for this burnt-offering?
> Then Abram bound the youth with belts and straps,
> and builded parapets and trenches there,
> And stretchèd forth the knife to slay his son.
> When lo! an angel called him out of heaven,
> Saying, Lay not thy hand upon the lad,
> Neither do anything to him. Behold,
> A ram, caught in a thicket by its horns;
> Offer the Ram of Pride instead of him.
> But the old man would not so, but slew his son,
> And half the seed of Europe, one by one.[134]

For Owen, the image of a father laying his son upon a sacrificial pyre became an image for the horrors of the First World War.

In his version, with the changed ending, it becomes a symbol of the way he felt the older generation had ordered the young men of Europe into senseless carnage. In the process, the future of the European nations seemed to have been devastated: the reference to 'half the seed of Europe' picks up and reverses God's promise to Abraham that his descendants, his 'seed', will be a great and populous nation.

Lewis takes the remarkable step of including elements of the Binding of Isaac in a children's novel. The first echo I want to examine is that promise made to Abraham about the future of his children and their descendants. When Aslan leads Peter up to a hill which overlooks the countryside, *The Lion, the Witch and the Wardrobe* gives the reader a panoramic view of Narnia:

> There a beautiful sight met their eyes. The sun was setting behind their backs. That meant that the whole country below them lay in the evening light – forest and hills and valleys and, winding away like a silver snake, the lower part of the great river. And beyond all this, miles away, was the sea, and beyond the sea the sky, full of clouds which were just turning rose colour with the reflection of the sunset. But just where the land of Narnia met the sea – in fact, at the mouth of the great river – there was something on a little hill, shining. It was shining because it was a castle and of course the sunlight was reflected from all the windows which looked towards Peter and the sunset; but to Peter it looked like a great star resting on the seashore.
>
> 'That, O Man,' said Aslan, 'is Cair Paravel of the four thrones, in one of which you must sit as King. I show it to you because you are the first-born and you will be High King over all the rest.'[135]

The key echo which links the two passages together is the image of Peter seeing the light reflected from the castle of Cair Paravel and 'it looked like a great star resting on the seashore'.

DEEP MAGIC FROM THE DAWN OF TIME

(If this phrase appeared in Tolkien, it would be tempting to interpret it through the title 'Stella Maris' or 'Star of the Sea', one of the names accorded to the Virgin Mary in Catholic devotional tradition. But 'shore' and Lewis's own religious tradition steers the echo in the direction of Abraham rather than Mary.) This combines the two metaphors with which God promises Abraham that he will be the father of a great nation: 'I will multiply thy seed as the stars of the heaven, and as the sand which is upon the sea shore'. Peter is shown the destiny which he is to achieve, though it is reframed within a rather different kind of narrative. Given that few young boys are likely to have their imagination thrilled by the notion that they will be the ancestor of a large number of families, and that the idea of a 'nation' has changed somewhat in the intervening years between Genesis and *The Lion, the Witch and the Wardrobe*, Lewis changes Peter's role from patriarch of a people to king of a nation. This still contains the idea of being part of a chosen and important family (Aslan mentions that he will be 'High King' because 'you are the first-born'), and of being the leader of all those around him. But Lewis has fitted the promise to Abraham into a chivalric set of ideas, where Peter can be an adventuring warrior and lead his people into battle, before taking his place as High King of Narnia.

The other, and longer, part of the Genesis passage concerns the near-sacrificing of Isaac by Abraham and the rescue by the angel. Both Peter and Edmund are in danger in these chapters, though Peter's risk is in single combat with the wolf. No one directly endangers him, unless in the sense that Aslan orders the others to let him fight the wolf alone, with the admonishment 'Back! Let the prince win his spurs'[136] Edmund's peril is a much clearer echo of the Isaac story. The witch decides to kill him, in order to prevent the prophecy being fulfilled that there will be four descendants of Adam on the thrones of Cair Paravel. Several details provide a parallel here:

'Now!' she said. 'We have no table – let me see. We had better put it against the trunk of a tree.'

Edmund found himself being roughly forced to his feet. Then the dwarf set him with his back against a tree and bound him fast. He saw the Witch take off her outer mantle. Her arms were bare underneath it and terribly white. Because they were so very white he could see them, but he could not see much else, it was so dark in this valley under the dark trees.

'Prepare the victim,' said the Witch. And the dwarf undid Edmund's collar and folded back his shirt at the neck. Then he took Edmund's hair and pulled his head back so that he had to raise his chin. After that Edmund heard a strange noise – whizz – whizz – whizz. For a moment he couldn't think what it was. Then he realised. It was the sound of a knife being sharpened.[137]

The arrangements to kill Edmund become chillingly ritualised in this passage. The witch's pondering on where they should do it clearly imply that a 'table' would be better, for some reason. She refers to him as 'it' and 'the victim', telling the dwarf to 'prepare' him. This is clearly more than a straightforward killing to stop him becoming king: Edmund could have been killed many times over by the time he is rescued, if it were not for this ceremonial element. The whole atmosphere is less of a murder than of a ritual sacrifice, which provides connections to the climactic moment in Genesis:

> And they came to the place which God had told him of; and Abraham built an altar there, and laid the wood in order, and bound Isaac his son, and laid him on the altar upon the wood. And Abraham stretched forth his hand, and took the knife to slay his son.

Putting the two passages next to each other, we might notice the near-killing as a sacrifice with its ceremonial air, the use of the word 'bound' for both Isaac and Edmund and the fact that the last thing mentioned before the rescue is the knife in the hand of Abraham and the White Witch. Even a small divergence underlines the connection: Abraham builds an altar whilst the Witch regrets that there is no 'table', and thus Isaac ends up bound to the wood on the altar and Edmund ends up bound to a tree. This near-killing is Lewis's version of the Binding of Isaac, and it is worth considering how he reworks the material, as well as how that affects the meaning of the novel.

The most obvious difference is that the near-sacrifice is not carried out by a deeply devout man who will be the father of the nation, but by the White Witch, the antagonist of the story. It is not an unbearably painful act of sacrifice but an attempt by the Witch to prevent the line of Narnian kings and queens from appearing, and to extend her own domination over the land. This makes the episode rather more morally straightforward for a children's novel, and keeps attention focused on the adventurous aspect of the story. The rescue by Aslan's company of animals and birds does not substitute another creature in Edmund's place – something which would raise even thornier questions in a Narnia full of talking beasts – but simply takes him away from the clutches of the White Witch. Another alteration in the echoes of this passage suits it to the moral landscape of a children's book: the dislocations of the order of events. In Genesis, the promise to Abraham, of descendants like the stars of the sky and the sands of the shore, comes after the near-death of Isaac, and is framed as a result of Abraham's act of renunciation and God's mercy. In *The Lion, the Witch and the Wardrobe* the promise to Peter, of kingship and a castle like a star on the sea-shore, comes before any of the danger to the brothers. Aslan has already told Peter of his royal destiny by the time he faces the wolf in single combat, and the wolf is already dead before the Witch tries to sacrifice Edmund. This rearrangement of events decouples the threat from the promise, and ensures that the Pevensies' royal destiny cannot be read as a 'reward' for Peter fighting the wolf or, more concerningly, for Edmund's near-death.

In fact, the way Lewis rewrites the Abraham and Isaac narrative appears to draw on a very different genre of fiction. Just as the promise to Abraham was reframed within a set of images from chivalric adventure, the Binding of Isaac is briefly reshaped within a much more contemporary mode of fiction: the occult thriller. This genre would become a very successful form in British cinema from the late 1950s, with Hammer Film Productions producing works like *Frankenstein's Revenge, Dracula, The Mummy's Tomb, The Brides of Dracula* and *The Devil Rides Out*. The author of the book which produced that last film, however, Dennis Wheatley, had been writing novels in the occult thriller genre since the 1930s. Stories of supernatural threats, sinister cults and Satanic rites were familiar on the bookstalls of Britain in the 1940s and 50s. Indeed, the plot of *The Devil Rides Out* involves a Satanic group whose rites involve blasphemous parodies of the mass, and who kidnap a child in order to use it in a sacrificial ritual. One of the heroes of the story exchanges himself for the child: this is obviously an echo of the Gospels themselves, but provides a striking parallel to the situation in Lewis's novel. One of the most dramatic scenes of *The Devil Rides Out* involves a Satanic ritual taking place amidst some 'ancient stones' on Salisbury Plain. This area, which is the site of the prehistoric monument known as Stonehenge, also echoes *The Lion, the Witch and the Wardrobe* with its ritual sacrifice taking place on an ancient 'stone table'.

Lewis's reworking of the biblical material is extensive here. Indeed, it requires some close textual comparison to argue that there is a refraction of the earlier text taking place. He splits up the order of events, recasts some roles and motives and adapts the two parts of the story via two different genres. The result, nonetheless, is a combination of scenes which bring images from the book of Genesis into the narrative of Aslan and the Pevensies. This helps build the literary theology of the novel, by placing biblical narratives closely together. Just as the New Testament uses images and ideas from the Hebrew Scriptures to understand the meaning of Jesus' life and death, Lewis brings symbols from Genesis into the story of rescue and sacrifice which is unfolding on the hill of the Stone Table.

CHAPTER FOURTEEN

THE TRIUMPH OF THE WITCH

THE GIRLS AND THE GOSPELS

s I have suggested before, Lewis's echoes of the Bible
are often more precise than we might notice at a first
(or second) glance. At the risk of labouring a point
made earlier, if we simply use a biblical parallel to underline
the supposed fact that Aslan is Jesus, then we miss a lot of
the depth and subtlety in the story. We also, potentially, miss
some of the religious inspiration and challenge which *The
Lion, the Witch and the Wardrobe* might present us with, if
we are already Christians when we read it. An association
between the two characters which merely notes similarities
in order to underline that we should read 'Jesus' where 'Aslan'
is mentioned is likely to supply the meaning of 'Jesus' from
our own pre-existing knowledge and assumptions. If we read
the lion as a disguise for the rabbi of Nazareth, then we are
not challenged to rethink anything we know about the latter.
On the other hand, if we treat Aslan as a more substantial
figure, with his own coherence and – crucially – some notable
differences from Jesus, then we are encouraged to clarify in
our own mind what we believe about Jesus. (In spiritual terms,
this nudges us to answer, if only to ourselves, one of the most
challenging lines of the entire Bible: 'What think ye of Christ?')

The story of Aslan's death and resurrection is obviously
soaked with biblical imagery and parallels. Indeed, to risk
a paradox, there are times when it is more pervaded with
biblical imagery than the Gospels themselves. After all, anyone
who has imagined these scenes in their mind has seen images
which translate easily into the symbolic language of the
Bible. They have seen 'the Lion of Judah bound to the tables

of stone'. In this chapter I will be paying close attention to echoes from, and allusions to, the Gospel accounts of Jesus' crucifixion, death and resurrection. I will be as interested to see where they differ and diverge as when they repeat familiar material. Lewis's allusive technique in these chapters is remarkable: he repeatedly seems to make allusions which insist we read the story in terms of the Gospels, and then alters or entirely reverses the expected image. There are other points when events and characters are telescoped into each other, or when the same thing happens for a different reason. We have already seen this kind of reworking of the earlier material in Edmund. He is clearly 'Adam' in some sense, since he has committed a sin for which Aslan has to atone, and his transgression was connected to eating something delicious which a woman gave him. But he is also 'Judas', since his crime is betraying those close to him to the illegitimate rulers of the land, and he literally got up and left a shared meal in order to enact his betrayal. This kind of blending of figures and events becomes a major feature of Lewis's novel in these chapters.

The earliest of these echoes in 'The Triumph of the Witch' comes when Peter wants to discuss battle plans with Aslan. While the future king is concerned with encampments and marches, with the mustering of forces and likely routes of attack, Aslan is not as interested. He commends Peter for thinking as a soldier should but comments that it does not really matter. Aslan knows, as Peter Pevensie does not, that this conflict will not be solved by military skill. There is a suggestion here of the series of misunderstandings which are displayed by Peter's namesake in the Gospels. The most famous example would be when Peter tries to persuade Jesus not to go to his death in Jerusalem, prompting the reply 'Get thee behind me, Satan' (Mat 16:23) and an even more dramatic episode happens when the armed guards come to arrest Jesus in the Garden of Gethsemane:

THE TRIUMPH OF THE WITCH

> Then Simon Peter having a sword drew it, and smote the high priest's servant, and cut off his right ear. The servant's name was Malchus. Then said Jesus unto Peter, Put up thy sword into the sheath: the cup which my Father hath given me, shall I not drink it?
>
> (John 18:10-11)

There is nothing so violent in this scene, either in terms of action or words. Aslan does not rebuke the young Pevensie openly. However, there is still a character called Peter who believes the situation is essentially a conflict of arms, whilst Aslan knows it is something more metaphysically profound. The Garden of Gethsemane is evoked again by the events of that night, when Susan and Lucy find themselves unable to sleep. They get up and find Aslan leaving the camp, looking dejected: '[h]is tail and his head hung low and he walked slowly as if he were very, very tired'.[138] When they ask if they can go with him, he agrees, saying he will be grateful for their company, but that they must stop at the point when he tells them. The parallel passage occurs in three Gospels, but I have chosen Matthew:

> Then cometh Jesus with them unto a place called Gethsemane, and saith unto the disciples, Sit ye here, while I go and pray yonder. And he took with him Peter and the two sons of Zebedee, and began to be sorrowful and very heavy. Then saith he unto them, My soul is exceeding sorrowful, even unto death: tarry ye here, and watch with me.
>
> And he went a little further, and fell on his face, and prayed, saying, O my Father, if it be possible, let this cup pass from me: nevertheless not as I will, but as thou wilt. And he cometh unto the disciples, and findeth them asleep, and saith unto Peter, What, could ye not watch with me one hour? Watch and pray, that ye enter not into temptation: the spirit indeed is willing, but the flesh is weak.
>
> (Matt 26:36-41)

It is always risky to speculate about why an artist made a particular choice, as if we could have unmediated access to their thoughts and intentions aside from the work they have produced. (Indeed, some artists have remarked that they are not always themselves in charge of the work's meanings: they did not plan and execute it as a set of abstract ideas, and images or themes may bubble up which they 'meant' in some sense but did not consciously decide to put into the work.) So I would be wary of stating what Lewis intended by these biblical parallels. It is, though, perfectly reasonable to look at the effect it has in the novel. Aslan's experience of weariness and dread is emphasised, echoing Jesus' desperation in the Garden of Gethsemane. This brings into Narnia something of the human significance of Jesus' death, which Christian theology has often reflected upon. The Gospels do not relate the story of a superhero who did not really suffer, or a calculating mastermind who set a trap for his enemies and escaped unscathed from their attempts to defeat him. Jesus' fear is genuine, and he prays that 'the Father' will 'let this cup pass from me'. Aslan does not address the Emperor Over The Sea in his night-time walk (or at least not aloud), but the text does not allow us to see him as an invincible superhero in this scene. Perhaps that aspect needs emphasising in a children's book, not because the horror of the crucifixion should be impressed upon them, but because children's stories include invincible and invulnerable super-figures much more often than adult novels do. Including this echo of the Garden of Gethsemane makes it less likely that the audience will class Aslan alongside Superman or Asterix the Gaul. The way this biblical parallel is structured puts the Pevensie girls in the position of the Apostles. The motif of their not being able to sleep evokes the sleeping in Gethsemane, but reverses it. It might seem paradoxical to suggest that the Gospel scene is being evoked, when the characters are doing literally the opposite, but the allusion seems unmistakeable. It is because

Susan and Lucy do precisely the opposite to the Apostles, rather than something simply different, that the connection is noticeable. Their inability to sleep puts them into the same passage as Aslan, but modifies its meaning somewhat. They experience some of the sympathy and fear which surrounds the Apostles in the Garden, but it is not combined with guilt. Lewis's narrative takes away any sense that they have failed or disobeyed Aslan during this night (except potentially in their own anguish that they cannot help him or follow him). The version presented in Narnia stresses their shocked awareness of Aslan's vulnerability and danger, without involving the rather more complex and adult theme of their responsibility for his death. It is also a neat reversal for the intended audience, since most children are more likely to be familiar with the experience of not being able to sleep when they should be safely tucked away until morning, whilst most adults can probably empathise with the Apostles' failure to stay awake after a long and tiring day when they still have responsibilities to fulfil. The motif of sleep is thus oddly inverted in a way which still conveys much of the impact of the scene, but is better suited to the emotional experiences of the audience.

When Aslan arrives at the Stone Table, the novel produces more of these altered or even reversed echoes. Aslan is humiliated by being tied up and having his mane shaved off, whilst the witch's followers taunt and jeer at him, calling him 'pussy' and asking if he wants a saucer of milk. This evokes the scenes of torment during Jesus' trial, such as Mark 14: 65: 'And some began to spit on him, and to cover his face, and to buffet him, and to say unto him, Prophesy: and the servants did strike him with the palms of their hands.' Matthew 27 gives a lengthier account:

> Then the soldiers of the governor took Jesus into the common hall, and gathered unto him the whole band of soldiers. And

they stripped him, and put on him a scarlet robe. And when they had platted a crown of thorns, they put it upon his head, and a reed in his right hand: and they bowed the knee before him, and mocked him, saying, Hail, King of the Jews! And they spit upon him, and took the reed, and smote him on the head. And after that they had mocked him, they took the robe off from him, and put his own raiment on him, and led him away to crucify him.

(Matt 27:27-31)

As with the Gethsemane sequence, there are clearly borrowings here, but they have been modified. Rather than putting on a crown of thorns, the White Witch's minions take off Aslan's mane, depriving him of a visible symbol of his kingly qualities. Instead of addressing him as 'king', they call him by the name of a much smaller version of his species, one which is not known as the king of the beasts. These emphasise the humiliation Aslan undergoes, but without the layers of irony which are present in the Gospels. Mockingly pretending to believe in Jesus' miraculous powers, by hitting him and then telling him to guess who delivered the blow, or pretending to recognise his kingship with a crown of thorns and a reed sceptre, are acts centred on the incongruity between the position of a prisoner and the grandiose rhetoric surrounding him. (They are also, obviously powerful symbols of the Christian understanding of Christ's identity and sacrifice.) The mockery is made clearer in Narnia by the more straightforward insult of depriving the lion of his kingly attributes and titles. Rather like Susan and Lucy's wakefulness, it may be that many children are more used to being belittled by being treated as younger and smaller than they feel themselves to be, and less familiar with being mocked for being pretentious or grandiose. The biblical image is modified in order to tap into recognisable emotions. We might recognise here a similar technique to the handshakes which replaced the holy kiss in Phillips' *Letters to Young Churches*: the reworking of the text does not move all the same gestures and movements across into Narnia, but instead recreates the emotional and symbolic meaning of them. As so often, Lewis's most deft and interesting literary parallels occur at the moment when the biblical passage is not directly followed, but refracted or modified in ways which produce a poignant experience for the reader.

CHAPTER FIFTEEN

DEEPER MAGIC FROM BEFORE THE DAWN OF TIME

DEEPER MAGIC RISING

A s the night of Aslan's death continues on towards the dawn, so does the reworking of recognisable Gospel material. The story describes Susan and Lucy's mourning over Aslan's body, and the contribution which the mice make to setting him free from the ropes. Then the moment of dawn appears:

> They walked to the eastern edge of the hill and looked down. The one big star had almost disappeared. The country all looked dark grey, but beyond, at the very end of the world, the sea showed pale. The sky began to turn red ... Then at last, as they stood for a moment looking out towards the sea and Cair Paravel (which they could now just make out) the red turned to gold along the line where the sea and sky met and very slowly up came the edge of the sun. At that moment they heard from behind them a loud noise – a great cracking, deafening noise as if a giant had broken a giant's plate.[139]

This account of Aslan's resurrection alludes to several details in the Gospels. The moment of Jesus' death is described thus in Luke: 'And it was about the sixth hour, and there was a darkness over all the earth until the ninth hour. And the sun was darkened, and the veil of the temple was rent in the midst' (Luke 23: 44-5). The Gospel of Mark also mentions the tearing of the veil, whilst Matthew adds that there was an earthquake, the graves of holy people opened, and they climbed out. The Narnian scene also provides portents, but at the moment of

237

resurrection rather than crucifixion. The sun is the focus of intense attention, but centred on its rising rather than being darkened. The earthquake and the symbolic tearing of the temple veil (read in Christian theology as marking the removal of the veil between God and humans) are combined in the cracking sound, which will soon be revealed as the breaking of the Stone Table. These reworkings of the biblical images continue the reshaping we have seen so far: presenting a less troubled (and troubling) picture of the Passion for a young audience, and adapting the narrative to their experience. The portents are moved to the moment of resurrection, throwing more emphasis on the wonder of Aslan's rising again as the moment when the 'Deeper Magic' happened, and less on the suffering and despair of his death. The attention to the rising sun, in place of the darkened sun, presents Aslan's return in the context of Christian notions of Creation. In place of a single miraculous event, the daily appearance of the sun itself is offered. It certainly reproduces the major impression of the darkened sun: that Jesus and Aslan are something more significant than the celestial firmament itself. When Jesus dies, the sun itself disappears, as if it is robbed of its light without him present. Susan and Lucy's gazing at the dawn develops this idea, since behind them (though they do not yet know it) Aslan is rising from the Stone Table. On rereading, this scene seems to offer the image of the dawn as a reflection of the light of Aslan himself. Thus a similar metaphysical image is produced in Narnia, by once again reversing the details of the biblical echo.

The girls' first response is not of joy, but that something else awful is being done to Aslan. As they return to the Stone Table, they echo the opening of the resurrection scenes in which Mary Magdalene and others go to tend Jesus' body (a parallel already set up by their care for Aslan in the night). In the Gospel of John:

The first day of the week cometh Mary Magdalene early, when it was yet dark, unto the sepulchre, and seeth the stone taken away from the sepulchre.

Then she runneth, and cometh to Simon Peter, and to the other disciple, whom Jesus loved, and saith unto them, They have taken away the LORD out of the sepulchre, and we know not where they have laid him.

(John 20:1-2)

Mary then meets two angels and mistakes the risen Jesus for a gardener:

But Mary stood without at the sepulchre weeping: and as she wept, she stooped down, and looked into the sepulchre, And seeth two angels in white sitting, the one at the head, and the other at the feet, where the body of Jesus had lain. And they say unto her, Woman, why weepest thou? She saith unto them, Because they have taken away my Lord, and I know not where they have laid him.

And when she had thus said, she turned herself back, and saw Jesus standing, and knew not that it was Jesus. Jesus saith unto her, Woman, why weepest thou? whom seekest thou? She, supposing him to be the gardener, saith unto him, Sir, if thou have borne him hence, tell me where thou hast laid him, and I will take him away. Jesus saith unto her, Mary. She turned herself, and saith unto him, Rabboni; which is to say, Master.

(John 20:11-6)

Neither Susan nor Lucy mistake Aslan for another animal, but I have quoted these verses because they emphasise the sorrow which attends the first events of the resurrection. Just as Mary Magdalene, even when she meets angels, is desolate that Jesus' body is gone, the Pevensie girls immediately think that some of the White Witch's followers have returned to desecrate Aslan's body further. It is also worth noticing how many scenes and characters have been shifted around and telescoped into each other. Susan and Lucy have occupied the position of the Apostles in the Garden of Gethsemane, the women standing at the foot of the cross, and now Mary Magdalene at the garden of the tomb. Just as the figures of Adam and Judas are layered over Edmund's character, the Pevensie sisters take on a series of roles in turn which combine the themes and images of the biblical material. Bringing Judas and Adam together into one character emphasises the idea of sin as betrayal of others and rejection of God. The figures whom Susan and Lucy echo share themes of faithfulness, adoration, pity and rejoicing. They also provide a focus and a coherence to the various people who witness the various stages of the crucifixion and resurrection: our perspective as audience is clarified by being presented through just two characters.

When they do meet the risen Aslan, the girls are understandably full of questions. In answer, Aslan relates that there is a 'deeper magic from beyond the dawn of time' which is greater and more profound than the deep magic which the White Witch cited. Here the borrowing from the Gospel accounts of the Passion is paused for a moment, and Lewis's attention turns more to theology than narrative, gesturing towards other biblical passages. To state the obvious, Jesus does not sit down with Mary Magdalene and give a coherent theory of the Atonement, but the Pevensies (not to mention Lewis's readers) need some explanation of what has happened. As a plot point, this 'deeper magic' might seem a little unconvincing. Or perhaps not unconvincing, since in a story so full of marvels we have had to become fairly flexible on what we accept during the foregoing chapters. But it could still be objected that the appearance of the 'deeper magic from beyond the dawn of time' lacks the kind of persuasiveness which we expect from a fictional plot. It does not seem to flow logically from what has gone before. We cannot look back – as we can in many detective stories, or in several Jane Austen novels – and see that of course this is the answer, we were shown hints and clues of it all along. There was little or no hint in the story that the girls should not have been sad at Aslan's death because he was going to come back to life. It seems almost arbitrary that, having been told about some Deep Magic which put Aslan to death, we are now told that there was a Deeper Magic which brought him back to life.

Theologically, however, this is one of the most crucial details of the story, and one of the most significant aspects of Aslan's character. I do not mean that it makes it even clearer that Aslan is Jesus. That argument could be made, incidentally. It would be perfectly possible to read the apparently unsatisfactory plot device of the 'deeper magic' as part of Lewis's fictional technique. If Aslan's return does not seem to develop naturally from the story of talking animals and sacrifice on a stone slab (this reading would run), then the reader has to look around for something which will make more sense of this episode. The parallel story of Jesus provides a solution to the problem: Aslan's story makes more sense if Jesus' name is substituted for his, and so the plot is 'restored' by a biblical parallel. From this point of view, the surprising and even unpersuasive nature of the surface story is part of the text's theological impetus: it becomes thinner and less distracting here so that the audience's attention can slip past Aslan to see the figure of Jesus shining through the story. This is, as I say, a possible reading. But it is not one which I think makes most sense of the chapter. As I have insisted before, I think it is too simplistic to swap in Jesus' name for Aslan's as if that solves the story and makes its real meaning clear. Instead, I would like to read the 'deeper magic' as part of Narnia's theology in a different way.

Aslan explains the White Witch's failure to finally defeat him by referring to an older magic:

though the Witch knew the Deep Magic, there is a magic
deeper still which she did not know. Her knowledge goes back
only to the dawn of time. But if she could have looked a little
further back, into the stillness and the darkness before Time
dawned, she would have read there a different incantation.[140]

The mild irony of 'if she could have looked back a little further'
than the beginning of time itself may distract us from a major
metaphysical point here. Aslan is claiming that he is older than
the Witch, indeed that he is older than the thing by which we
measure age. If I read this passage correctly, then Aslan is claiming
to be the Logos, the Word which begins the Gospel of John:

In the beginning was the Word, and the Word was with God,
and the Word was God. The same was in the beginning with
God. All things were made by him; and without him was not
any thing made that was made. In him was life; and the life was
the light of men. And the light shineth in darkness; and the
darkness comprehended it not.

There was a man sent from God, whose name was John.
The same came for a witness, to bear witness of the Light, that
all men through him might believe. He was not that Light, but
was sent to bear witness of that Light.

That was the true Light, which lighteth every man that
cometh into the world. He was in the world, and the world
was made by him, and the world knew him not. He came
unto his own, and his own received him not. But as many as
received him, to them gave the power to become the sons of
God, even to them that believe on his name

(John 1:1-12)

This passage is itself the New Testament reworking of the opening
of the Hebrew Scriptures or Old Testament. John's imagery of
beginnings and light picks up the opening symbols of Genesis:

In the beginning God created the heaven and the earth. And the earth was without form, and void; and darkness was upon the face of the deep. And the Spirit of God moved upon the face of the waters.

And God said, Let there be light: and there was light. And God saw the light, that it was good: and God divided the light from the darkness. And God called the light Day, and the darkness he called Night. And the evening and the morning were the first day.

(Gen 1:1-5)

John's Gospel, via its literary parallels with Genesis, makes the claim that the Logos (or Word), the second person of the Trinity, was present at the making of everything. It goes on to identify that Logos with the rabbi known as Jesus of Nazareth. This was part of the early theological thinking which built an intellectual groundwork for a Christian account of the universe. Like the children's questions about Aslan, posed in the earlier chapter, this was not a process which reasoned from first principles and arrived at Christ. Rather, it was the intellectual reaction to the revelation of God which was felt to have happened in the life, death and resurrection of Jesus of Nazareth. John's Gospel seems clear that the Word is not part of the world, and pre-existed time and space. Aslan's wry comment about the White Witch's knowledge only stretching back as far as time itself sounds like a joke or a poetic hyperbole. Surely someone whose knowledge went back as far as that would know everything. That is both true and exactly the point. To know every-thing is not to know God, because God is not a thing. The 'little further' the Witch would have to go back to know about the 'deeper magic' marks the boundary between the created order and uncreated divinity. It crosses the category between things, people, objects, and that which is beyond categorisation. We might say that the plot wobbles at this point, not because it is a badly-written story, but because the story evokes a presence which cannot be treated in the same way as other characters in any novel. It is not failing to live up to the standards of a normal children's book, it is gesturing towards something greater. Time and space, the usual parameters for fictional action, and the absolute requirements for our common understanding of causality, do not quite apply in the same way. This is another moment where *The Lion, the Witch and Wardrobe* produces a sense of the mysterious, rather than the magical or fantastic. The White Witch appears in the story as the most powerful magical person which the Narnian world has yet seen, but it is clear that Aslan is not simply a character with a greater quantity of magical power. He is a different kind of person entirely.

CATCH ME IF YOU CAN

As the story of this chapter continues, the romp which Aslan shares with the girls is another moment where biblical material is reworked, and independent Narnian material is used to develop Lewis's image of the risen lion. Susan has a terrible thought when looking at Aslan's figure, asking if 'You're not – not a – ?' and the narrator supplies the missing word by telling us that she could not bring herself to say 'ghost'.[141] Aslan's response, understanding what she means, is to lower his head and lick her forehead, asking if he looks like one. This establishes the reality of Aslan's presence, in the same form in which they knew him before. (Susan's idea that he is a ghost might be a doubly horrific thought, since the White Witch's company included 'Wraiths' and 'Incubuses', and no such ghostly creatures were seen on Aslan's side. For Susan, who has only just found out that such things are definitely real, an Aslan who came back as a ghost might be worse than an Aslan who remained dead.) There is no particular line being echoed in Susan and Aslan's conversation, but we can draw parallels with the passages in the Gospels which seem to be making the same point after Jesus' resurrection. The most famous is the story of St Thomas, who came to be known as 'doubting Thomas':

> But Thomas, one of the twelve, called Didymus, was not with them when Jesus came. The other disciples therefore said unto him, We have seen the Lord. But he said unto them, Except I shall see in his hands the print of the nails, and put my finger into the print of the nails, and thrust my hand into his side, I will not believe.
>
> And after eight days again his disciples were within, and Thomas with them: then came Jesus, the doors being shut, and stood in the midst, and said, Peace be unto you. Then saith he to Thomas, Reach hither thy finger, and behold my hands; and reach hither thy hand, and thrust it into my side: and be not faithless, but believing. And Thomas answered and said unto him, My Lord and my God. Jesus saith unto him, Thomas, because thou hast seen me, thou hast believed: blessed are they that have not seen, and yet have believed.
>
> (John 20:24-9)

Aslan does not show the girls the wound where the White Witch stabbed him (indeed it is not clear that Aslan's body after he reappeared bore any marks in the way that Jesus' body did.) There is something about the immediate and very physical act of a lick which echoes the same idea, if in a much less disturbing and visceral way. A lick demonstrates the sightly messy physicality of the leonine body in a way which immediately removes Susan's momentary doubt.

The same physicality is evident in the romp which they share immediately after Aslan has explained the 'deeper magic'. This is another moment when Lewis adapts biblical material by reversing its surface meaning. Aslan tells the girls that he can feel his strength returning and exclaims 'Catch me if you can!' There follows an ecstatic game in which Aslan keeps just out of their reach as the girls dash breathlessly after him, until he suddenly stops and they all tumble on the grass together. Lucy mentally compares it to playing with both a kitten and a thunderstorm. Aslan's invitation to the game almost exactly inverts Jesus' speech to Mary Magdalene in the continuation of a passage of John's Gospel I quoted above:

> And when she had thus said, she turned herself back, and saw Jesus standing, and knew not that it was Jesus.
>
> Jesus saith unto her, Woman, why weepest thou? whom seekest thou? She, supposing him to be the gardener, saith unto him, Sir, if thou have borne him hence, tell me where thou hast laid him, and I will take him away.
>
> Jesus saith unto her, Mary. She turned herself, and saith unto him, Rabboni; which is to say, Master.
>
> Jesus saith unto her, Touch me not; for I am not yet ascended to my Father: but go to my brethren, and say unto them, I ascend unto my Father, and your Father; and to my God, and your God.
>
> (John 20:14-7)

Jesus' injunction, even rebuke, 'Touch me not', has become especially famous in its Latin form in the Vulgate Bible: 'Noli me tangere'. The enigmatic phrase, whose precise significance is still discussed by scholars, became the title of the scene when depicted in art. Just as Christian painters over the centuries produced tens of thousands of examples of the 'nativity', showing Jesus and the holy family in Bethlehem, and of the 'pieta', depicting the dead Jesus in Mary's arms, there are very large numbers of the 'noli me tangere' scene. Michelangelo Buonaroti painted one, as did Fra Angelico, and Titian, and Hans Holbein, and scores of less famous artists. The phrase also made its way, though much less frequently, into poetry and other forms of literature. The sixteenth-century courtier poet Sir Thomas Wyatt wrote a famous (or notorious) sonnet entitled 'Whoso list to hunt', which includes the fateful words. It is apparently about a man talking about a female deer who is very difficult to catch, but many people have interpreted it through the rumours that Wyatt had a love affair with Anne Boleyn, before she became Henry VIII's queen:

> Whoso list to hunt, I know where is an hind,
> But as for me, hélas, I may no more.
> The vain travail hath wearied me so sore,
> I am of them that farthest cometh behind.
> Yet may I by no means my wearied mind
> Draw from the deer, but as she fleeth afore
> Fainting I follow. I leave off therefore,
> Sithens in a net I seek to hold the wind.
> Who list her hunt, I put him out of doubt,
> As well as I may spend his time in vain.
> And graven with diamonds in letters plain
> There is written, her fair neck round about:
> Noli me tangere, for Caesar's I am,
> And wild for to hold, though I seem tame.[142]

Lewis would have known this poem well, given his familiarity with the poetry of this era, which included his monumental study *English Literature in the Sixteenth Century (Excluding Drama)*. Aslan's 'catch me if you can!' is, according to my reading of this scene, an inverted 'noli me tangere'. It turns the admonition into a game, inviting touch rather than forbidding it, but still remaining out of grasp for the moment. The game they play emphasises Aslan's physical reality, rather like the echoes of the story of Doubting Thomas, but it also stresses the delight and pleasure of the physical. Aslan's return in the body is not simply a fact about him, but something which can give consolation and fun. Their game even contains, perhaps, a joyful recapitulation of the tragic events of the last day and night. Aslan is out of their reach, and then returns delightfully and they are reunited as they tumble over each other. I quoted the Wyatt poem above because I also wonder whether it had some role in inspiring this scene. The lines from John's Gospel provide the basis for the inversion of 'noli me tangere' into 'catch me if you can', but the idea of 'noli me tangere' being embedded in a scene of chasing appears in 'Whoso list to hunt'. The Pevensie girls' game with Aslan has nothing of the romantic obsession or frustration which Wyatt depicts in his poem, but his very well-known work did combine 'noli me tangere' with the image of teasing pursuit. The recasting of this imagery in terms of delight and fun rather than frustration also chimes with the accounts which the Gospels provide of Jesus' appearances to the disciples after the resurrection. These are often scenes of eating and sharing food, which similarly highlights the combination of real, substantial physicality and companionable delight. The turning of the 'noli me tangere' into Aslan's 'catch me if you can!' is probably the boldest and most outrageous rewriting of an image from the Gospels in these chapters. It follows the same pattern of entirely reworking a significant symbol from the biblical texts, but using it to shape a theological meaning which carries an important strand of the New Testament's ideas, and is framed for the emotional world of a young reader. These images are, of course, still available when the reader is no longer young. Rereading the Narnia books, and noticing these parallels with the Gospels, is an experience which draws the adult readers' attention to the individual details. The divergences may do this even more dramatically than the similarities, as I suggested above. A general sense that 'Aslan is suffering and rising, which is very much what happened to Jesus', may enliven the imagination less than the sudden realisation that the sun is rising, not setting, or that the children are being challenged to grab the lion, not warned off touching him.

248

CHAPTER SIXTEEN

WHAT HAPPENED ABOUT THE STATUES

A TINY STREAK OF FLAME

This chapter can perhaps feel a little like an afterthought, given the narrative drama of Aslan's death, and the even greater drama of his resurrection. Even the title, 'What happened about the statues', has a slightly off-hand air, as if tidying up some loose ends. It is certainly true that the most transformative events of the novel have taken place, but there is still plenty of action left in the book. This chapter unfolds some of the effects produced by the scenes at the Stone Table, and dramatises two moments which Christian thought has connected with the story of Christ's death and resurrection. They are the descent of the Holy Spirit at Pentecost, and the legend of the Harrowing of Hell.

Reading this chapter alongside the story of Pentecost in the New Testament depends on the symbols which appear in 'What happened about the statues'. The two episodes have rather different narrative positions: if we are drawing direct parallels between Aslan and Jesus, then we might expect a Pentecost-like event to take place when Aslan has left Narnia. However, Lewis seems to be layering Pentecostal images onto the sequence in which Aslan wakes up the petrified Narnians, through the mentions of breath, fire and an outburst of speech. When Aslan begins to bring the statues in the witch's castle back to life, the narration describes the process in some detail. It mentions that he does this by breathing on each one in turn, but that he moves on immediately to the next. It then elaborates:

> I expect you've seen someone put a lighted match to a bit of newspaper which is propped up in a grate against an unlit fire.

And for a second nothing seems to have happened; and then
you notice a tiny streak of flame creeping along the edge of the
newspaper. It was like that now.[143]

The stone lion has a 'tiny streak of gold 'running along his
back and 'then the colour seemed to lick all over him as
the flame licks all over a bit of paper', before he comes alive
completely.[144] This comparison has a homely, everyday feel
to it: the spreading of the fire is not compared to a flaming
torch in a Classical myth or a brazier on Hadrian's wall. It's the
sort of domestic detail which we have seen in the portrayal
of the Beavers' house, and which Lewis remarked upon in
the work of John Bunyan. It is worth pointing out, in passing,
that the act of lighting a fire probably has a slightly different
significance for most of Lewis's contemporary readers than
for most of his modern readers. Open fires provided the bulk
of heating in British homes during the middle of the twentieth
century, and central heating did not become usual until the
later decades. There was in increase in other heat sources,
such as radiators or electric heaters, during the 40s and 50s,
which led writers like George Orwell to write in defence of
the traditional hearth-side with the family gathered round
(in his newspaper essay 'The Case for the Open Fire'.) Most
people, however, would be used to a fire as the source of
heating, and as the focal point of the main living room. This
means that Lewis's comparison is more literally homely, and
closer to the quotidian routine than it might be for twenty-
first-century readers. Building a fire with wood or coal was an
everyday chore for the majority of people in his time, rather
than a mildly enjoyable activity connected with barbecuing or
fashionable indoor woodstoves. This is not to say that many
modern readers will not be using practical woodburners or
open fires themselves, simply that the general cultural meaning
of the image has changed over the decades.

WHAT HAPPENED ABOUT THE STATUES

This domestic comparison provides an easily-imaginable image for the magical transformation which is taking place as Aslan breathes upon the stone animals. The combination of breath and fire brings this chapter into juxtaposition with the apostles in the upper room at Pentecost, as told in the book of Acts:

> And when the day of Pentecost was fully come, they were all with one accord in one place. And suddenly there came a sound from heaven as of a rushing mighty wind, and it filled all the house where they were sitting. And there appeared unto them cloven tongues like as of fire, and it sat upon each of them. And they were all filled with the Holy Ghost, and began to speak with other tongues, as the Spirit gave them utterance.
>
> (Act 2:1-4)

The wind and fire imagery, as well as being the central image of these verses, has become part of the symbolic language of Christian devotion. To pick only two examples from myriad possibilities, we could look to John Cosin's seventeenth-century hymn, translated from a medieval original, 'Come, Holy Ghost, our souls inspire/ and lighten with celestial fire;/ thou the anointing Spirit art,/ who dost thy sevenfold gifts impart', or Edwin Hatch's nineteenth-century verses, 'Breathe on me, Breath of God,/ fill me with life anew,/ that I may love the way you love,/ and do what you would do'.

> And there were dwelling at Jerusalem Jews, devout men, out of every nation under heaven. Now when this was noised abroad, the multitude came together, and were confounded, because that every man heard them speak in his own language. And they were all amazed and marvelled, saying one to another, Behold, are not all these which speak Galilaeans? And how hear we every man in our own tongue, wherein we were

born? Parthians, and Medes, and Elamites, and the dwellers in Mesopotamia, and in Judaea, and Cappadocia, in Pontus, and Asia, Phrygia, and Pamphylia, in Egypt, and in the parts of Libya about Cyrene, and strangers of Rome, Jews and proselytes, Cretes and Arabians, we do hear them speak in our tongues the wonderful works of God.

(Acts 2:5-11)

This miraculous outpouring of language has been a key symbol for Christians' understanding of what happened at Pentecost, and the way humanity was affected by the resurrection. The Anglo-Saxon preacher Ælfric described it as the reversal of the scattering of people at the Tower of Babel. To him human pride had led to the building of that tower, as an attempt to rival God, with the resulting punishment that humankind was scattered and given different languages which stopped them understanding each other. The gathering of the disciples at Pentecost, with their obedience and humble witness to the works of God, was blessed by the undoing of Babel's curse. For a moment, the common language returned and humanity could tell each other of God's glory. For other Christians, Pentecost has been interpreted as a sign of the renewing of creation. The appearance of the Holy Spirit, and the marvellous speech, can be paralleled with the very opening verses of the Book of Genesis. The spirit of God brooded upon the deep, and God began to create via divine speech: 'And God said, let there be light: and there was light.' This parallel encourages a reading of Pentecost as an echo of creation, and an anointing of redeemed humanity. For others, the wind and fire in the room, followed by the miraculous speech, is a pattern for the experiences and mission of the Church. The knowledge of the presence of God in a small group, breaking out into the speech to everyone outside, is an image for many of a Christian duty to proclaim the Gospel wherever it is not being heard. The particular quality of this speech, that it can be understood in whatever language the person themselves speaks, is read as an assurance that the Gospel is for everyone, and will speak personally and meaningfully to individual people. Of course, there are forms of Christian practice which do not simply use Pentecost as a symbol or pattern, but which arrange their common life around the reception of the same kinds of gift. The Pentecostal churches emphasise the 'baptism of the Holy Spirit' as an experience repeated in the lives of believers, and it is often associated with 'speaking in tongues'. This variety of interpretations of Pentecost (which are not mutually exclusive, of course) all emphasise the outburst of speech as part of the spirit's descent on the disciples. Turning to Aslan's actions in the Witch's castle, we find that the revived Narnians in the courtyard are described as colourful and lively, and as very vocal: 'And instead of the deadly silence the whole place rang with the sound of happy roarings, braying, yelpings, barkings, squealings, cooings, neighing, stampings, shouts, hurrahs, songs and laughter'.[145] The combination of the breath, the fire and the outburst of 'speech' establishes the parallel for the reader between what is happening in the castle and the story of Pentecost. This dramatises the effects of Aslan's resurrection: it is the undoing of the Witch's apparent triumph, and the working of the deeper magic from before the dawn of time, but it is also the undoing of the Witch's power over individual Narnians. The isolated, frozen figures come back to life, and are able to give voice again.

LIFT UP YOUR HEADS, O YE GATES

The setting within which all this happens provides another layering of Christian imagery. I have laid out parallels with the story of Pentecost, which is probably familiar to most modern Christians, but the second narrative is somewhat more obscure. The 'harrowing of hell' is the name for the idea that during the three days between Jesus' death and resurrection, he visited the dead and rescued some of them from hell. The Dunbar poem,

'On the Resurrection', which I quoted in the introduction, uses imagery of the harrowing in several lines, when it declares that 'the presone [is] broken', 'the fetteris lowsit and the dungeon temit ... the prisoneris redeemit'. (In modern English: the prison is broken, the fetters are loosed, the dungeon is emptied, the prisoners are redeemed.) There is no narrative episode in the Bible which corresponds to this doctrine, and it was partially derived from lines in the New Testament and from speculation on how Christ's atonement affected those who had lived before he was born. The harrowing of hell was a popular part of medieval Christian and Renaissance Christian imagery, and was depicted in paintings, poems and plays. The version of the Apostles' Creed which appeared in the 1662 Book of Common Prayer, the version which was used during Lewis's lifetime (and still is by many Anglicans) includes a clause which gestures towards the harrowing:

> I believe in God, the Father Almighty, Maker of heaven and earth: And in Jesus Christ his only Son our Lord, Who was conceived by the holy Ghost, Born of the virgin Mary, Suffered under Pontius Pilate, Was crucified, dead and buried. He descended into Hell, The third day he rose again from the dead. He ascended into Heaven, And sitteth on the right hand of God the Father Almighty. From thence he shall come to judge the quick and the dead. I believe in the holy ghost, The holy Catholic Church, The Communion of Saints, the forgiveness of sins, The resurrection of the body, And the life everlasting. Amen[146]

The phrase 'He descended into Hell' in this creed would not necessarily have conjured up for 1950s Christians the same set of images of Christ breaking down the gates and hell and raiding the underworld which are provided by medieval wall-paintings. Nonetheless, these words were still in the Creed, and were repeated by those taking part in the standard services of the Church of England at the time. The harrowing is also mentioned in a text which I have already argued has echoes in *The Lion, the Witch and the Wardrobe*: Dante's *Divine Comedy*. As might seem reasonable for a poem which deals with hell, the *Inferno* mentions Christ's appearance in that region. It happens whilst Dante is being conducted by Virgil through the upper realms of hell, which are inhabited by souls who were not saved by Christ because they did not have an opportunity to meet his Church or hear his gospel. Dante, as an Italian of the Renaissance, admired the great figures of Classical history, and could claim them as part of the cultural and even spiritual inheritance of his own society, but could not pretend they had been devout worshippers of Christ. Thus the upper realms contain philosophers like Plato and Socrates, as well as political figures such as Caesar and Lucrece and poets including Homer and Ovid. They inhabit a stately and noble place, which is described as containing a castle and meadows, but one which seems cold and unwarmed by the glorious love which bathes the descriptions of paradise. Dante, taking in this arrangement of those who lived before Jesus, raises a question to his Roman guide. I will quote the passage in the version translated by Dorothy L. Sayers:

> Tell me, sir – tell me, Master, I began
> (In hope some fresh assurance to be gleaning
> Of our sin-conquering Faith), 'did any man
>
> Of his self-merit, or on another leaning
> Ever fare forth from hence and come to be
> Among the blest?' He took my hidden meaning.
>
> 'When I was newly in this state,' said he,
> 'I saw One come in majesty and awe,
> And on His head were crowns of victory.

Our first great father's spirit He did withdraw,
And righteous Abel, Noah who built the ark,
Moses who gave and obeyed the Law,

King David, Abraham the Patriarch,
Israel with his father and generation,
Rachel, for whom he did such deeds of mark,

With many another of His chosen nation;
These did He bless, and know, that ere that day,
No human soul had ever seen salvation'[147]

The lines deliberately do not name Jesus, referring only to 'one come in majesty and awe' with conqueror's crowns on his head: this may be to signal Virgil's inability to truly understand who Jesus was. He talks about salvation as someone who is outside it, and can see what has happened externally but not recount the experience or identify the meaning of the conqueror.

The harrowing of hell was thus an established part of the medieval literary world-view, and mentioned in one of the texts which so much fantasy literature drew upon. However, the account in Dante is rather distant and explanatory. To explore the parallels between the scene in the Witch's castle and the imagery of the harrowing of hell further, I will look at the scenes of a Mystery Play cycle which stages it in a much more dramatic and dynamic way. I am not arguing that Lewis is specifically quoting this particular play, nor that he intended readers to recognise references to it, but rather using it to demonstrate the characteristic images and ideas which clustered around the doctrine. The medieval Mystery Cycles were collections of short plays which depicted the whole arc of biblical history, from Creation to Apocalypse. They were performed outside in the streets, on platforms or wagons, and the performers were members of the various trade guilds of the town.

WHAT HAPPENED ABOUT THE STATUES

The groups which performed each episode often had an ironic or bizarre relationship to the story they were depicting. Thus in the York Mystery Plays, it seems that the fishermen performed the play of the Flood, the pinners (who made nails and other small metal objects) performed the Crucifixion, and the tilehatchers took care of the Nativity. The guild's everyday jobs, and their pride in their craft, mingles oddly with plays which appear to dramatise their fears (the Flood), the times when their craft was misused (the pinners) or when their job was simply done very badly (the leaky roof of the stable.) The plays themselves were written in lively and often funny vernacular language, with jokes and local references woven through the biblical story. For example, the 'Second Shepherds' Play' from the Wakefield cycle shows the familiar tale of the shepherds who are told by the angels to visit Jesus in the manger. However, it also involves a magic spell, a lamb which is stolen and hidden in a cradle, and sundry jokes along the way. The harrowing of hell, from the same cycle shows Jesus appearing onstage to explain that now he has died on the cross

> ... till hell now will I go
> *I will now go into Hell*
> To challenge that is myne,
> *To demand those who belong to me*
> Adam, eue, and other mo,
> *Adam, Eve and others as well*
> They shall no longer dwell in pyne
> *They shall no longer live in torment*

He sends a light before him into hell, which Adam and Isaiah notice. John the Baptist recognises it as well, as does Simeon and Moses. Two devils called Rybald and Beelzebub begin to worry that the souls might escape. To prevent this, they call up other devils and Beelzebub sends Rybald to report to

Satan what is happening. Jesus appears and declaims 'Attolite portas, principes, vestras et eleuamini porte eternales, et introit rex gloria'. This is the Latin version of the Psalm verse which the King James version renders as: 'Lift up your heads, O ye gates; and be ye lift up, ye everlasting doors; and the King of glory shall come in'. Beelzebub tells Rybald to 'go, spar the yate ... And set the watches on the wall' (Go, bar the gates, and put sentries on the walls). When Satan arrives, Beelzebub complains that 'we ar beseged about', continuing the imagery of hell as a physical castle with its gates, sentries and now a hostile force besieging it. Jesus demands the gates be opened again, and announces that he is coming in:

> Ye prynces of hell open youre yate
> And let my folk furth gone;
> A prynce of peace shall enter therat
> Wheder ye will or none

The scene continues on to discussions of prophecy, Jesus' parentage and whether Satan himself can get out of hell. Throughout the play Christ's action, and the devils' resistance to it, is framed in terms of locking gates, bursting through walls and conquering a fortified place.

Thus the bringing back to life of the Narnians who had been petrified by the White Witch blends two sets of imagery from Christian tradition. The lively (even wild) impact of Aslan's breath upon them, and the joyful cacophony which results, draw on the narrative of Pentecost. The castle where they have been kept, and through which Aslan bounds to bring them back, borrows from the Harrowing of Hell. The resulting scenes give a sense of the exultant liberation which both infuse both sets of imagery, and dramatise the feeling of life set free.

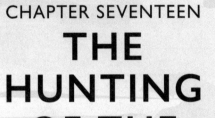

CHAPTER SEVENTEEN

THE HUNTING OF THE OF THE WHITE STAG

THE TRICK OF WORDS

During this chapter the children's reign in Narnia is briefly described. Or, at least, a general impression is given of what kinds of monarch they became. Lewis makes a point of giving us the titles which they became known by in Narnia:

> And they themselves grew and changed as the years passed over them. And Peter became a tall and deep-chested man and a great warrior, and he was called King Peter the Magnificent. And Susan grew into a tall and gracious woman with black hair that fell almost to her feet and the kings of the countries beyond the sea began to send ambassadors asking for her hand in marriage. And she was called Queen Susan the Gentle. Edmund was a graver and quieter man than Peter, and great in council and judgement. He was called King Edmund the Just. But as for Lucy, she was always gay and golden-haired, and all princes in those parts desired her to be their Queen, and her own people called her Queen Lucy the Valiant.[148]

Those titles – the Magnificent, the Gentle, the Just and the Valiant – are worth pausing on. Lewis makes clear that these are not names which the children chose for themselves, but which were given to them by other people in Narnia, to sum up their qualities. I would like to suggest that Lewis is playing a linguistic game in this passage, which highlights the apparently archaic virtues which the children gain whilst ruling Narnia. He does this by using words which exist both in modern English and in medieval English, but which have slightly different meanings in the two versions of the language.

We know Lewis had a particular interest in language and its changing forms, since he published an entire book on the subject. *Studies in Words* may not be his most famous volume, particularly amongst those who mostly see him as a fantasy novelist or a Christian apologist, but it contains some revealing insights about the way Lewis thought about the world. In the book, he takes a series of words which have existed in English for a long time, such as 'nature', 'wit', 'sad', 'free', 'sense', and traces their shifts in meaning over the centuries. He notes, for example, the way 'sad' meant 'serious or weighty' rather than 'unhappy' in earlier usage. Whilst doing so, he suggests how the different meanings of a word might be connected to each other, and what caused them to alter into later meanings. For example, he comments that 'virtue' and 'vice' came at one point in the language's history to mean almost entirely 'chastity' and 'lechery', rather than the wider range of characteristics they had previously signified. Lewis suggests, cynically but persuasively, that '[t]hese are the forms of virtue and vice which both the prudish and the prurient most want to talk about. And since most of us have a dash of prudery or prurience and many among us of both, we may say simply which most people most want to talk about' (16). When people said 'I fear she has been immoral' they most often meant 'I fear she has been involved in sexual transgression', and so the terms came to be essentially synonymous. Another drive for words to slip between meanings is provided by what he calls the 'moralisation of status-words':

> Words which originally referred to a person's rank—to legal, social, or economic status and the qualifications of birth which have often been attached to these—have a tendency to become words which assign a type of character and behaviour. Those implying superior status can become terms

of praise; those implying inferior status, terms of disapproval. Chivalrous, courteous, frank, generous, gentle, liberal, and noble are examples of the first; ignoble, villain, and vulgar, of the second.[149]

This particular aspect of language change has implications for how we read the Pevensies' titles, as I will suggest in a moment. Lewis also explains the origin of his interest in the way words change, saying in the introduction that *Studies in Words* 'has grown out of a practice which was at first my necessity and later my hobby; whether at last it has attained the dignity of a study, others must decide', and that '[i]n my young days when I had to take my pupils through Anglo-Saxon and Middle English texts' they became absorbed in how different meanings 'could have radiated out from a central meaning'.

> Once embarked, it was impossible not to be curious about the later senses of those which survived into Modern English. Margins and notebooks thus became steadily fuller. One saw increasingly that sixteenth- and even nineteenth-century texts needed such elucidation not very much more rarely, and in a more subtle way, than those of the eleventh or twelfth; for in the older books one knows what one does not understand but in the later one discovers, often after years of contented misreading, that one has been interpolating senses later than those the author intended.[150]

Thus language change provided a trap for the unwary reader, since anyone straying beyond their immediate time period risks meeting words which they think they understand, but which bear quite different meanings for the author and original audience. At the same time, the study of words provides a means for modern people to explore the worlds in which people in the past lived, to see how they thought and felt.

It even gives an opportunity for speakers of modern English to feel the richness and weight within their own words. The terms and phrases which they use so casually may turn out to have a deep sediment of meaning within them, like discovering that the chair one sits on at breakfast every morning is actually an important antique. Reading Lewis's notes on language, I get the impression that the shifting significance of words could be a way of connecting to a deeper past for him. It was both a practical necessity for someone who did not want to misunderstand the old texts he dealt with every day, and an opportunity to experience the world with a broader horizon and greater depth of colour. It could even be a way of giving respect to those who had used the language before the modern era, and appreciating that we owe them some sort of recognition.

The fact that words in English have this history, and this slipperiness, allows Lewis to set a mild trap for the reader in a later Narnia novel, *The Silver Chair*. In this story, the hero and heroine (both human children) and their Marshwiggle companion (a Narnian creature like a part-human, part-frog that lives in the Narnian region most closely equivalent to Norfolk) are travelling through wild country. They have recently escaped from some giants who threw huge boulders at them (or threw rocks around the hillsides with insufficient care whether it was at them or not), and so are pleased when they meet a lady who tells them they are on the road which leads to a more pleasant place:

> 'This road leads to the burgh and Castle of Harfang, where dwell the gentle giants. They are as mild, civil, prudent, and courteous as those of Ettinsmoor are foolish, fierce, savage and given to all beastliness. And in Harfang you may or may not hear tidings of the City Ruinous, but certainly you shall find good lodgings and merry hosts. You would be wise to

winter there, or, at the least, to tarry certain days for your ease and refreshment. There you shall have steaming baths, soft beds, and bright hearths; and the roast and the baked and the sweet and the strong will be on the table four times in a day.'[151]

She also advises them to say to the giants of Harfang that she sent them: 'Only tell them … that She of the Green Kirtle salutes them by you, and has sent them two fair Southern children for the Autumn Feast.' That last line contains the most obvious play on words, which should have put the adventurers on their guard. The giants of Harfang regard humans as a delicacy, and being sent to them 'for the Autumn Feast' means that the children are more likely to end up as one of the dishes than as one of the guests. A game of words is also happening in the lady's description of these man-eating giants. She calls them 'gentle', 'mild', 'civil', 'prudent' and 'courteous', painting a very pleasing picture to a modern reader of giants with excellent morals and manners to match. But if we look back into the earlier meanings of those words, a different image emerges. As mentioned above, 'gentle' has become moralised: we tend to use 'gentle' to indicate tenderness, softness and a sensitivity to others. In its earlier meanings it meant simply 'of noble birth', just as 'gentleman' earlier did not mean someone who was thoughtful and honest, but someone who came of an upper-class family. A giant can be 'gentle' and still violent or harsh, if it is descended from giant aristocracy. 'Mild' might be associated by a contemporary ear with doves and milk, another word implying softness, kindness, etc. But one of the OED's definitions renders it as 'Of language or speech: gentle, moderate, measured. Of appearance or mien: kindly, pleasant, placid.' Giants can be 'mild' in their speech and still want to eat the person they are talking to. 'Civil' has also moved from its original meaning, of relating to the 'civitas', or 'city-state'. We still have this meaning: a civil war is one that happens within a state and a civil partnership is a union recognised by the state (rather than the Church). The 'civil' giants live in a city rather than on a hillside. If they are 'prudent' they take care of their resources and manage them with foresight, showing the virtue of 'prudence', which could include not wasting tasty children who wander into their castle. And 'courteous' giants do not necessarily behave well, they need only behave as people do 'at court', and the history of England is full of examples showing how a 'courtier' need not be a virtuous or abstinent person. This string of fine-sounding adjectives sounds as if it is assuring us of the excellent moral character of the giants of Harfang. In fact it is doing nothing of the sort, so long as we listen to it etymologically. A modern reader will be taken in, but one who has tuned their ear to the earlier meanings of words will see that the lady is telling a different story. (Or indeed, a reader who has continued on to the part where they find a recipe book in Harfang which includes directions for cooking humans, and has then turned back and reread the lady's description of the giants.)

The stakes are less drastic for the Pevensies, who are not in danger of being eaten at an Autumn Feast. Their titles are, nonetheless, part of the same verbal game. They exist both in modern English and in older states of the language, and if we only hear them with modern ears then we will not appreciate the way these children have grown into their role as Narnian monarchs. Peter the Magnificent has a title which sounds odd in contemporary English. By the twentieth century it had come mostly to be a general term of approbation, or to mean splendour in decoration. A theatre might have a magnificent façade, a restaurant serve a magnificent pudding, or a cricketer make a magnificent stroke with the bat. Earlier senses of the word, however, surely hang around Peter's title. (I draw these earlier definitions from the Oxford English Dictionary, which not only records the multiple meanings of words, but notes when in history they were prevalent, and gives short quotations to illustrate them.) Medieval English usage included 'magnificent' as meaning a person of great achievements and princely bearing. Killing the wolf could be regarded as 'magnificent' in this sense, as could leading the army into battle against the White Witch's minions. The entry for the allied word 'magnificence' notes that it is the term given to the virtue of fortitude, quoting Chaucer to the effect that 'Magnificence, that is to seyn, whan a man dooth and perfourneth grete werkes of goodnesse'. Peter's status as the Magnificent brings together an outward appearance of kingship with achieving great things, and being steadfast.

'Edmund the Just' is even more nuanced. It appears to mean that Edmund acts with justice, and judges well, which fits with the description of him as a grave and quiet man who gave good advice. Read in a longer historical context, however, the word 'just' means both that and the inverse. Not the opposite – Edmund is not 'unjust' – but the inverse, in that Edmund is 'justified'. He is able to act justly and judge things correctly because he has been acted upon by a justifying power. After all, the Christian tradition has always stressed that being just is not something which humans can achieve on their own. Certainly they cannot make themselves just in the greatest and most metaphysical sense: just in the eyes of God. In the New Testament, the Epistle of Paul to the Romans focuses strongly on this question of being made just. In one particularly well-known passage from the third chapter of Romans, Paul insists that 'by the deeds of the law there shall no flesh be justified in his sight' and 'all have sinned, and come short of the glory of God', but they can be 'justified freely by his grace through the redemption that is in Christ Jesus', and '[t]herefore we conclude that a man is justified by faith without the deeds of the law' (Rom 3:28). A couple of chapters later, Paul declares that '[t]herefore having been justified by faith, we have peace with God through our Lord

Jesus Christ' (Rom 5:1). The question of justification, being made 'just', is a key term in Paul's theology, and became a major point of contention during the Reformation. It remains a central issue in all Christian thought. In the nineteenth century the poet Gerard Manley Hopkins reflected on the 'just man' who is able to do justice because he has been imbued with that quality by Christ, in his luminously knotty sonnet, 'As kingfishers catch fire':

> As kingfishers catch fire, dragonflies draw flame;
> As tumbled over rim in roundy wells
> Stones ring; like each tucked string tells, each hung bell's
> Bow swung finds tongue to fling out broad its name;
> Each mortal thing does one thing and the same:
> Deals out that being indoors each one dwells;
> Selves — goes itself; *myself* it speaks and spells,
> Crying *Whát I dó is me: for that I came.*
>
> I say móre: the just man justices;
> Keeps grace: thát keeps all his goings graces;
> Acts in God's eye what in God's eye he is —
> Chríst — for Christ plays in ten thousand places,
> Lovely in limbs, and lovely in eyes not his
> To the Father through the features of men's faces.[152]

Though less intense and tangled in its form than this poem, Lewis's title for Edmund embodies a similar insight: Edmund is 'just' because he has been justified. It is evidence of the paradox at the heart of salvation that Edmund, the character who has bullied his sister, betrayed his family, indulged in gluttony and pride, and joined with the forces of evil in Narnia, is the one who gains the title 'the Just' at the end. He is not 'the Just' because he has done good things, but because he has been saved by Aslan's atoning self-sacrifice.

THE HUNTING OF THE WHITE STAG

The double meaning in the title belonging to Susan the Gentle has already been revealed above. 'Gentle' did not always mean meek and quiet, but signified noble birth and the manners which went with it. Susan could be 'gentle' when sitting on her throne at Cair Paravel or riding out hunting with her brothers and sister. She could be 'gentle' when – as we see in another later Narnia novel, *The Horse and His Boy* – rejecting the advances of a foreign prince who wanted to marry her. 'Gentle' here does not necessarily carry the implications of pliable, soft and low-voiced. A more modern and more democratic outlook might wince at the idea of moral terms being connected to the social status of the person involved, but Lewis suggested in *Studies in Words* that there was a more positive way to see this function of language change:

> It will be diagnosed by many as a symptom of the inveterate snobbery of the human race; and certainly the implications of language are hardly ever egalitarian. But that is not the whole story ... A word like nobility begins to take on its social-ethical meaning when it refers not simply to a man's status but to the manners and character which are thought to be appropriate to that status. But the mind cannot long consider those manners and that character without being forced on the reflection that they are sometimes lacking in those who are noble by status and sometimes present in those who are not. Thus from the very first the social-ethical meaning, merely by existing, is bound to separate itself from the status-meaning. Accordingly, from Boethius down, it becomes a commonplace of European literature that the true nobility is within, that villanie, not status, makes the villain, that there are 'ungentle gentles' and that 'gentle is as gentle does'.

In Lewis's view, the word 'gentle' coming to mean 'noble behaviour' rather than 'nobly born' worked against an assumption that all aristocrats were morally better than the common people. In his view, the separation of the moral and social senses allowed the word to be used to criticise the well-born. Either way, Susan's status as 'the Gentle' offers a much wider range of virtues and activities in the medieval-inflected world of Narnia than it might at her English school.

Lucy's title is 'the Valiant', and this might seem surprising. Just as 'the Just' is apparently an unlikely name for someone who betrayed everyone close to him, 'the Valiant' does not seem to fit the youngest of the siblings who did not fight in any battle. In the twentieth century, 'valiant' had narrowed in meaning to military bravery. One of the word's strongest associations for most British people in the early 1950s would probably have been the medal known as the 'Victoria Cross', which is the highest award which can be given under the British system of decorations. It is awarded for 'most conspicuous bravery, or some daring or pre-eminent act of valour or self-sacrifice, or extreme devotion to duty in the presence of the enemy', and the medal itself, which carries an emblem of a lion and a crown, is inscribed with the words 'For Valour'. Nothing which Lucy has done in the novel fits with this sense of the word. Once again, however, older usages provide other shades of meaning. The OED records as an obsolete meaning 'strong, firm', and gives some intriguing examples: in 1542 'the name of the Lorde is a stronge Tower and a valeaunt Bulwarke' and in 1607 'a Lyon hath a most valiant and strong head'. This meaning does make sense in Lucy's case, indeed she has been 'valiant' in this sense ever since she first entered Narnia. She was 'valiant' in standing firm when Edmund taunted her, and when she did not say she had made up Narnia for the sake of an easier time. She was 'valiant' when she and Susan walked with Aslan when he went to the Stone Table, and then stayed there all night. Lucy has not shown bravery on the battlefield, but she has been valiant in the older sense. The King James

Version of the Bible includes a verse in which the prophet Jeremiah criticises those who 'bend their tongues like their bow for lies: but they are not valiant for the truth upon the earth' as well as a line from 2 Samuel, which refers to he 'that is valiant, whose heart is as the heart of a lion' (Jer 9:3; 2 Sam 17:10). I am intrigued by the coincidence that quotations about being valiant often occur near the mention of lions in the Bible, and that the medal 'For Valour' has a lion on it. Both are explicable, since a lion is part of the heraldry of the monarch who bestows the Victoria Cross, and lions were the deadliest animal in the region where the Hebrew Scriptures were written. Nonetheless, there may well have been a subconscious association in Lewis's mind between Lucy's steadfastness for the truth and the image of the lion Aslan. Indeed, in the next book of the series, Queen Lucy the Valiant will have to insist to her sceptical siblings that she has seen Aslan, and will be rewarded by him telling her 'now you are a lioness'. The final resonance of the word 'valiant' which seems relevant to Lucy comes in a song entitled 'He Who Would True Valour See'. It originally appears in Bunyan's *Pilgrim's Progress*, the seventeenth-century tale which allegorises the spiritual life as an adventurous journey. It became a popular hymn in the nineteenth century (with words slightly adapted), and combines its praise of steadfast Christian virtue with fantastical quest imagery:

> Who would true valour see,
> Let him come hither;
> One here will constant be,
> Come wind, come weather.
> There's no discouragement
> Shall make him once relent
> His first avowed intent
> To be a pilgrim.

Whoso beset him round
With dismal stories,
Do but themselves confound;
His strength the more is.
No lion can him fright
He'll with a giant fight
But he will have a right
To be a pilgrim.

Hobgoblin, nor foul fiend
Can daunt his spirit;
He know he at the end
Shall life inherit.
Then fancies fly away,
He'll fear not what men say,
He'll labour night and day
To be a pilgrim.

Having traced the various meanings which cluster around the Pevensies' titles – the Magnificent, the Just, the Gentle and the Valiant – it is worth considering what effect these meanings have. I have suggested that Lewis was playing a bit of a linguistic game with the words, hiding older meanings under modern words just as he did with the Lady of the Green Kirtle's speech about the gentle giants of Harfang. However, I think it is more than a private trap set for the linguistically unwary. Firstly, recognising the older meanings of the titles allows the reader to see the Pevensies existing in two worlds at the same time. In our world, where they are schoolchildren, gentleness may be associated with a soft touch and a low voice, justice may look like simple fairness in sharing something out, magnificence may be the showy façade of a cinema and valour may mean a medal for a soldier. In Narnia, however, the children (and it is doubtful whether it is strictly accurate to call them 'children' at this point) have experienced something of the longer and deeper meanings of these words. They have experienced them from the inside, as royal virtues which other people recognised and praised. At the same time, though these words may have different shades of meaning in their lives in both worlds, they are still the same words. They provide a linguistic connection between the two lives they lead. After all, the 'length' and 'depth' of the titles which I have explored comes from the words' continual usage through the centuries. The medieval thought-world which we are plunged into when we pore over the aristocratic meaning of 'gentle' or the religious meaning of 'just' is some distance away from our everyday use of those terms. It is still the thought-world which shaped them, and traces of which can be seen in their modern sense. One of the impulses which drove Lewis to write *Studies in Words* was a desire to understand that linguistic history, and to see the words as connected through time. The modern meaning may be different to the medieval meaning, they may be at different ends of a historical stretch of time, but they are not different words. For Lewis, they provide a means of contact across the centuries, perhaps a recognition that using the English language involves plunging ourselves into a river of implications and associations which is not subject to control by our own momentary intention. Put another way, it is joining a game which has been going on for centuries, and which we cannot fully understand by declaring what we think the rules should be today. From this point of view, the Pevensies' titles emphasise the distinction between their identities as schoolchildren and their identities as Narnian royalty. But it also offers the possibility of inhabiting those identities at the same time, or at least being aware of them both.

This idea appears in more physical form at the end of *The Silver Chair*, when the two human children in that story return from Narnia. One of them, a girl called Jill, is still wearing the Narnian dress that she has been adventuring in. The story mentions that she changes back into her school uniform, but keeps the dress secretly, and only wears it when she goes to a fancy-dress ball in the holidays. When she dresses up for these festivities, she is in fact putting on her own clothes. As one of my Narnia Club put it, 'but Jill's cosplaying as herself'. She is a pupil at school, that is not a disguise or a cover, but she also exists in another world. Paradoxically, it is only when she puts on what appears to be a fancy-dress outfit that she is outwardly proclaiming that existence, though it is part of her memory and her personality the rest of the time. This parallel, where Jill's clothes point up the meaning of the Pevensies' titles, might cause us to return to the coronation scene a few pages earlier. The narrative states that 'Aslan solemnly crowned them and led them to the four thrones amid deafening shouts of, "Long Live King Peter! Long Live Queen Susan! Long Live King Edmund! Long Live Queen Lucy!"'. The lion himself then adds his own acclamation to their crowning: 'Once a king or queen in Narnia, always a king or queen. Bear it well, Sons of Adam! Bear it well, Daughters of Eve!'[153] Without wanting to get too involved in science-fictional speculation on the precise effect on a person of travelling between Narnia and our world, this certainly implies that the Pevensies will not simply stop being their royal selves when they return. They are, in some sense, always to be kings and queens now they have been crowned at Cair Paravel. Indeed, at the moment of their coronation, Aslan addresses them by titles which they have always possessed, though they have not always been conscious of the fact: sons of Adam and daughters of Eve. At the beginning of the adventure, when Lucy first entered Narnia and met Tumnus, she was surprised when he asked her if she was a daughter of Eve. As I suggested in an earlier chapter, the moment implied that to be a girl in the English countryside was potentially more fantastical and magical than being a faun or a witch. Here, as the Pevensies are crowned, they are shown the full splendour and potential of their status as humans, of the line of Adam and Eve. Their titles, which exist in both worlds, imply that the cry of the crowd will come true: 'Long Live King Peter ... Long Live Queen Lucy!' It is a conventional shout of respect to a monarch, but it is also truer for the Pevensies: there is a sense in which their life-spans have been made longer. They now participate in a deeper and older way of being themselves, to which their royal titles attest, and which will not be taken away when they leave Narnia.

THE SOUND OF THE HORNS AND HOUNDS

The way the kings and queens of Narnia find their way back to the wardrobe borrows from one of the classic medieval collections of myth and legend: the stories which surround King Arthur. As we have seen earlier, Thomas Malory's prose collection *Le Morte d'Arthur* provided a standard synthesis of many of the tales in English, and inspired much of the later Arthurian writing in English. When Alfred Lord Tennyson wanted to write a cycle of poems on the theme of Camelot in *Idylls of the King*, when Mark Twain wanted to satirise the tradition in *A Connecticut Yankee at King Arthur's Court*, when T. H. White explored the bleak parallels between medieval legend and the violence of the twentieth century in *The Once and Future King*, they all returned to *Le Morte d'Arthur*. The first suggestion that Malory may be an influence on this chapter comes in the title. There is no hunting of a white stag in *Le Morte d'Arthur*, but there is a hunting of a white hart, and the words are synonymous in medieval English. The beginning of this adventure is described in the third book of the collection:

Then was this feast made ready, and the King was wedded at Camelot unto Dame Guenivere in the church of Saint Stephen's, with great solemnity.

Then as every man was set as his degree asked, Merlin went to all the knights of the Round Table and bade them sit well, 'that none of you remove, for ye shall see a strange and a marvellous adventure.'

Right so as they sat there came running in a white hart into the hall, and a white bratchet next him, and thirty couple of black running hounds came after with a great cry; and the hart went about the Round Table, and as he went by the side boards the bratchet ever bit him by the buttock and pulled out a piece, wherethrough the hart leapt a great leap and overthrew a knight that sat at the side board. And therewith the knight arose and took up the bratchet and took up the bratchet, and so went forth out of the hall, and took his horse and rose his way with the bratchet.

Right so came in a lady on a white palfrey, and cried aloud unto King Arthur and said 'Sir, suffer me not to have this despite, for the bratchet is mine that the knight hath led away.'[154]

This is a somewhat more boisterous opening to a hunt than the news brought to the monarchs of Narnia that the white stag had been sighted. It does, however, take place just after the marriage of Arthur and Guinevere, just as the hunting of the stag is the next scene described after the Pevensies' coronation. In Malory the white hart leads the knights on a dramatic and ultimately tragic quest, and luckily nothing similar happens to the Pevensies. The similarity of the two episodes, however, points up the way Malory appears to influence this chapter.

The narrator's own voice is distinctively different in these passages, after the Pevensies have been crowned and before they return to our world. Some of this is noticeable in the kind of vocabulary used: King Edmund is not a serious man who gives good advice, he is a 'graver man ... great in council and judgement'. The monarchs do not set out to find the stag, rather 'these two Kings and two Queens with the principal members of their court, rode a-hunting with horns and hounds in the Western Woods to follow the White Stag'. In that last example the style as well as the vocabulary is strikingly archaic. The verb 'hunting' has a prefix, so it becomes 'a-hunting', and there is a formal repetition in the phrase 'these two Kings and two Queens'. The grammatical arrangement of this passage becomes noticeably different. It contains a feature which scholars have identified as particular characteristic of Malory's prose: a 'paratactic' style, in which clauses are added to each other in a string with conjunctions like 'and' or 'then', rather than being subordinated by logical connections and explanatory terms such as 'because' or 'but'.[155] This style is not unique to Malory (it can be seen, for example, in the King James Bible, especially in the historical books), but it is especially visible in his work. Comparing a passage from Lucy's entrance into Narnia with one describing the hunting party about to leave it highlights the difference:

> 'Nothing there!' said Peter, and they all trooped out again – all except Lucy. She stayed behind because she thought it would be worth trying the door of the wardrobe, even though she felt almost sure that it would be locked. To her surprise it opened quite easily, and two moth-balls dropped out.[156]

> And they had not hunted long before they had a sight of him. And he led them a great pace over rough and smooth and through thick and thin, till the horses of all the courtiers were tired out and these four were still following. And they saw the stag enter into a thicket where their horses could not follow.[157]

Many readers will probably just recognise the latter passage as archaic or old-fashioned in its style without being able to isolate elements such as the paratactic style, but Lewis constructs his pseudo-medieval narrative from exactly this sort of textual detail. Another touch characteristic of Malory is the way the narrative relates multiple people speaking as if they were all saying the same words in unison. In Malory, the scholar Jeremy Smith gives an example, when 'seven score knights' all give the same reply:

> Then they seyde all at onys with one voice:
> 'Sir, us thynkis beste that ye knightly rescow the queen.'[158]

The same rhetorical trick happens twice in Lewis's description of the hunt:

> 'Fair consorts, let us now alight from our horses and follow this beast into the thicket; for in all my days I never hunted a nobler quarry.'
> 'Sir', said the others, 'even so let us do.'[159]

> 'I know not how it is, but this lamp on the post worketh upon me strangely. It runs in my mind that I have seen the like before; as it were in a dream, or in the dream of a dream.'
> 'Sir,' answered they all, 'it is even so with us also.'[160]

In contrast, when Lucy comes out of the wardrobe for the first time, her siblings are united in disbelieving her stories, but they each speak individually. Lewis does not tell us that 'they all answered to her, 'I say, come off it Lu, stop talking such absolute rot.''

Even the arrangement of sounds within the sentences is strongly medieval in this passage. The heavy use of alliteration, repeating the initial letters of words, is more typical of medieval prose and poetry than their modern equivalents. The bulk of the poetry which survives from the Anglo-Saxon period is arranged by alliteration rather than by rhyme, and alliterative poetry continues into the later medieval period. The sentence I quoted above repeats 'k', 'h' and 'w' sounds to an extent which we would not expect in a twentieth-century novel: 'So these two Kings and two Queens, and the principal members of their court, went a-hunting with horns and hounds in the Western Woods, to follow the White Stag.' In fact, we can go further, and place this sentence alongside some of the alliterative poetry of the Middle English writer known as the Gawain-poet. His work known as *Sir Gawain and the Green Knight* includes a description of the court of Camelot in its early pages. I have selected some lines and added capital letters to the translation, to show how the metre uses alliteration to set up a pattern of three in each line:

Þis kyng lay at Camylot vpon Krystmasse
This King lay at Camelot / at Christmas
With mony luflych lorde, ledez of þe best,
With many Lovely Lords / and the best knights

...

Justed ful jolilé þise gentyle kniȝtes,
Jousted full Jollily / these Gentle knights

...

For þer þe fest watz ilyche ful fiften dayes,
 For there the Feast lasted / Full Fifteen days
With alle þe mete and þe mirþe þat men couþe avyse;
With all the Meat [food] and Mirth / that Men could devise

PATHS IN THE SNOW

With this poetic metre in mind, the sentence about the Pevensies going hunting sounds more than simply heavy on alliteration. It appears to be written in a medieval alliterative metre:

> These two KINGS and two QUEENS / and the principal members of their COURT
>
> rode a -HUNTING/with HORNS and HOUNDS
>
> in the WESTERN WOODS/to follow the WHITE stag.

All this gives a distinctively Arthurian feel to this part of the chapter. Though, as I mentioned, most readers are probably not noting down grammatical and alliterative elements in order to compare them with medieval authors, the style feels archaic and chivalric. The elements which Lewis has borrowed for his pseudo-medieval few pages evoke the feeling of Malory and the Gawain poet, wrapping his characters in an Arthurian atmosphere. This intensifies just at the moment when the Pevensies are about to stumble back into our world. That fact seems significant to me. Lewis does not give us a last chapter or so of fantasy novel in which the Pevensies act and speak like medieval monarchs, and then move them gradually back towards our world until they find the lamp-post again. Literary counter-factuals are always risky, and often unrewarding, but he could have written the novel that way. It wouldn't be too difficult to imagine a version of this story in which, after having various chivalric adventures, one of the Pevensies had a dream about their life back in England. In this version they might become nostalgic and melancholy, and catch themselves calling Narnian things by their modern names, until they realised it was time for them to return to their own world. This is not how Lewis wrote it. They end up back in England at their most

THE HUNTING OF THE WHITE STAG

Narnian time of life. They speak pseudo-medieval English, they undertake a quest to hunt the white stag, they delve deeper into a mysterious wood, and when faced with an unexpected sign they decide to plunge onwards with their quest. It is the Pevensies' success in acting like Arthurian royalty which lands them back through the wardrobe door. In plotting the novel this way, Lewis achieves something which we saw at the other end of *The Lion, the Witch and the Wardrobe*: he re-enchants our world. When Lucy first enters Narnia, she meets a faun who talks as if being a Daughter of Eve is the most magical and remarkable status he can imagine. When Queen Lucy the Valiant leaves Narnia, she has set her face to follow the quest of the white stag wherever it may lead, and it leads her back to the spare room. Returning to the world in which the reader has been sitting all this time is not a failure of the adventure, it is the quest's mysterious and triumphant end. As the last words of the novel ambiguously declare, ' ... that is the very end of the adventure of the wardrobe. But if the Professor was right it was only the beginning of the adventures of Narnia'.

ENDNOTES

1   C. S. Lewis, *The Lion, the Witch and the Wardrobe* (1950, repr Diamond Books 1997), p.58
2   Lewis, *Lion*, p.59
3   Francis Hodgson Burnett, *The Secret Garden* (1911, repr. Simon and Schuster, ebook), p.7
4   Burnett, *Garden*, p. 27
5   Burnett, *Garden*, p. 30-1
6   Burnett, *Garden*, p.81
7   Burnett, *Garden*, p.100-1
8   Lancelot Andrewes, *Selected Writings*, ed. Hewison (Carcanet, 1995), p.101-2
9   All quotations from the Bible, unless otherwise noted, are from the Authorised Version, also known as the King James Bible or King James Version. This is because the KJV was the dominant version in British culture from the early seventeenth to the mid twentieth century (except for the Psalms, which were most familiar in Coverdale's translation), and is the text which most English-speaking writers would think of as 'the English Bible' during these years. This is not to suggest that Lewis necessarily thought it the only or the best version, as we shall see in a later chapter, but it is the text which he would have been brought up on, and which he would have heard read at services.
10 C. S. Lewis, *English Literature in the Sixteenth Century (Excluding Drama)* (Cambridge University Press, 1954) p.96
11 Lewis, *Lion*, p.9
12 Beatrix Potter, *The Tale of Peter Rabbit* (Frederick Warne, 1902), n.pag.
13 C. S. Lewis, *An Experiment in Criticism* (Cambridge University Press, 1961, repr. 1979), p.8
14 C. S. Lewis, 'High and Low Brows', in *Essay Collection: Literature, Philosophy and Short Stories*, ed. Lesley Walmsley (HarperCollins, 2000), p.13
15 The (very rough) translation is mine, but based on those done by Dorothy L. Sayers and Robin Kirkpatrick.
16 Lewis, *Lion*, p.12-3
17 Farah Mendlesohn and Michael Levy, *Children's Fantasy Literature: An Introduction* (Cambridge University Press, 2016), p.106
18 Lewis, *Lion*, p.11
19 Lewis, *Lion*, p.11
20 In Laskaya and Salisbury, eds., *The Middle English Breton Lays* (Medieval Institute, 1995), p.26

ENDNOTES

21   *Breton*, p.26
22   *Breton*, p.26-7
23   *Breton*, p.35
24   Rudyard Kipling, *Puck of Pook's Hill*, (Macmillan, repr.1964) p.12
25   William Shakespeare, *A Midsummer Night's Dream*, 2.1.31-41.
26   Kipling, *Puck*, p.13
27   Kipling, *Puck*, p.17-8
28   Christin Ditchfield, *A Family Guide to The Lion, the Witch and the Wardrobe* (Crossway, 2005), p.116
29   Kenneth Grahame, *The Wind in the Willows*, (repr. Puffin, 1983) p.128-30
30   See Ronald Hutton, *The Triumph of the Moon: A History of Modern Pagan Witchcraft* and Paul Robichaud, *Pan: The Great God's Modern Return*.
31   Edmund Spenser, *The Shepheardes Calendar*, quoted in Robichaud, *Pan*, p.56
32   John Milton, 'On the Morning of Christ's Nativity', in *The Major Works*, ed. Orgel and Goldberg (Oxford, 2003), p.5-6
33   Lewis, *Lion*, p.32
34   Lewis, *Lion*, p.33
35   'A Visit from St. Nicholas', anon, *The Troy Sentinel*, 1823
36   Lewis, *Lion*, p.33
37   Lewis, *Lion*, p.95
38   Lewis, *Lion*, p.97
39   Lewis, *Lion*, p.98
40   Lewis, *Lion*, p.99
41   Lewis, *Lion*, p.92
42   Quoted in Alan Jacobs, 'The Chronicles of Narnia', in Ward and MacSwain, eds. *The Cambridge Companion to C. S. Lewis* (Cambridge, 2010) p.273
43   Lewis, *Lion*, p.99
44   In *The Lion's World*, (SPCK, 2012)
45   https://exhibits.lib.utexas.edu/spotlight/great-britain-ministry-of-information/catalog/61-2102 *Great Britain Ministry of Information: Daily Press Notices and Bulletins, No. 14: December 30, 1939*
46   Humphrey Carpenter, *The Inklings* (HarperCollins, 1978, repr. 2006) p.209
47   Carpenter, *Inklings*, p.210
48   It's even tempting to speculate that the stress laid on the Witch's very white face, and her very red lips, implies luxury cosmetics which would have been difficult to get in the post-war years. Make-up was an ambiguous topic during rationing, as it was never technically controlled by regulation and some government publicity encouraged women to contribute to the war effort by looking pretty and maintaining their morale with some cosmetics. Nonetheless, they were difficult to acquire, and this led to a consciously 'natural' look becoming popular, so being heavily made-up in striking shades might be a signal that a woman had access to shady sources of supply.
49   *Derby Daily Telegraph*, 21st February 1949
50   *Evening Telegraph* (Dundee), 21st February, 1949
51   *Derby Evening Telegraph*, 26th July, 1949
52   *Evening Telegraph* (Dundee), 16th July 1949

53   *Dundee Courier*, 19th August 1949
54   Dorothy L. Sayers, *Strong Poison* (1930, repr. Hodder 2003) p.48
55   Sayers, *Poison*, p.139
56   Sayers, *Poison*, p.276
57   Lewis, *Lion*, p.38
58   C. S. Lewis, *Mere Christianity* (1952, repr. Harper Collins, 2016) p.52
59   Lewis, *Experiment*, p.71-2
60   Lewis, *Experiment*, p.73
61   Lewis, *Lion*, p.48-9
62   J. W. Dunne, *An Experiment in Time*, (1927, repr Rare Treasures ebook) p.4
63   Dunne, *Time*, p.5
64   J. B. Priestley, *Time and the Conways and Other Plays* (repr. Penguin, 1969) p.59-60
65   Agatha Christie, *Sleeping Murder*, (1976, repr Harper Collins ebook), p.20-1
66   Lucy M. Boston, *The Stones of Green Knowe* (1976, repr Oldknow Books, 2003) p.118-9
67   Lewis, *Reflections on the Psalms* (1958, repr. Collins) p.137
68   Lewis, *Lion*, p.148
69   Lewis, *Lion*, p.54
70   Lewis, *Lion* p.126
71   Lewis, *Lion*, p.26
72   J. B. Phillips, *Letters to Young Churches* (Collins, 1947, repr. 1956) p. 53-4
73   Phillips, *Letters*, p. 11
74   Phillips, *Letters*, p.11
75   Phillips, *Letters*, p.79
76   Phillips, *Letters*, p.12
77   In Phillips, *Letters*, p.7
78   In Phillips, *Letters*, p.7
79   In Phillips, *Letters*, p.7
80   In Phillips, *Letters*, p.7-8
81   In Phillips, *Letters*, p.8
82   In Phillips, *Letters*, p.8
83   J. W. C. Wand, *The New Testament Letters* (Oxford University Press, 1944, rept. 1947), inside cover.
84   One of the best and most accessible discussions of this distinction can be found in John Barton's *The Word: On the Translation of the Bible* (Allen Lane, 2022).
85   Michael Ward, *Planet Narnia: The Seven Heavens in the Imagination of C.S. Lewis* (NY: OUP, 2010) p.63; Farah Mendlesohn and Edward James, *A Short History of Fantasy*, (2nd ed. Faringdon: Libri, 2012), p.54.
86   Grahame, *Willows*, p.12
87   *Hull Daily Mail*, 17th October, 1947
88   *Nottingham Evening Post*, 13th October, 1947
89   *Aberdeen Journal*, 15th March, 1949
90   *Cheltenham Chronicle*, 16th July 1949
91   *Aberdeen Journal*, 16th July, 1949
92   Evelyn Waugh, *Brideshead Revisited* (1945, repr.2016 Penguin, ebook) p.19-20

ENDNOTES

93   J. K. Rowling, *Harry Potter and the Philosopher's Stone* (Bloombury, 1997) srepr. 92-3

94   Lewis, *Lion*, p.65

95   In Schaff and Wallace, eds. *Nicene and Post-Nicene Fathers* (repr. Cosimo, 2007) p.440

96   St. Athanasius, *On the Incarnation*, tr. Behr (repr. SPCK, 2011), p.97

97   Anon, in Silverstein, ed. *Medieval English Lyrics* (Edward Arnold, 1971) p.100

98   Lewis, *Lion*, p.76

99   Lewis, *Lion*, p.75

100 William Shakespeare, *The Complete Sonnets and Poems,* ed. Burrow (Oxford: 2008) p.163

101 Lewis, *Experiment*, p.32-3

102 *Sir Thomas Malory, Le Morte d'Arthur* (Winchester Manuscript), ed. Helen Cooper, p.390

103 Lewis, *Mere*, p.121

104 Lewis, *Mere*, p.121-2

105 Milton, *Major*, p.357

106 Lewis, *Lion*, p.101

107 Cyril Hare, *When the Wind Blows* (Faber and Faber, 1949, repr.2007) p. 188-9

108 Lewis, 'The Vision of John Bunyan' in *Selected Literary Essays* (1961, repr. Canto 2012) p. 207

109 Lewis, 'Bunyan', p.208

110 Lewis, 'Bunyan', p.208-9

111 Lewis, 'Bunyan', p.209-10

112 Lewis, 'Bunyan', p.210

113 Lewis, *Lion*, p.102

114 In *Chaucer's Dream Poetry*, eds. Phillips and Havely, (Longman, 1997) p.242-3

115 Chaucer, *Dream*, p.267-8

116 Lewis, *Lion*, p.111

117 Chaucer, *Dream*, p.248-9

118 Lewis, *Lion*, p.105

119 Lewis, *Lion*, p.113

120 Lewis, *Lion*, 167, 168-9

121 This is apt, since in *The Silver Chair* Jill and Eustace, two later visitors to Narnia, will be taken to the gathering of the 'Parliament of Owls'. This is the correct collective noun for a group of owls in English, but it also feels slightly like a joke about medieval dream poetry by Lewis.

122 Eric Crozier, *Albert Herring: A Comic Opera in Three Acts* (Hawkes and Son, 1947)

123 A similar comment could be made about sovereignty: Alan Jacobs has suggested that the repeated theme or narrative situation of the Narnia novels is that of 'an unacknowledged but true King and the efforts of his loyalists to reclaim or protect his throne from usurpers' (274). This is another theme which preachers have touched on, particularly to young audiences, perhaps: that in a corrupt and materialist society the truest rebellion is going to the church and the most authentic unconformist

is the devout Christian. Lewis's novels dramatise this idea, so that it becomes part of most readers' attitude to the narrative without them even registering it.

124 Michael V. Fox, quoted in Cheryl Exum, *The Song of Songs: A Commentary* (Presbyterian Publishing, 2011) p.19

125 Origen, quoted in Christopher J. King, *Origen on the Song of Songs as the Spirit of Scripture* (Oxford, 2005), p.16

126 Lewis, *Lion*, p.106, 107

127 Lewis, *Lion*, p.107

128 Lewis, *Lion*, p.32

129 Lewis, *Lion*, p.115

130 Lewis *Lion*, p.115

131 See Ronald Hutton, *The Triumph of the Moon* (Oxford University Press, 1999) and *Blood and Mistletoe* (Oxford University Press, 2009)

132 *Daily Mail*, 16th June, 1948

133 Lewis, *Out of the Silent Planet* (1938, repr.1952) p.125

134 Quoted in Merryn Williams, *Wilfred Owen* (Seren, 1993) p.137

135 Lewis, *Lion*, p.119

136 Lewis, *Lion*, p.119

137 Lewis, *Lion*, p.123-4

138 Lewis, *Lion*, p.135

139 Lewis, *Lion*, p.146

140 Lewis, *Lion*, p.148

141 Lewis, *Lion*, p.147

142 Sir Thomas Wyatt, *The Complete Poems*, ed.Rebholz, (Penguin 1997), p.77

143 Lewis, *Lion*, p.152

144 Lewis, *Lion*, p.152

145 Lewis, *Lion*, p.153

146 *The Book of Common Prayer* (Cambridge University Press) p.48

147 Dorothy L. Sayers, *Dante: Hell* (Penguin 1949, repr. 2001) p.22-3

148 Lewis, *Lion*, p.166-7

149 Lewis, *Studies in Words* (Cambridge University Press, 1960, repr. 2013) p.21

150 Lewis, *Words*, p.1

151 Lewis, *The Silver Chair* (1953, repr. Collins 2001) p.102-3

152 In *The Poetical Works of Gerard Manley Hopkins*, ed. MacKenzie (Clarendon Press, 1990) p.141

153 Lewis, *Lion*, p.165

154 Malory, *Morte*, 55

155 See Jeremy Smith, 'Language and Style in Malory', in Archbald and Edwards, eds. *A Companion to Malory*, Arthurian Studies 37 (Cambridge: Boydell and Brewer, 1996)

156 Lewis, *Lion*, p.12

157 Lewis, *Lion*, p.167

158 Quoted in Smith, p. 102.

159 Lewis, *Lion*, p.167-8

160 Lewis, *Lion*, p.168-9